A Scotch Paisano in
Old Los Angeles

A Scotch Paisano in Old Los Angeles

Hugo Reid's Life in California, 1832-1852
Derived from His Correspondence

By SUSANNA BRYANT DAKIN

University of California Press
Berkeley • Los Angeles • London

UNIVERSITY OF CALIFORNIA PRESS
BERKELEY, CALIFORNIA

UNIVERSITY OF CALIFORNIA PRESS, LTD.
LONDON, ENGLAND

FIRST PAPERBACK PRINTING 1978
ISBN 0-520-03717-0

PRINTED IN THE UNITED STATES OF AMERICA

PREFACE

ABOUT ten years ago I first heard of Hugo Reid, the mysterious Scotch *paisano*,[1] from an old friend of my father's. John Tracy Gaffey, himself an Irish *paisano,* was then living the gracious life of a past generation in his time-worn *adobe*[2] residence, Hacienda la Rambla, at San Pedro. On one of our frequent visits to the Gaffey home, "Don Juan" drew me into a dim recess of his library which was a cache of early Californiana almost as fascinating as his own mind. Burrowing into a pile of papers and manuscripts, he miraculously found what he was looking for—a bundle of letters yellowed by age but easily legible. Handing them to me, with no cautioning, he said they were mine to use as long as I liked, adding that an interesting study might be made from them, of an "original" who had played an important part in the California scene during the colorful *hacendado*[3] period ended by the great Gold Rush in 1849.

Careful perusal of the letters revealed that they had been written between 1836 and 1852 by Hugo Reid, an educated Scotchman with a keen sense of humor, to his *estimado amigo,* "Don Abel" Stearns, originally a New Englander. The whole correspondence seemed like an intimate conversation between friends who were equally at home in the English and Spanish languages. And I soon found out that Reid and Stearns had been two of the most influential men

---

[1] Superior figures refer to notes on pp. 287–290.

of their day. Their careers ran parallel, so far as they came to
the Pacific coast in the 'twenties, engaged in trade at a time
when individual enterprise was rewarded by possessions and
power as seldom before or since, settled down within a few
miles of each other as *hacendados* in southern California—
Reid in San Gabriel and Stearns in Los Angeles,—and held
public office repeatedly. Both became Mexican citizens and
Catholics in order to own land and marry native Californians. Reid's wife was an Indian woman named Victoria, of
the once-powerful Comicrabit family; and Stearns married
the lovely Arcadia, daughter of Don Juan Bandini.[4] Both
men played parts in the Mexican War, mined for gold,
and attended the constitutional convention which achieved
statehood for California. Hugo Reid died in '52, twenty
years before his *compadre*.[5]

Such a correspondence as theirs could not be duplicated
today, when messages usually are transmitted in a more
transitory manner—over the telephone and in casual conversation. Automobiles, moving swiftly on smooth streets,
have cut distances into a fraction of what they seemed a
hundred years ago. Most of the letters exchanged between
Don Abel and Don Hugo traveled only the few leagues[6]
between San Gabriel and Los Angeles, and were carried by
Indian runners, friends on horseback, or in *carretas* drawn
by oxen plodding slowly over bumpy roads, dusty in summer and muddy in winter.

With the passing of the years, the Scotchman became
more impregnated with the spirit of *poco tiempo*[7] than his
friend, the "Yankee trader," ever did. Hugo enjoyed the leisurely life of a gentleman rancher and literary dilettante far

more than a competitive business career. As a result, he
never made a fortune to compare with Stearns's land empire;[8] but it is his letters, rather than the busy Don Abel's,
that reveal in a witty, intimate way the life they lived. Both
men had received a good education—Don Abel in Salem,
Massachusetts, and Hugo Reid in Scotch schools and two
years at Cambridge University.[9] They remained freethink-
ing citizens of the world, beyond the day of becoming
paisanos by settling in Mexican territory and swearing alle-
giance solely to a Catholic mother country. Always their
conversation had remarkable scope, and never was limited
for long to local affairs. It would dart from South America to
the Sandwich Isles (Hawaii)[10] and back again to Boston, as
likely as not, because they were familiar with such far-away
places, as captains of their own trading vessels—Don Abel's
American Ranger and Don Hugo's Mexican schooner, the
Esmeralda.

John Gaffey tried to give me the proper background for
such a study as he had suggested, by devoting most of his
Saturdays for a year or so toward my education in early
California history. Frequently his own eloquence would
carry him away, beyond the bounds of exact dates and docu-
mentary evidence, but always he was seeking the "essential
truth" and knowledge of the spacious, happy way of living
which vanished so suddenly at Midas' touch.

In time I completed a sketch—which only lately I have
attempted to amplify—of Hugo Reid's life as derived from
his letters: a hundred twenty-one of them written to Abel
Stearns; twenty-two others published the year of his death,
in the *Los Angeles Star;*[11] and miscellaneous Reid items

in the John Gaffey, William Heath Davis, Pío Pico, Antonio Coronel, and Henry Raup Wagner collections of Californiana.[12]

Mr. Gaffey seemed pleased with my work, but I felt that affection obscured his critical sense. The original sketch only skirted the essential truth which he had hoped I could reach. The result of my research, accurate as far as it went, had not been illumined by the use of informed imagination, indispensable in the re-creation of an unfamiliar way of life. To be sure, Helen Hunt Jackson and William Heath Davis before me had each felt an interest in this adventurous Scotchman; but neither had given Hugo Reid's character and influence their due.

Davis once paid a two months' visit to Don Hugo and Doña Victoria, the Indian wife, in their most prosperous days when they were living off the fat of the land. They offered gay and unstinting hospitality from their beautiful Rancho de Santa Anita to whoever came that way. This was in 1844, and later Davis collected much written information about the Reids while working on his classic *Seventy-five Years in California*. Most of what he knew he left out of the final draft, retaining hearsay in place of vivid, revealing passages from his own account of the long visit at Santa Anita. Fortunately the full account is preserved among the Davis manuscripts in the Huntington Library.

Mrs. Jackson used the extraordinary Reid family as prototypes for leading characters in *Ramona,* but to our way of thinking—Mr. Gaffey's and mine—the fictional characters hold less interest than the originals. "H. H." saw some of Hugo Reid's own letters and heard the true story of his life from Don Antonio Coronel, who had been his friend.[13] She knew that Reid left Scotland at the age of eighteen, when his first love jilted him and "forever" embittered him against women; and that the impulsive youth sailed for an unknown destination in the New World. He spent some six years of compassless wandering in South America and Mexico, learning several languages and seeking color, gold, romance, before being drawn north to settle in California. She also knew that there he met and fell in love with a beautiful Indian woman who had four children by an early, Indian marriage. He gave them all his name and lifelong devotion, and became a pillar of society in San Gabriel.

In spite of this information—hers for the asking—in drawing the character of Angus Phail (Ramona's Scotch father), Mrs. Jackson yielded to the popular prejudice that a white man marrying an Indian inevitably became a drunken "squaw man." Many of Hugo Reid's friends had feared just such a sordid outcome of his marriage; but it seems strange that, in the book, Ramona's mother should have remained a nameless squaw, when Doña Victoria herself was recognized by whoever came to know her as a person of consequence. The faithless Ramona Gonzaga, Angus' first love, receded into the shadowy character of a Scotch girl from Cardross who played her part before Hugo was twenty.

From Reid's own letters and the diary of a young dragoon[14] now emerges the true story of Doña Victoria's daughter, María Ygnacia, who grew up to have such charm that the *paisanos* called her the "Flower of San Gabriel." It is less passionate, less eventful, than the romance of *Ramona,* but has a delicacy and a pathos quite lost in the novel.[15]

Ramona's imaginary lover, the long-suffering Alessandro, must yield his place in real life to John McHenry Hollingsworth, a boyish officer of dragoons, who came West with the New York Volunteers at the time of the Mexican War and greatly admired María Ygnacia. Since she died at twenty-one, hers is only a minor rôle in the strictly historical drama, while Hugo and Victoria effectively play the leads.

Occasionally, in order to interpret the meaning of Hugo's own words or to fill a gap in the correspondence, I have supplemented the Reid letters with information drawn from contemporary accounts and reminiscences of a later date. There are three specific passages, in the beginning of the book, where I have attempted to find the essential truth through the use of informed imagination. To the best of my knowledge, no eyewitness account has survived of (1) Hugo Reid's first visit to California in '32 (2) his meeting with Victoria in '34; and (3) his *paisano* wedding in '37. Around the dates given by Don Hugo himself, entries in the San Gabriel Mission records, and contemporary census lists, I reconstructed three probable scenes, with the idea of placing Hugo and Victoria in the surroundings in which they lived and breathed throughout the period of the Reid-Stearns correspondence. Hugo did not commence writing regularly to Don Abel until just after the marriage. Indeed, among the first items in the correspondence are a number of *cartas de orden* informing Don Abel of materials needed from his Los Angeles *tienda* (store) in the construction of the Reids' first home, Uva Espina, in San Gabriel.

John Gaffey was not old enough to have known Hugo Reid, as did Charles Jenkins,[16] "Lalita" Evertson King,[17] and

Don Antonio Coronel, but Reid's letters to Stearns came to
"Don Juan" in a direct way. Don Abel's beautiful wife, Doña
Arcadia, was only fourteen when she became mistress of
El Palacio de Don Abel,[18] the undisputed social center of
Los Angeles for a long time after their marriage. She hero-
worshiped her big husband, so much older and more experienced than she, and spent many hours in appreciative
silence, listening to vital conversations between him and his
cronies—such men as her own father, who was Don Abel's
contemporary, Hugo Reid, Jacob Leese, Alfred Robinson,
the Pico brothers Andrés and Pío, Nathaniel Pryor, Captain John Cooper, William Hartnell, William Heath Davis,
José Antonio Carrillo, Captain Sutter, Don José de la Guerra
y Noriega, Henry Mellus, Robert Semple, Captain John
Wilson, Richard Laughlin, J. J. Warner, "Don Benito" Wilson, John Temple, Henry Fitch, Thomas Larkin, William
Leidesdorff, William Wolfskill, Louis Vignes, and others of
that informal oligarchy which guided California's destiny
through a difficult transition period and laid the foundations
for her later, astounding growth.

Some of these men played a part in California politics
during each of the three successive decades that covered her
transformation from a Spanish missionary colony whose
"currency" in trade was Indian shell money[19] or bullock
hides; through a pastoral Mexican interlude when the
power of the Church was sharply curtailed; into an American territory known to possess one of the richest deposits
of gold in the world. A few *paisanos,* notably Don Abel and
Don Hugo, can be remembered most of all for their part in
securing full state rights for California in 1850, when all law

and order seemed to have been submerged by the horde of unruly "miners" who participated in the Gold Rush.

After Don Abel's death, his letters and papers went into the keeping of his brother-in-law, Don Arturo Bandini. For years they were stored in an office in the Arcadia Block.[20] When Don Arturo also died, Doña Arcadia insisted that her husband's most valuable papers be turned over to John Gaffey. She had been intensely gratified when this delightful, scholarly Irishman married her favorite niece and namesake. They had started family life in a way that pleased her, offering oldtime hospitality from Hacienda la Rambla.

Doña Arcadia outlived most of her contemporaries, not dying until 1912, and John Gaffey, such a great storyteller himself, spent many hours in her company listening tirelessly to tales of life in the Land of *Poco Tiempo,* the vanished land in which she had spent her youth. Three years ago, "Don Juan" followed her in death, and his valuable collection of Californiana, including Hugo Reid's letters to Don Abel, has passed into the keeping of the Huntington Library. This is as it should be, for the library was founded by Mr. Gaffey's lifelong friend, Henry E. Huntington, and it stands on ground once owned by Hugo Reid and his Indian wife.[21]

SUSANNA BRYANT DAKIN.

San Marino, California,
February 1, 1939.

NOTE OF ACKNOWLEDGMENT

THE AUTHOR *feels deeply indebted for constructive criticism offered from time to time, during a period of research at the Huntington Library, by Messrs. Lindley Bynum, Robert Cleland, Godfrey Davies, Allan Nevins, and Allen Chickering. The translation of difficult and obsolete Spanish phrases in Hugo Reid's correspondence, by Miss Haydee Noya; the notes compiled for the author's use by Thomas Workman Temple II, after many hours spent in deciphering mission records at San Gabriel; and the painstaking edition of A SCOTCH PAISANO by Miss Olive Burchfiel—these services, done with equal zeal, are acknowledged with equal thanks.*

CONTENTS

[xv]

Contents

ILLUSTRATIONS

CHAPTER ONE

The Land of Poco Tiempo

SOMETIME in the summer of 1832, the brig *Ayacucho* put in at the port of San Pedro. Being a large vessel of some three hundred tons, she did not risk anchoring closer than a league offshore; and the shoreline, low and monotonously level, appeared even farther away than it actually was. Landing was difficult, and loading more so, but few traders could afford to pass by the best place on the whole West Coast for hides and tallow. Ten leagues inland, in the center of a fertile plain pasturing great herds of cattle, was El Pueblo de los Ángeles, the largest town in Alta California, and near by was the most flourishing mission community, San Gabriel.

The *Ayacucho* was a long, sharp-nosed brig with raking masts and square yards; and as the custom was, her hatches were battened down in anticipation of a sudden, dangerous sou'easter. Several of the ship's officers, a passenger, and chosen members of the crew, impatient for the feel of earth underfoot after months at sea, crowded into the longboat until little freeboard showed above the surface of the water. After pushing off for shore, the Kanaka seamen assigned to the oars needed all their fabulous strength to pull the heavy load. An assortment of nationalities filled that small boat, and a babel arose each time she threatened to sink.

[1]

The *Ayacucho* hailed from Callao, port of Lima. Built in Peru and named for the battlefield where the Peruvians had won their independence from Spain, she was now flying the British colors, being owned and commanded by a native of Scotland, one John Wilson. Under his fine seamanship she had gained the reputation of being the fastest sailing ship in trade on the coast. The other ship's officers were Scotch, English, and American, commanding a crew of twenty Sandwich Islanders.

The sole passenger on this trip was Hugo Reid, a handsome young Scotchman with sandy hair and keen blue eyes, intent on seeing the world. He had impulsively come aboard in Mexico at the invitation of his friends and fellow countrymen, Captain Wilson and James Scott, the supercargo.[1] As Reid had a lively spirit, a fund of anecdote, and a splendid singing voice, his presence on board must have broken the monotony of daily life on a long sea voyage. A thorough knowledge of accounting must have made him of value to the supercargo, whose duty it was to attend to the business detail of coastal trading, keeping the books and checking cargoes taken aboard or put ashore.

The smiling, brown Kanakas propelled the longboat with smooth, even strokes of their oars across the open sea until, drawing in toward a landing place, they found the tide low and the rocks covered only with exposed sea life: kelp, starfish, sea urchins, mussels, crabs, and barnacles. It was necessary to fasten the boat to a jutting rock and pick their way barefoot over some three hundred yards of knife-edged or slippery footing. Startled sea gulls and pelicans circled con-

---

[1] Superior figures refer to notes on pp. 291–305.

tinuously overhead, squawking their resentment at the invasion, and smooth, brown sea lions slithered down from sun-warmed rocks and swam lazily away.

Finally the wayfarers arrived at what would be the landing place at high tide. A low *adobe* sitting on a little hill seemed a sign of human habitation. But no one came down to meet them, and when the passenger and the supercargo went exploring, they found the place unoccupied. From the smell, it appeared to have been used as a storehouse for hides. It consisted of a single dirty room with a cold fireplace, cooking utensils, a rough-hewn table, and a few chairs.

Fortunately Scott had been to San Pedro before, and he remembered that the Mexican customs official lived at the Domínguez *hacienda,* only a league distant. It was this man's business to inform all the *hacendados* in the vicinity that a trading vessel was anchored offshore. There would be great excitement over the news that the well-known *Ayacucho* had an exotic cargo from Peru to trade for California's perennial products—hides and tallow, tallow and hides.

Reid was surprised to learn that the horses nibbling dry grass near the hovel, each with a lasso dangling from its neck, were there for anyone's convenience. Horses being plentiful, whoever could catch and ride one was welcome. He had only to let it go again when he reached his destination. Even the poorest *peón* owned a mustang, and the best blooded horse seldom commanded more than ten dollars, or five bullock hides, at a sale.

Reid watched his friend the supercargo set out in search of the customs official, riding bareback along the shadeless, dusty road that wound by way of the Domínguez *rancho*

inland to the Pueblo. Returning to the warehouse, Reid removed two chairs from the depressing interior and, with
Captain Wilson, settled down on the shady side of the *adobe*
to await Scott's return. Everyone, especially the Kanaka
crew, was reveling in physical freedom and the spaciousness
of the beach after so long a time spent in cramped ship's
quarters. A day of leisure seemed like a miracle after the
rigorous routine of life at sea.

It would be at least a day before the Mexican *capitán* could
be found, and Indian runners dispatched by his orders to
all the *haciendas* for miles around. Those *hacendados* who
had worked like the proverbial ant, laying in a supply of
hides, would at once commence to load them, along with
the tallow already stored in huge vats. Others, victims of
the grasshopper's philosophy, must go out into the fields
and kill the cattle, then prepare the hides and tallow; and
the delay might result in their missing the boat.

Early next morning the first large oxcarts, called *carretas,*
and droves of mules loaded with hides could be seen coming
over the flat country, raising clouds of dust. They also could
be heard from afar, for the wooden *carretas* creaked and
shrieked at each turn of solid oak wheels. California fashion,
two Indian boys accompanied each ox team and continually
urged their charges on with shouts and the pricking of sharp
sticks. Snatches of Spanish song rose on the air, vying with
the melodious songs of meadowlarks, which flew up from
underfoot as the procession passed.

Squirrels, rabbits, and gophers were continually scurry-
ing down into their holes, out of harm's way. Indeed, these
tiny animals had so honeycombed the surface of the ground

as to make it dangerous to ride anywhere off the roadway faster than at a walk. The caravan stretched out in a thin line along a road the surface of which seemed no smoother than the open field. Only in this way was it possible to avoid stumbling, dropping a load, and perhaps breaking a leg.

At high tide the longboat came inshore again, loaded this time with boxes and barrels. Hugo Reid, taking advantage of his status as "passenger," did not stop even to watch the trading and the difficult reloading of the longboat with bulky hides. Following Scott's example of the previous day, he caught a nondescript mustang and set out along the one road leading to the Pueblo. He had almost a week in which to learn the customs of the country.

The ride might have seemed monotonous to another, less observing person, but an abundance of wild life held the young Scotchman's interest. From the ship at anchor, and later from the waterfront, he had seen the countryside as bare of trees and shrubs. Even Palos Verdes, as the *paisanos* called some rolling hills on a promontory northwest of the "harbor," seemed a misnomer in the summertime. Under a drying sun, and without rainfall for months at a stretch, the grass and wild oats that grew luxuriantly there had turned the same yellow-tan color as the characteristic, clayey soil. But a little way inland the traveler was surprised to see frequent clumps of trees, and evidence, in marsh reeds and grasses, of water close to the surface.

Though the dry season in California lasted a long time, compensation always came with the heavy winter rains. Rain water would remain from one winter to the next in lowlands like those the Los Angeles road crossed for sev-

eral leagues after leaving San Pedro. Along either side of the
hard-packed dirt roadway, only a few feet above sea level,
stretched marshes filled with *tules* and cattails, yellow snap-
dragons, and the star-flowered plants used by the Indians in
making soap; also *álamos* (cottonwoods) and weeping willows which had more the size and appearance of shrubs than
of trees. These extensive lowlands were the breeding places
of a great variety of birds.

With the coming of spring, the ducks and wild geese had
winged their way north, toward Canada and Alaska, leaving
only a few of their adventurous kind to spend the summer
at home with the more domestic mudhens. Most beautiful
of the many water fowl that the horseman saw were snowy
white herons standing like storks, on one leg, to watch him
pass by.

On dry land, pheasant-colored birds with long tails—
which Reid later learned were called *churreas* (roadrun-
ners)—constantly crossed and recrossed the road in front
of him. From the entrance of innumerable underground
homes, furry creatures peered out with curiosity in their
bright eyes, and little brown owls took a last look around
before going to sleep for the day.

Starting so early, Hugo had seen the landscape sparkling
with dew. The whole world seemed fresh and new in the
clear morning light. Jack rabbits, full of high spirits, had
sprinted across the plain with the speed of greyhounds. Occasionally a coyote, seeming half wolf, half dog, would start
in pursuit, but the day soon turned too warm for continued
exertion. Gradually a sultry haze dispelled all dewy fresh-
ness from the air, and the earlier activity subsided. As the

birds and animals retreated into their homes, human beings commenced to come out into the open, having slept through the beauty of early morning.

The traveler could now turn his attention to such sights as a *hacendado* and his family creaking slowly toward the Pueblo in a *carreta* padded in calico for comfort; or a lone *caballero* riding with a message from one *hacienda* to another. Always Hugo would be recognized as an *extranjero*, and usually greeted with the question:

"Buenos días, señor. Cuánto tiempo va a demorar el buque en San Pedro?" (Good day, sir. How long will the vessel remain in San Pedro?)

As Reid approached Los Angeles, he found that it completely lacked the bustle and activity to which he had recently become accustomed, living in the Mexican city of Hermosillo.[2] He had heard that there were fifteen hundred residents, but, arriving about noon, could not see a soul; it must be that everyone took a *siesta*.

The Pueblo was not prepossessing in appearance, being mud colored and built without plan. Hugo did not see a wooden house in the place; only low, one-story *adobes* with bituminous pitch covering flat roofs. Since the foundation, on September 4, 1781, of El Pueblo de Nuestra Señora de los Ángeles de Porciúncula by Governor Felipe de Neve, landholders had built where they pleased. Originally, small plots had been granted to colonists by the Spanish government; within the past ten years, by Mexican masters. Always, a fine disregard for streets had been shown. Very narrow ones existed, but the independent *adobes* backed up on them, retired, and only occasionally fronted on them as was proper.

There were no sidewalks, and now during the dry season dust stood a foot thick in the streets. Of course, when it rained, the mud seemed far worse, being of sticky *adobe* consistency. It was the custom to ride horseback, even across the Plaza.³ Finding himself forced to walk a few steps, a *paisano* invariably would stroll down the middle of the road; in winter to enjoy the sunshine, and in summer to escape the trickling of black *brea* from roofs with which the heat played havoc. Innumerable dogs lounged about the streets, as sleepy looking as most of the citizens. A river, El Río de Porciúncula, almost dry now, meandered through the center of town, and along its banks, a short distance away, grew acres of welcome green vineyards. The Mexican flag flapped desultorily from an impressive pole in the Plaza.

Presently Hugo discovered someone of whom to ask directions. A *tendero* (storekeeper) was sitting in the sun outside his *tienda,* on a chair tilted back against the *adobe* wall. A large *sombrero* covered his eyes, and at first Hugo thought him asleep, like everyone else in town. He therefore took the liberty of looking in through the one, barred, window of the store. To his great surprise he saw little else but watches— watches and clocks,—which were rather a rarity in the West. Hugo was startled when the man suddenly came to life and addressed him in excellent English, asking what he could do for the stranger in town.

It followed that purely by chance Hugo had come upon the one person in town with accommodations for *extranjeros.* This was Nathaniel Pryor, a Kentucky silversmith and clockmaker who had come to California in '28 as a trapper in the ill-fated Pattie party.⁴ Being a genial soul, a bachelor with extra rooms in his home, he was by way of becoming a boarding-house keeper in a town where there was no hotel. At the moment it appeared that he had only one guest, Don Abel Stearns, the traveling representative of Captain Cooper's Monterey trading company.[5]

Hugo accepted the man's cordial invitation to lodge with him. The house, as he soon observed, was of the style most favored by the Pueblo.

The material used in its construction was *adobe* mud mixed with straw and made into large bricks, then baked in the sun. *Adobe* bricks were cemented together with a mud mortar, to form very thick walls resistant alike to heat and to cold. In Monterey and occasionally in Los Angeles they were whitewashed, but Pryor's house remained dirt colored. The floors were no more than dirt, hard packed and worn to the shine and color of slate. Only in the living room had Pryor laid down a plank floor, of which he seemed very proud. His grated windows also were rather remarkable, having glass in them. Each bedroom opened through one door into the living room and through another on a spacious veranda. Pryor owned a minimum of hard-used furniture, except beds, which were plentiful—constructed of rawhide stretched over a frame, neatly made up and surprisingly comfortable. Since he had no wife, the walls were bare of holy pictures, and the windows, of lace curtains.

In Pryor's home, as in everyone else's, all the cooking was done in a separate cookhouse containing a stone oven, and the food was served out of doors under a *ramada* roofed with *tules*. Indians did all the work, indoors and out, in return for food and clothing. This usually consisted of *frijoles* (red beans) three times a day, and a small piece of coarse cloth with a belt, for the men; *frijoles* and a shapeless gown, without shoes or stockings, for the women.

On Hugo's first evening another resident, "Handsome Dick" Laughlin,° dropped in at Pryor's for a friendly game of whist, Don Abel's favorite game. The four men sat down by the light of a tallow candle with a pack of precious Spanish cards, greasy from frequent use, and a bottle of locally distilled *aguardiente* (brandy) to keep up their spirits.

Hugo found the others very congenial company. Like himself, they were full of vitality, strong spirited, and accustomed to an outdoor life of adventure and physical hardship. Dick Laughlin immediately became the center of any gathering he attended, having a lively wit and a charming smile, in addition to manly good looks. Like Pryor, he was an American and had been a member of the Pattie party. They were all young men, ranging from Hugo's twenty-two years to Don Abel's thirty-two or -three.

The four players resembled each other in yet another way—this the most subtle. Each had lived a period of years in Mexican territory and had absorbed more than he realized of Mexico's customs and habits of thought. These men, three Americans and a Scotchman, might easily have been mistaken for Mexicans, by a casual observer. Their skins had turned brown under the sun; their clothes were alike; and their speech, whether originally a Scotch burr or a Yankee drawl, by now had absorbed so much of the Mexican-Spanish idiom as to take on a softer, more melodious tone.

Deeper than such surface changes went their impregnation with the spirit of *poco tiempo,* less marked in the New

Englander, Abel Stearns, than in the others. *"Poco tiempo"* was an expression often used by those *paisanos* who were living a pastoral life in Alta California a few years before Reid's visit, when the first white trappers and traders came over the mountains and around the Horn. Freely translated, it meant "Too little time"—too little time today to do anything that could be done tomorrow. One heard the word *"Mañana"* as often on a Californian's lips as in Old Mexico. They all had hoped to make their fortune out of a rich land and a lazy people—those true pioneers who came to California in the 'twenties from the other side of the world, surviving great hardships on the way. But only in a handful did ambition live to conquer the carefree spirit that prevailed, especially in the southern, semitropical section of California. One by one the most adventurous souls turned into typical Californians, adopting Mexico as their mother country and embracing the Roman Catholic religion. These acts entitled a man to own land and to marry a native daughter, usually a beautiful dark-eyed maiden of sixteen summers. Educated only to please, she could make life so delightful that the struggle for "success," in which the rest of the world was endlessly engaged, seemed a futile way of life.

Life in California, business opportunities, and beautiful women—of such absorbing subjects the Angelenos talked. The whist game was abandoned, for they soon became more interested in what the newcomer had to say than in trying to take his money away from him. Quite casually Reid mentioned being the Hermosillo representative of Henry Dalton's trading company, headquarters in Lima—showing business interests similar to Don Abel's. They all knew that

Hermosillo, the capital of Sonora in upper Mexico, was passing through a period of great prosperity from the discovery of gold in the vicinity. Hugo admitted that only the need of a vacation made him entrust a thriving young business, temporarily, to the supervision of a subordinate.

Answering Don Abel's questions, Hugo told them that Hermosillo's *adobe*-lined streets now swarmed with people from all over the world, for the cry *"Oro! Oro!"* had appealed with equal force, as it always does, to soldiers of fortune, cutthroats, and gentlemen. At the time of Hugo's own arrival there were four fine buildings of which the citizens felt exceedingly proud—a stone prison, a mint, and two churches. Naturally, a town going through a mining boom also sported numerous saloons and places to dance and gamble.

The lively atmosphere and exciting proximity to a gold mine had appealed to Hugo. Having had experience in merchandising as a boy in his father's shop in Scotland and, later, in working for Dalton in Peru, he saw a splendid opportunity for "striking it rich" by selling supplies to inadequately equipped "miners." Hastily arranging a partnership with Dalton, who was well known on the West Coast, he had opened a store in time to profit by the gold rush and still was finding business good. Encouraged by the Angelenos' interest and the total suspension of the whist game, Hugo went on to describe certain persons whose acquaintance he had made when he lived in Hermosillo—Sonoreñas famous for their beauty, and adventurous young men drawn westward by various magnets. He felt that he had found a true and lasting friend in an American doctor, William

Keith. This young man was enjoying a flourishing practice in Hermosillo, having no competition there—indeed very little in all his part of the world.

Hugo's present companions were all too familiar with the dearth of accredited M.D.'s. Pryor pointed out that Los Angeles still had no doctor. Each of the three as a "foreigner" had at some time or other been endowed by his Mexican *vecinos* with strange curative powers. This led the conversation into "cures" often far worse than the original complaints, but always accepted with blind faith by importunate patients. The medicine kit that almost every white trapper or trader carried with him was regarded by gullible Mexicans and Indians as a talisman, long after the original contents had been exhausted. As Reid himself remarked:

I know not why, but an Anglo-Saxon is synonymous with an M.D. Many an *extranjero* who never before possessed sufficient confidence in himself to administer even a dose of Epsom, after killing God knows how many, has at length become a tolerable empiric. One thing in favor of the sick is, that after a lapse of years the greater part of the drugs lose their virtue.

It was almost dawn, and a good deal of *aguardiente* had been drunk, before the foursome went to bed.

A few days later they met for another memorable evening, at the weekly *merienda* given by the beloved Padre Sánchez for the whole community. According to long-established custom, the picnic place was El Molino (the mill) near the San Gabriel Mission, and a yearling heifer was to be baked underground. Pryor, having appointed himself mentor to the young Scotchman, assured him that all the food would be delicious, the atmosphere gay; and as Hugo had a good voice, there would be a chance to exercise it to the tune of a guitar. Always, after *cena* (supper), all the guests sat round a blazing fire and sang or told stories, with the old padre's encouragement and frequent participation—indeed, he was the best storyteller of them all.

Riding over the fertile plain eastward toward San Gabriel, three leagues or more, the newcomer must have seen much to interest him. They were approaching a high range of mountains, the Sierra Madre, and Hugo always was curious about trails taken by early pathfinders. He knew that the already legendary figures of Portolá and Junípero Serra had passed through the San Gabriel Valley, coming from Baja California; and Pryor told him that only six years previously, on November 28, 1826, the placid mission community at San Gabriel had been startled by the appearance of a rough-looking little band of fur traders, led by Jedediah Smith. Though hungry, and exhausted in body, these men were jubilant in spirit, for they knew themselves to be the first white conquerors of the forbidding Sierra Madre.

Following close on the heels of this heroic expedition came other fur traders, blazing their own trails toward the fabulous West Coast. Pryor launched into a saga of terrific hardships conquered by courage. He himself had traveled overland to California from Kentucky, as early as '28, in a party led by James Ohio Pattie. And he named other well-known residents of southern California, good friends of his, who had braved equal hazards and won the right to be known as pathfinders. Such men were William Wolfskill and J. J. Warner, who had arrived in 1831, with separate parties of trappers.

An extraordinarily interesting diary has survived from those adventurous years, kept during the Jedediah Smith expedition by Smith's clerk, Harrison Rogers. He described the region of San Gabriel as "a country whose face changed hourly," and Hugo Reid, coming a few years later, knew this to be true. The Los Angeles *mesa* was edged on the east by oak groves and casual clumps of sycamores, the natural haunt of deer and tiny antelope and grizzly bear; but Reid and Pryor often found the shade preëmpted by fat black mission cattle shunning the hot sun. The heat seemed more oppressive in midafternoon than at any other time, to men as well as beasts; and the *caballeros* were relieved to see the mill in the distance, shortly before sundown, and soon afterward to hear cool water rushing over the dam.

Hugo Reid has described Sánchez' picnic site as the old priest first saw it:[7]

The water, which now composes the lagoon of the mill (one mile and a half distant from the mission), being free, like everything else, to wander and meander where it pleased, came down into the hollow nearest the mission, on the Angeles road. This hollow was a complete thicket, formed by sycamores, cottonwood, larch, ash, and willows; besides brambles, nettles, palma cristi, wild roses, and wild grapevines lent a hand to make it impassable, except where footpaths had rendered entrance to its barriers a matter more easy of accomplishment. This hollow, cleared of all encumbrance, served to raise the first crops ever produced at the mission, and . . . at that time it rejoiced in a rich, black soil.

The appearance of an attractive *extranjero* caused some excitement among the *señoritas,* already assembled for the *merienda.* But Hugo was absorbed, for the moment, in Pryor's talk of pioneers and overland trails and the first colo-

nists of California. Appreciating an unusual interest in the
past, Hugo's host, the jovial padre, was easily persuaded to
describe the selection of the mill site by his own colleague,
the powerful Padre Zalvidea. Under Zalvidea's supervision,
Sánchez himself had labored in construction of the mill and
dam, clearing of undergrowth, and planting of crops, orchards, and vineyards—these last from cuttings made many
months previously in Baja California. Closer to the mission
they had planted protective *tuna* (cactus) hedges, and even
a flower garden around a sun dial. With Indian labor, which
they trained to many trades, a herculean task had been completed, and now Sánchez was reaping his reward in the
knowledge that San Gabriel was known in both Baja and
Alta California as the "Pride of the Missions." A look of
sadness passed over the padre's face at the thought that Zalvidea, the man of iron who had originated the mission's progressive policy, should have suffered a complete mental
breakdown only a few years previously, after being transferred to San Juan Capistrano.

   Reid found an extraordinary personality in Fray José Bernardo Sánchez, and described the revered churchman as
follows:

He was of a cheerful disposition, frank and generous in his
nature, although at times he lost his temper with the strange,
unruly set around him.

He was a great sportsman and capital shot, both with rifle
and fowling piece. Although no one could complain of Zalvidea
in regard to his kind treatment, still there was a certain restraint
in his presence, arising from his austerity and pensiveness, which
even custom did not erase from the mind. Padre Sánchez was
different; his temper was governed according to circumstances.

In ecclesiastical affairs, his deportment was solemn; in trade he was formal; in the government of the mission, active, lively, and strict; in social intercourse he was friendly, full of anecdote, fond of a joke, even to a practical one....

The same regulations which had been observed by his predecessor [Zalvidea] were still in force under Sánchez, but more lenity was shown to the failings of the neophytes. Although the lash was ever ready, yet many other modes of chastising were adopted in its stead for minor offenses.

The general condition of the Indians was rendered better, and a more healthy state prevailed even in their morals. Many an Indian who had previously stolen and committed other acts of insubordination, from a vindictive spirit, now refrained from such deeds, through the love and good will held to their spiritual and temporal ruler.

During the *merienda,* which was all Pryor had promised, Padre Sánchez repeatedly urged his guests from Los Angeles, including the visiting Scotchman, to spend the night at the mission, where there were ample accommodations and plenty of food on the long table always set for travelers. This invitation appealed to them all, since it was growing late and the ride home would seem long and dark and full of pitfalls. The hours had flown by while they sat with a spell upon them, around a cheerful fire, listening to Sánchez' stories of his intrepid, pathfinding Brothers.

In the course of the evening, the good Fray José Bernardo, who had learned something of the Indian language during his long service at San Gabriel, observed that when the Spaniards first appeared in the vicinity, the aborigines gave them the name of *"Chichinabros,"* meaning "reasonable beings." For Reid's benefit, he had told a story familiar to the

other guests, about the pioneer Franciscans who were sent
to select a site for the new mission. It was to be the fourth in a
chain of twenty-one strung along the Alta California coast—
preceded only by the missions of San Diego, San Carlos, and
San Antonio. In August and September, 1771, the Brothers
Ángel Somera and Pedro Benito Cambón had traveled toward the north, on foot and unarmed, following the trail
taken the preceding year by the Portolá expedition, and
finally had arrived at their destination—El Río de los Temblores (the River of the Earthquakes).

Just as they were deliberating about the choice of a site, a great
multitude of savages, armed and headed by two chiefs, appeared
and with frightful yells attempted to prevent the founding of
the mission. Fearing that a battle might ensue and that some
might be killed, one of the Fathers produced a canvas picture of
Our Lady of Sorrows and put it in view of the savages. No
sooner had he done this than all, overcome by the sight of the
beautiful image, threw down their bows and arrows. The two
chiefs quickly ran up to lay at the feet of the Sovereign Queen
as tokens of their greatest esteem the beads they wore on the
neck. By the same action they manifested their desire to be at
peace with us. They called upon all the neighboring *rancherías,*
who in large numbers flocked together, men, women, and children, and came to see the Most Holy Virgin. They also brought
seeds, which they left at the feet of the Most Holy Lady, imagining that she would eat like the rest.[8]

After listening to Padre Sánchez' account of the savages'
original "conversion," Reid, being something of a skeptic,
became anxious to see for himself how much of the miracle
had survived the sixty years of the mission's establishment.
Could he ever penetrate the neophyte's impassive surface,

he feared he would find resentment—over the humiliating loss of independence, depredations of the lawless soldiery, and the lash of Zalvidea—counterbalancing the appealing piety of many of the padres. However, on this visit Hugo was not to have the opportunity, because several *hacendados* had warned him, in the course of the evening, that the *Ayacucho's* hold was almost full. The sailing would not be postponed for more than a day or so, and it seemed necessary for him to set out at once for San Pedro.

Later, Hugo was to regret deeply that he had seen so little of life at San Gabriel while it reigned as Pride of the Missions. Great changes were to occur before his return, and this glimpse of the prosperous and happy days at San Gabriel was always to gleam in his memory in contrast with the dark, unhappy years of despoliation, which came so quickly and lasted so long.

After Hugo Reid had reluctantly left Sánchez' *merienda* and started back alone over the rough, dark road, the affectionate farewells of his newly found friends—Pryor, Don Abel, and Dick Laughlin—echoed in his heart. And up to the moment that he swung into his saddle, the kind Padre Sánchez had continued to urge him:

"No se apure. Siéntese, hijito!" (Don't be in a hurry. Sit down, little son!)

Life in southern California must have seemed like heaven on earth to a young man who so loved life and color, music and leisure. Indeed, he had half promised to return; to close his Hermosillo office, and persuade William Keith to accompany him north. Within one short week Hugo himself had been persuaded that there were great and increasing opportunities for a young merchant and a doctor to establish themselves in Los Angeles. The bitter spirit of competition, which so often seemed to corrode life in other parts of the world, apparently had been banished from the happy Land of *Poco Tiempo*.

CHAPTER TWO

Trial and Error

For a time after Hugo Reid's return to Hermosillo the business boom continued, and he was too busy selling mining *anchetas*[1] to consider departure from such a lucrative area. He also found his friend William Keith inclined to laugh at his enthusiasm for the fabulous Land of *Poco Tiempo*. "*Mañana*," Don Guillermo would say; "*Mañana* we shall go."

But presently the gold excitement subsided; most of the "miners" drifted away, having had no luck; and Hugo's stories at last stimulated Keith's interest in Los Angeles. The doctor himself began to talk of setting up practice in a town of fifteen hundred permanent residents, with as many more Gabrielenos close by. In contrast to the transients who had been his recent patients, the majority would pay their bills, if only in hides or *aguardiente;* and Hugo assured him that he need fear no serious competition. Indeed, Hugo had gathered that the few *extranjeros* and overworked padres would be relieved to shed the responsibility of doctoring the community.

Letters from the Angelenos, Pryor and Stearns, encouraged Hugo to take the first steps toward moving north. But the year 1834 was well under way before a date could be set for departure. There had been the inevitable Mexican delay in getting a passport from the *jefe político* at La Paz, Poliano Monterde, and it also required more time than Hugo had expected to wind up his own affairs by closing the Hermosillo branch of Dalton's trading company. William Keith watched his friend's actions with increasing interest, and finally decided to go along.

The trip north must have been uneventful, since it apparently passed without comment. There is a record of their appearance in San Diego in August, and it is certain that they received a warm welcome from all the friends that Reid had made, in Los Angeles, two years previously. As they expected, plenty of opportunities awaited them in Alta California. From the moment that Keith hung out his shingle as a practicing M.D., there were more patients than hours to treat them in. Reid, deciding to form a new trading company with Jacob P. Leese, persuaded the doctor to invest some money and become a partner.

The firm of Reid, Keith, and Leese opened a *tienda* on the Angeles Plaza in September. Leese, a native of Ohio, born in 1809, had engaged in the Santa Fé trade since '30 and appeared to be shrewd and fairly well educated. Hearing of fortunes to be made in trade on the coast, he had joined a small party traveling along the southwestern trail and braving the natural perils of the desert and the constant danger of attack by Indians on the warpath. Leese reached Los Angeles a few months before Reid and Keith.

In the rear of their one-story *adobe* building was a large warehouse lined with long wooden shelves where they piled large bags of tallow and stacks of bullock hides, each doubled lengthwise down the middle and dried stiff as a board. The hides were brought in mostly by the mission Indians from San Gabriel in exchange for household commodities, personal ornaments, and farming tools; then used again by the firm in trade for ships' cargoes.

The front display room was a fascinating place, especially to curious Indians and ladies of the *gente de razón*.[2] Ships from San Blas, Mazatlán, and Acapulco brought them silk and cotton *rebozos*, cotton and woolen *sarapes,* pointed shoes, *panocha,* sugar, and rice. Boston cargoes mainly attracted housewives, bringing groceries, furniture, crockery, cutlery, cooking utensils, drygoods, and hardware. The most exotic articles came from China, the Sandwich and South Sea islands, and South America; but British cargoes were the most varied and most longed for.

From British ships' holds onto Hugo's counters came prints of brilliant fast colors, silk handkerchiefs, velveteen, brown fustian, cambric muslin and bishop's lawn, lace, cashmere shawls, silk stockings, cassimere, cassinet, *bayeta,* Irish linen, red and white flannel, new dress patterns—not more than two years old,—hats, boots and shoes, ready-made clothes, sewing supplies, tea trays, tea and coffee, spices, molasses, window glass, carpeting and nails, artificial flowers, perfumery, gold and silver lace, beads, bracelets, and earrings; even fine furniture and silver candlesticks. Sometimes the sailors had old newspapers and magazines which they were willing to part with, for a price. Spirits of all kinds were sold by the cask. Indeed, as Richard Dana once remarked, one found "everything from Chinese fireworks to English cartwheels" in a California *tienda* like that of Reid, Keith, and Leese.

Of course the Californians could have manufactured many of these articles themselves, had they so desired. The land was rich in natural resources; but the inhabitants lacked initiative and energy. For example, owing to favorable climatic and soil conditions, they were able to grow good grapes; yet it was the custom, for a long time, to buy expensive, inferior wine made in Boston and brought around the Horn, rather than to make their own *vino del país* in sufficient quantity.

The *paisanos* would often exchange bullock hides, valued at two dollars apiece, for objects costing less than a dollar in Boston. They bought clumsy shoes, made of their own hides carried to Boston and back again, for three or four dollars; and fancier "chicken-skin" boots with high heels for as much as fifteen dollars a pair. Articles sold in California cost about three hundred per cent more than like articles displayed in eastern stores. This was due partly to excessive duties imposed by the Mexican government and partly to the ruinous expense of the long sea voyage.

The necessity of heavy capital investment explains why more than two-thirds of all cargoes coming around the Horn during the 'twenties, 'thirties, and 'forties were carried by ships of the one wealthy house, Bryant, Sturgis, and Company, headquarters in Boston. Indeed, most Sandwich Islanders knew the entire United States by no other name than "Boston." It was on a vessel of this house, the *Pilgrim*, that Richard Henry Dana, Jr., spent his memorable "two years before the mast," sailing from Boston in '34, the year that Hugo Reid opened his Los Angeles *tienda*. Alfred Robinson, a lifelong friend of Reid and Stearns, who became famous as the author of *Life in California,* acted as the company's confidential agent on the coast for a period of years commencing in 1829.

Robinson and Dana both commented on the excessive cost of articles sold on the coast, but high prices never changed the Californians' attitude. They always preferred to let others accomplish the miracle of manufacture, being content to wait, and to pay, for the privilege of exclaiming over finished products, *"Qué hermosa! Qué útil!"*

One day in the fall of '34, a distinguished member of the *gente de razón*—an old woman wearing a black lace *mantilla*—came into Reid's store. This was Señora Eulalia Pérez y de Mariné, from San Gabriel, who wished to see the latest shipment and to make a few purchases.

Hugo had been in the warehouse, directing a stupid Indian in the stacking of smelly hides, and he welcomed an opportunity to wait on an interesting-looking customer. She spent a long time over lengths of drill and brown fustian, finally deciding to take a half-dozen spoons and a large platter. With the courteous manner that endeared him to women, old and young, Hugo offered to carry the package to a *carreta* awaiting her outside.

Sunshine, striking suddenly on Hugo's eyes, seemed unbearably bright for a moment. He had become so accustomed to a half light, from the one small window in the warehouse and the one other in the display room, that he could scarcely see before him. For a few seconds he followed, blinking after a blurred shape, out to the street. When his vision cleared, he was startled to see who was driving the oxcart for Doña Eulalia. Instead of the stolid Indian boy whom he subconsciously expected, an intelligent-looking young woman sat on the hard board seat, holding the reins in shapely brown hands.

She was beautiful, seeming rather tall and slender, and dressed like a Castilian lady of quality. A *mantilla* covered her glossy black hair and shadowed immense dark eyes. To Hugo they seemed full of sensibility—even sorrow. He stared at this lovely, unexpected apparition beyond the point of politeness, hardly hearing the introduction. Perhaps it was then that he first thought of her as his *rosa de Castilla,*[3] never dreaming—because of her olive complexion and air of real refinement—that she belonged to another, "inferior" race. Later he could remember only that her name was Victoria, and apparently she lived with Doña Eulalia at the Pérez place near the mission. Before the oxen lumbered off, he received an invitation from his customer, Doña Eulalia:

"*Venga,* take *cha* [tea] with us some afternoon, Señor Hugo Reid. A ride in the open air will do you good."

Hugo thought he heard a laughing remark about an owl blinking in the sunlight, as the ladies drove away.

The arrival of a new cargo at San Pedro delayed his little "ride in the open air" for a week or so. But finally one day Hugo found time to saddle up his mustang and set out over El Camino Real toward San Gabriel. The first part of the ride was as he remembered from attending Padre Sánchez' *merienda,* only two years earlier, but as he neared the mission a strange and terrible sight met his eyes. Stretched on the parched, brown plain were the bleaching bones of innumerable cattle, and over the mission buildings—the church itself, the neophyte dormitories, workshops, grana-

ries, and storehouses which formerly had resembled a bee-
hive in hum of activity—over the whole community hung
an indefinable air of desolation and life suspended. Hugo
wondered at the sad change, but reserved his questions for
Doña Eulalia. He had no difficulty in finding the Pérez
place, situated as it was on the edge of the extensive mission
garden and accessible to the mission itself.

Doña Eulalia had long served the padres in an official
capacity as *llavera* (housemother). Born in Loreto, Baja
California, she had come to Alta California with her first
husband, Antonio Guillen, in the service of the King of
Spain. They lived in San Diego until his appointment to the
garrison at San Gabriel—long before Hugo's day—when
Padre Zalvidea ruled that vast mission domain. At the time
of Doña Eulalia's arrival, the "old mission" was still in use,
although the permanent, "new" church was under construction. She could remember the new walls as being then about
three feet high.

It was the wise Padre Zalvidea who chose Doña Eulalia
as *llavera* because she showed an interest in the lowly Indians that was rarely to be found in a member of the *gente
de razón*. He entrusted her with all his keys and put her di-
rectly in charge of the girl neophytes. She proved indefatigable in her duties—nursing, scolding, advising—and won the
complete confidence of her charges. Occasionally, through
the years, she had taken a very promising Indian girl into
her home.

Before Zalvidea's tragic transfer to San Juan Capistrano,
he had used his influence to obtain a grant of land for Doña
Eulalia and "her heirs forever"—three and a half square

leagues of fertile land near the mission. It was called San Pascual, final receipt of the deed being signed at Eastertime by Eulalia's second husband, Juan de Mariné. Her grandsons stocked the *rancho* with cattle and built her the spacious *adobe* in which she spent a renowned old age. Here she was living, already believed by the *vecinos* (neighbors) to be more than a hundred years old, when Hugo came to tea.

Wooden gates with massive iron locks at first barred him out. He could see through the cracks that the one-story house was built around a patio and that a fountain played in the center. There were pepper trees for shade, covered with bright red berries, and a profusion of plants—geraniums and carnations, roses and cactus flowers—growing in terra-cotta pots made by the Indians for their beloved *llavera*. Hugo rattled the gates, eager to enter, and his impatience mounted as no one came. Finally a long wait was rewarded as he had not dared to hope; Doña Victoria herself answered his summons, seeming no less fascinating than he had thought to find her.

For a week past he had inquired of his infallible friend Pryor concerning who and what she was, and had learned that she was a pure-blooded Indian whose ancestors had been chieftains of great pride and independence before the padres "converted" them to a life of servitude. She herself was a superior person, as shown by the fact that everyone called her *Doña* Victoria. Pryor said that Indian women seldom were addressed so respectfully, *Doña* being a title reserved for ladies of the *gente de razón*. He knew no more about Victoria than that she had become a ward of Doña Eulalia's and lived at the Pérez place with several half-grown children who were hers by an early marriage. He did not even know her status at the moment, whether wife or widow.

Save for shining black braids, Doña Victoria did not resemble the squat and humble Indian women whom Hugo had seen in service at Pryor's home and similar establishments in the Pueblo. She possessed a quiet assurance of good birth and self-respect which hardship and sorrow could never take from her. Her carriage was proudly erect, and her speech the purest Castilian Spanish, acquired from long and close association with the family of a Spanish officer.

"Doña Eulalia is not receiving just now. It is the hour of her *siesta*."

Hugo answered that he had hoped as much and, indeed, that he had not come for the one purpose of seeing the old lady. Victoria smiled and asked him in—to wait until Doña Eulalia should wake from her nap. Instinctively these two, the Scot and the Indian of such dissimilar backgrounds, felt a sympathetic understanding of each other, besides a strong physical attraction.

Hugo opened the conversation with the thought uppermost in his mind. He asked her to explain the change he had noticed in the atmosphere of San Gabriel. Desolation seemed to extend even to the plain, where he had seen so many bones of slaughtered animals. Victoria answered with reserve, for she knew neither his religion nor his politics. But when Hugo mentioned having met and admired Padre Sánchez, on a previous visit to San Gabriel, this released her confidence. She told him sadly that the good padre had been dead a year and that everything went wrong without him.

The Padre Tomás Estenaga succeeded him, and "never has there been a purer priest in California . . . but he believes every word that is told him."[4]

Hugo's quick sympathy encouraged Victoria to explain more fully that San Gabriel, when Padre Tomás arrived, was "in a flourishing condition," still the Pride of the Missions. But within the year—Padre Sánchez died in the middle of January, 1833—a long-disputed law had been passed by the Mexican Congress, the far-reaching Secularization Act. The power of the Church was sharply curtailed, and only the spiritual guidance of their neophytes was left to the Franciscans. As the first step in secularization of church property, civil administrators, usually two in number, were placed in charge of temporal affairs at each mission. These laymen used their power, all too often, to enrich themselves, as the padres had never done—by the rule of their order, the Franciscans were forbidden to acquire personal possessions. When Padre Tomás heard of the despoliation of church property in Baja California and elsewhere, he became deeply discouraged and permitted the *vecinos* to enter the San Gabriel precincts and, themselves, to commence the "work of destruction." Undoubtedly his idea was that the *vecinos* and his own neophytes were more entitled to the spoils than strange administrators from Mexico City. Indeed, in its original form, the Secularization Act had provided that "each Indian was to receive his share of land, gardens, and stock."

Whatever his reasoning, Padre Tomás unprotestingly allowed many of the mission buildings to be unroofed and the lumber converted into firewood. Fat mission cattle were killed for hides and tallow, and their bones left to bleach upon the plain. Tools and utensils were disposed of, and goods "distributed in profusion among the neophytes." From the depths of his despair, Padre Tomás even gave the order that the vineyards should all be razed to the ground. But this the Indians refused to do.

Victoria ended her sad recital with the words:

"It did not require long to destroy what years took to establish. Destruction came as a thief in the night. The whites rejoiced at it. They required no encouragement, and seemed to think it would last forever. Even the mere spectators were gladdened at the sight, and many of them helped themselves to a sufficiency of calves to stock farms."

Hugo could see that the mere thought of recent developments in San Gabriel was distressing to his lovely friend, and in order to lift the depression from her spirit he launched into a half-humorous account of his own life, saying it seemed a remarkable coincidence that all his wandering had been started by a girl named Victoria, across the world in Cardross,⁵ and that now it might be ended by someone of the same name. They went a long way in the two hours that were allowed them before the appearance of Doña Eulalia and afternoon tea.

The sun was setting as Hugo started back toward the Pueblo. The memory of Victoria remaining indelibly within him was her slow smile. From her ancestors she had inherited a sphinxlike quality which formed a large part of her fascination. Hugo often returned to San Gabriel, drawn by a force stronger than himself.

In the small community where he was now a familiar figure, Reid's attraction toward the Indian could not long remain a secret. Men in the Pueblo who did not know Victoria merely shrugged their shoulders. The women, disturbed over losing such a welcome guest at their *bailes* (parties)—since Hugo was tall and handsome and musical—were heard to speak witheringly of "that squaw man." Of course this was only to each other and their own menfolk. Reid himself had a final reserve which they did not dare to assault.

Dr. William Keith was as perturbed and bitter as any of the women, because he loved Hugo and could not bear to see him throw his life away. He had a mental picture of his friend living sloppily on the outskirts of town with a thickening, stupid wife, the whole place overrun by unhappy little half-breeds. No words of Hugo's could persuade him of the difference between Victoria and most other women of her race. He never cared to accompany Reid to the mission, nor did he believe the young Scotchman's insistent protest that the relationship was platonic—that the Indian already had a husband to whom she was devoted, the father of her children.

During frequent visits to San Gabriel, where Hugo found peace and happiness such as he had not known since his childhood at home, he naturally learned a great deal about Doña Victoria. It was a sad story that he heard in snatches, and pieced together for himself.

Victoria's ancestors had been chieftains of the Gabrielenos, men of power and wealth. Before the Franciscans came, they had been feared by all the neighboring Indians, the Serranos, the Allikliks, the Fernandeños, even the fierce Juaneños. It may have been because they became overbearing that retribution at last fell upon them, when the white men occupied the land and reduced them all to permanent subservience.

The Spanish padres came to California to "convert" the Indians. Victoria told Hugo bitterly that this meant baptizing them, putting the fear of God into men who had feared nothing, and adding a knowledge of Hell completely lacking in the aboriginal religion. The padres, aided by soldiers from Spain who often went beyond authority in abuse of the proud red men and women, stripped them of tribal paint and tribal possessions, saying it was "for the good of their souls." Miraculously they succeeded in transforming the mightiest chieftains into humble, confused neophytes doomed to live, from then on, at the very bottom of the social scale.

Victoria herself had lived on the Comicrabit *ranchería*° with her own family until the fateful age of six. Then, as the custom was, she had been locked into the girls' *monjerio* (dormitory) at the mission, and brought up by the padres. At thirteen they considered her sufficiently mature for marriage and allowed her to choose a husband, supposedly from the boys' *monjerio*. Of course she knew nothing of men, having only seen and smiled from a distance at the Indian page boys who carried messages and served at meals, adolescents who were never permitted to speak with anyone of the opposite sex. Girls and boys lived in their separate quarters, literally little monks and nuns.

While the other marriageable girls were choosing good-looking youths—occasionally being forced to draw lots, as when a fascinating *vaquero* named Caschuco was selected by ten young women simultaneously—Victoria listened to the whispered advice of Doña Eulalia. So, when her turn came, she shyly asked to marry, not one of the handsome young men, but rather one of their elders, Pablo María, of the Yutucubit *ranchería,* an Indian of lineage as ancient as her own, and of respected position in the community.

Victoria found kindness and security in her husband, a man twenty-eight years older than herself. Soon they had three children, whom they named Felipe, José Dolores, and María Ygnacia de Jesús. Felipe, the oldest, had been born in 1822, when his mother was only fourteen years old. During the years in the *monjerio,* Doña Eulalia had become attached to Victoria, and she permitted the whole family to live at San Pascual. Pablo relieved the old lady of many responsibilities, and Doña Eulalia derived great pleasure, in unfamiliar leisure, from the companionship of Victoria and her healthy, attractive children.

During the flowering of his friendship with the Indian woman, Hugo fell into hot water politically. He was accused of complicity in a revolution against Don José Figueroa, then governor of California. Probably he would never have been suspected had he not come so recently from Hermosillo. Historians refer to this incident as the Apalátegui Revolt, and it is typical of a number of abortive "revolutions" through which the Californians protested against the lax rule of Mexican governors.

Early in the morning of March 7, 1835, Juan Gallardo, a cobbler, and Felipe Castillo, a cigarmaker, assembled and armed some fifty Sonorans at Los Nietos, not far from the Pueblo. For reasons best known to themselves they were planning a revolution. The first step was to approach the *ayuntamiento* (city council) and get the keys to the city hall, by force if necessary. After a great deal of haranguing, the revolutionaries started out, stopping along the way for arms and provisions at the houses of several "foreigners." Both Hugo Reid and Dr. Keith happened to be among those honored, and along with the fact that Hermosillo, the capital of Sonora, so recently had been their home, this laid them open to the charge of being traitors to the Mexican government.

The Sonorans unlocked the city hall, having met no resistance at the *ayuntamiento,* and summoned the *alcalde,* Francisco Alvarado. They gave him orders to call a general meeting of all Los Angeles citizens in the Plaza. Gallardo, the cobbler, submitted a letter of grievances to the assembled multitude. It seemed that his chief grievance was Governor Figueroa, whose removal from office he respectfully requested "to save California from the evils which she had suffered and is suffering."

Brave members of the *ayuntamiento* decided that as he had no substitute for governor and they had no authority to remove Figueroa, they must formally disapprove the revolution. For several days the disappointed rebels did nothing, but lingered ominously in Los Angeles, refusing to go back across the river. Don Pío Pico, who was on the spot, asserted that they were waiting for money which *somebody* had promised them. At length, however, they grew tired of delay and surrendered Antonio Apalátegui and Francisco Torres, acknowledged instigators of the revolt. These men were thrown into jail. A few others like Reid and Keith, charged with complicity in a plot which they never fully understood, were heavily fined. But a little while later everyone was pardoned by Figueroa, who now could afford to be magnanimous.

Reid's troubles did not end with the Apalátegui Revolt. His store was doing badly, the chief cause being the incurably quarrelsome nature of Jacob Leese.[7] It became necessary to liquidate stock and dissolve the firm of Reid, Keith, and Leese less than a year after the revolt.

This was a keen disappointment to Hugo, who had expected to make a fortune out of the partnership, at least enough to buy land and become a *hacendado*—an ambition which he shared with Don Abel. But the canny New Englander had already laid the foundations for a future land empire. In '34 Stearns had bought a large lot in Los Angeles, on which he intended one day to build a *palacio;* and at the same time he had acquired property in San Pedro, including the site of that *adobe* warehouse which had aroused Hugo's curiosity on his first visit to California. The census taker of '36 found Reid living at San Pedro, assisting Don Abel with certain improvements of the "harbor" property.

In April of the same year, Hugo yielded to the persuasion of his friend William Keith that they should return on a visit to Hermosillo. The doctor was anxious to get him out of California, having worried incessantly of late over Hugo's intense attachment to the Indian woman. A temporary absence, he felt, would restore his friend's shattered perspective.

Don Abel, who had lived in the Pueblo since '33, acting as the Los Angeles partner of Don Juan Bandini, received a letter from Hugo Reid, dated "Hermosillo, 26 de Julio,

1836." No stamp or envelope was needed. Hugo had merely folded the notepaper and addressed it on the outside:

Al Señor
D. Abel Stearns
Síndico & Cía
Pueblo

My Dear Sir,

We arrived here after a pleasant journey on the 12 May, having been detained two weeks in San José and stopped a considerable time in the Altar to allow the doctor a little *descanso* [rest]. . . .

There has been hot work going on between the Republic and Texas; from the superiority of the Mexicans in number they were at the first always victorious, Santa Ana[8] at their head—he was called the omnipotent second Napoleon—but alas, Mr. Stearns, his fame has vanished; 412 Americans were by him put into a corral and shot, being rebels. It was his downfall; the United States troops which were on the line deserted and joined the Texonians, and every day brought them stragglers from New Orleans. The last battle was fought on Red River, and the Mexican army was "used up," Santa Ana, yes, the omnipotent Santa Ana and all his officers made prisoners. Uncle Sam for more security keeps him on board of a steamboat. When Santa Ana's *desgracias* were made known in the capital, you may easily imagine it made a stir among the people. They raged like grasshoppers and were determined to eat them up, stump and root.

Government has passed a decree for a forced loan of $2,000,000 to carry on the war, while Santa Ana had made a treaty with the Republic of Texas which will not be acknowledged in Mexico. By Santa Ana's treaty Mexico is to declare Texas a free and independent republic, grant it the territory of California, change the form of government to federalism *to please it,* and several other desperates.

General Houston, commander-in-chief of the Texas forces, was wounded in the leg and had gone to New Orleans to get cured.

Santa Ana has made him a present of his saddle and a gold-headed cane. He is not yet at liberty. I believe there are two commissioners gone from the new to the old republic to treat, but from all accounts they had better stop at home. The affair has nearly been breeding a war with the United States, and *quién sabe todavía*.

Dr. Keith is well. Forster and he are doing a little to see if by January or February at farthest he may be master of two or three hundred dollars so as to buy a small *ancheta* of nick-nacks to take to California; he is now in Guaymas or I am certain he would write.

Finding everything so dull here in the line of business, I saw nothing else to do but hang myself. At last my friends told me if I liked to open an establishment for teaching boys, they would support me. I have done so, *enseñando* English, a language they are fond of, arithmetic, writing, and geography, and at present have a salary of about four dollars, three meals per diem, but after *Agual* I shall have more. Therefore you have me now a sober, steady young man occupied from six in the morning until eight at night with a large house at your disposition, should you ever come this way, as I am certain you would honor me with your company before a stranger.

The King of France has been assassinated. . . . I forgot to mention that Mexico is raising an army of 20,000 men. I see it mentioned in the Mexican papers that some disturbances have occurred in California. Please give me the particulars. . . .

I shall have great pleasure in giving you any information you may require from this part of the world, and anything you may want executed shall be done to the best of my ability.

I have, since here, translated some of the most fashionable songs from English into Spanish, one of them *Home Sweet Home,*[9] so that my translations are now *all the go*.

If Silvestro Portillo owes you any money, you had better send on powers before he squanders away all he has, as I am pretty certain he never intends returning to California. This I tell you in *confianza*.

I shall give you more news on some other occasion. Remember
me kindly to Pryor and all friends, and believe, my dear sir,

Yours ever truly,

Hugo Reid.

Hugo taught school at Hermosillo for a little over a year,
with great success. Indeed he thought he would never return to California, where three distressing experiences had
been his lot in as many years—involuntary implication in
the Apalátegui Revolt, resulting in the payment of a heavy
fine; the failure of the Reid, Keith, and Leese company; and
falling in love with a married woman who was, besides, an
Indian and a Catholic. Distance clarified his vision, as Dr.
Keith had foreseen, and he realized, only too clearly, that his
feeling transcended friendship. He longed to see Victoria—
she lingered in the background of his thoughts and disturbed his rest; yet he knew that no happiness could be
found in return to San Gabriel.

Close on Hugo's decision to remain "a sober, steady young
man occupied from six in the morning until eight at night"
came the news from California that changed the whole
course of his life. Letters from friends must have informed
him, almost simultaneously, of the birth of another child
to Victoria,[10] and of the death of her Indian husband from
smallpox.

The visualization of Victoria's distress undoubtedly
warred, in Hugo's mind, with the realization that she would
regard him as a business failure, in no position to support a
wife and four children, should he return to San Gabriel and
ask her to marry him. It could only have been after a painful
struggle within himself that Hugo resigned his position of

schoolmaster, telling his Sonoran friends that he planned a
fresh start in the business life of Los Angeles.

Keith tried hard to dissuade him, suspecting more than
he was told of Hugo's object in returning to California. To
no avail. Hugo left Hermosillo without even waiting for the
doctor to complete his *ancheta,* and only a short time later
Keith received an urgent summons to hurry north. Hugo
wanted him to "stand up" at his wedding—to the Indian
woman. It was only with the hope of changing Reid's mind
at the last moment that his best friend sadly went aboard the
next northbound vessel.

CHAPTER THREE

The Festal Wedding

CUSTOM required that Hugo Reid should not marry Doña Victoria without becoming a Catholic. It was also necessary for him to produce four character witnesses who had known him for a long time; and to aid in the composition of an exhaustive "marriage investigation." First, he presented to the "superior political chief," Governor Juan Alvarado, the following, which is translated and in which he used the Spanish name "Perfecto" acquired in addition to his own "Hugo" at the time of his recent baptism:[1]

Perfecto Hugo Reid, native of Great Britain, Roman Catholic, resident of the City of Our Lady of the Angels, appears before your Lordship in the best legal manner to state: that during the term of three years he has lived in the above-mentioned city, engaged in business, *et cetera,* has benefited society in every way possible, and finding himself ready to enter into the state of matrimony with a native daughter of this country, respectfully requests and entreats your permission to contract this marriage.

Wherefore, I appeal to your justice to grant me this privilege. I assure you I intend no slight to your Lordship's dignity in submitting this petition on common paper, there not being any with the corresponding seal available in this city.

PERFECTO HUGO REID.

City of Los Angeles.
August 6, 1837.

Then he advised "the Reverend Father Fray Tomás Eleuterio de Estenaga, Clergyman in the former Mission of San Gabriel Archangel," that:

Perfecto Hugo Reid, native of Great Britain, legitimate son of Charles Reid and Essex Milchin, natives of Scotland in the County of Renfrew, resident of Our Lady of the Angels, before your Reverence, hereby makes known his intention to marry [Victoria] Bartolomea² Comicrabit, a neophyte of this mission.

I entreat your Reverence to order that the customary steps be taken to carry this out. I swear and promise, *et cetera*.

Mission of San Gabriel.   PERFECTO HUGO REID.
July 30, 1837.

Fray Tomás produced two witnesses: Santiago Suñer, native of Mallorca, and Nicolás Díaz, native of the city of Durango. Hugo's taking of the oath was recorded by the priest and incorporated in the "investigation":

Immediately after, there appeared at my request the above-mentioned Perfecto Hugo Reid, who took the oath, in the name of Our Lord and the Holy Cross, to answer truthfully all questions put to him, in the presence of assisting witnesses.

1. Question: What is your name, your parents' names, your age, and present condition. He answered that his name was Perfecto Hugo Reid, legitimate son of Charles Reid and Essex Milchin, natives of Scotland, Renfrew County, resident of Our Lady of the Angels; his age, 27 years old, single.

2. Question: If he is pledged to marry any other woman than the above-mentioned Bartolomea. He answered, no.

3. Question: Whether any force is being exerted on him to marry. He answered, no.

4. Question: If he is a blood relation of the above[-mentioned Bartolomea] or connected with her by affinity or some other spiritual bond. He answered, no.

5. Question: If he has taken a vow of chastity, of a religious or any other nature, and if there exist any other obstacles. He answered, no.

The foregoing having been read by him and confirmed by him, he signed together with me, that it be recorded, as well as of the assisting witnesses, the second placing his mark, not knowing how to write.

PERFECTO HUGO REID.   Fr[ay] TOMÁS ESTENAGA.
SANTIAGO SUÑER.   NICOLÁS DÍAZ.

Immediately afterward, there appeared as first witness, to attest the freedom and condition of singleness of the above mentioned, Santiago Dove, native of London and resident of the City of Los Angeles, who took oath in the name of Our Lord and the Holy Cross to answer truthfully, *et cetera.*

1. Question: If he knows Perfecto Hugo Reid and for how long. He answered that he has known him since 1831.

Dove was required to answer five more questions, substantiating the information that Reid had already given under oath. The three other character witnesses, all chosen by Don Perfecto himself, were Julian Pope, Joaquín Bowman, and Diego (James) Scott, former supercargo on the *Ayacucho.* Pope had known him longest—seven years.[3]

Victoria's age was given as twenty-nine, and her parents' names as Bartolomé and Petra, of the Comicrabit *ranchería,* adjacent to the Pueblo. She was described as the widow of the Indian, Pablo María "de Yutucubit, Partida 512," by whom she had had four children.[4]

The entire deposition was sent first to the highest secular authority in California, the governor; then to the "ecclesiastical judge of Alta California," Padre Narciso Durán.[5] Their necessary permissions for the marriage to take place were appended to the manuscript.

1. Santa Barbara, August 12, 1837. The author of this petition is hereby permitted to marry a native daughter of this country, as he wishes, to which end this decree will serve as a license for so doing.   ALVARADO.

2. Mission of San Fernando, August 20, 1837. Having examined the preceding marriage investigation and in spite of the fact that the attestation by the witnesses, of the bachelorhood of Perfecto Hugo Reid, is a guarantee covering only a few years, I grant the permission for the marriage *servatis servandis.*

Fr[ay] NARCISO DURÁN.
Ecclesiastical Judge of Alta California.

After Durán's permission for the alliance had been obtained, the banns had to be published on three successive feast days. During this period, Victoria and Doña Eulalia busied themselves with preparations for the wedding: fashioning the dress, trousseau, and household linen, and planning the customary *fiesta.* The date was set for the week of *la luna de la cosecha,* the harvest moon of September. A morning service in the mission would start a round of gaiety to which all San Gabriel and many out-of-town guests would be invited.

Few invitations were refused. Everyone loved and respected Doña Eulalia, and regardless of disapproval, in certain quarters, of the romance between Don Perfecto and Doña Victoria, no one wanted to miss a *fiesta* at the Pérez place, or the pageant of a *paisano's* wedding.[6]

Thick *adobe* walls stemmed a flood of morning sunshine, welcoming the wedding day; but it filtered in through the narrow, iron-barred windows of the mission, quickening to life and color all that it touched. Many eyes followed its shining path, along a crudely illuminated wall and across the bowed heads of the wedding guests. It stopped, sparkling, over a silver plate resting on the altar rail. From this plate the padre took two rings, blessed them, and slipped them on the wedding fingers of the *novios*. Then over the shoulders of the kneeling pair he threw a scarf, yoking them in eternal matrimony. Heads drooped deeper in prayer, till lifted by a welcome *"Dominus vobiscum"* and the minor notes of a hymn. Indian choirboys marched down the aisle, singing and playing stringed instruments. Padre Tomás followed after them, with the rest of his "children."

In the patio a *carreta* was waiting, scrubbed and garlanded. How thankfully the bride saw it; for Doña Victoria was exhausted from long hours spent in the mission, confessing and praying for happiness in her strange marriage. Everybody lingered awhile in the patio, and friends crowded around the bride and bridegroom with their *"Saludos," "Viva mil años,"* and "God follow you." Then all San Gabriel started toward the Pérez place, where a wedding feast awaited them.

It was a colorful, noisy cavalcade. Liberated choirboys led the way, with flute, violin, triangle, and drum, singing their own ribald songs more spiritedly than ever they sang the padres' hymns. After the Indians in their gaudiest blankets, came the bridal *carreta* drawn by two white oxen; then another garlanded cart containing Doña Eulalia and Padre Tomás Estenaga, who had changed the gorgeous vestments worn to conduct the church ceremonies, for the coarse and drab Franciscan robes. After these followed relatives and friends on horseback; and more *carretas* filled with women whose splendor of attire, age, or avoirdupois interfered with

mounting a horse. Brilliant sunshine emphasized the sheen
in blue-black hair and the colors in embroidered flowers on
dresses and shawls, although it wilted the real flowers that
most of the women wore. Trailing the procession were many
Indians afoot and childishly happy over a *fiesta*.

The most dashing *caballeros* had caught up maidens to
ride before them on their prancing steeds. The dun-colored
habits and tiny-brimmed "sugar-loaf" hats of the equestri-
ennes were foils for the gay velvet suits of the men. Metallic
embroidery sparkled on their jackets; brilliant sashes en-
circled their waists, and twisted silver, their *sombreros*.
Trousers were fitted skin tight above the knee, widening
below and laced with gold cord. Or else knee breeches were
worn, with deerskin *botas* wrapped around the leg and fastened by a long-tasseled garter. Red was insistent in the mas-
culine array; black, blue, green, and yellow, too.

But the bride outshone them all. White lace cascaded
down from her high Spanish comb to little white slippers,
for she wore a *mantilla* that dissolved in the lace of her dress.
Pearls were her jewels, and her flowers, white Castilian roses.
This slender Indian and her tall, blue-eyed Scot were the
magnetic center of attraction.

Though Doña Eulalia lived near the mission, everyone
took the long way round. The wedding procession moved
so slowly that it was more than an hour on the road. Horses,
impatient at the pace of oxen, plunged and danced, showing their fine leather saddles, intricately carved and silver
adorned; their stirrups, ending in *tapaderas* that reached
to the ground; and beautiful, cruel-bitted bridles, clanking
and jangling. Californians usually displayed their silver on

horses, rather than on sideboards. The whole cavalcade reflected wealth and freedom from care, but there were holes in the gayest Indian blankets, and some *caballeros* wore or rode their entire fortunes.

The Pérez place soon overflowed with the arriving throng. At one o'clock, Indian girls from the *monjerio* began to serve everyone with hot Spanish dishes and San Gabriel wine and fruit. A long refectory table had been set up in the patio for the most intimate friends. Doña Eulalia honored the bridal pair by seating herself next to the bridegroom, and Padre Tomás on the bride's right hand. Toasts and compliments launched the delicious, three-hour meal.

By the time the last *dulce* had been eaten, and the last glass of *vino del país* had been drained by appreciative guests, everyone was ready for a nap. The bride was the first to excuse herself, since she must dance the whole night through. Others followed her gladly for a *siesta* out of the sun. A few young people danced, rather desultorily, but the real festivities were to commence that evening.

A hundred years ago, people came punctually to parties. The sun had scarcely disappeared when the first company came. Their hostess broke the awkwardness of early arrival by requesting the musicians, two violins and a guitar, to tune up and two pleased young *paisanos* to start *el jarabe*.

Crowded rooms would have been intolerable on a warm September evening, and Doña Eulalia expected the town; so she had ordered a pavilion out of doors for dancing. It was simply made, of boughs from the river willows and rough cloth, and enclosed on only three sides and decorated with artificial flowers and colored ribbons. The musicians played in a corner while the impromptu entertainers moved out on the floor facing each other and keeping time to the music by a monotonous heel-and-toe drumming. The *señorita* remained always erect, her head tilted a little toward the right. Lowering her eyes with unconvincing modesty, she lifted her skirt to show twinkling feet. Her partner rattled his with extraordinary agility. His arms, crossed carelessly at his back, kept the *sarape* down, and not once did he upset his *sombrero*. Just as *el jarabe* was growing tiresome, they edged off the floor.

Before the girl had stopped tapping her pretty foot, a man came up behind her and clapped his hat on her head, singing a song in several verses; declaring that he would feel like a king who had crowned his queen, if she should accept his *sombrero*. Though it disturbed her comb and roses, the dancer laughed and left it on, indicating that she preferred this humble hat to a golden crown. The new cavalier must give her a present to retrieve it; he had shown by his act that he admired her intensely.

By now, people were lining the walls and crowding in on the dance floor. Some of the men stayed on their horses, to see over the crowd. It was time for general participation. The band played a waltz, then an intricate *contradanza,* and again a waltz. Doña Eulalia encouraged her humbler guests to mingle with the others; and threw down doubloons from time to time, for laughing neophytes to scramble for.

A more lively tune, and Don Juan Bandini, *el tecolero* (master of ceremonies) for the evening, approached a young lady to dance *la bamba*. Clapping his hands with the music, he brought her to the center of the room, made her step into a silken hobble, and balanced a full glass of water on her head. Always tapping the floor with her feet, she must raise the hobble to her knees and lower it again, without spilling the water. Miraculously successful, she gave two or three whirls besides. As she left the floor, she was showered with coins, and received also the crowning compliment of having her smiles extinguished under a man's *sombrero*.

Doña Eulalia asked Don Juan himself, a slight and darkly handsome man of thirty-seven, to choose a partner and waltz; having introduced this dance to California, six years before, he had become its ablest exponent.

Then there were more general dances, some peculiar to San Gabriel and others popular in all Alta California and Mexico: several *jarabes, la jota, los camotes,* and *el borrego,* which was danced by a couple impersonating a bull and his tormentor, with much waving of handkerchiefs and reversal of rôles. *El burro* provoked the most mirth of all, for as many men as women grabbed hands to make a circle. Another man or woman went inside the circle. When the music commenced, they danced around the odd one while two or three verses were sung. Then at a signal everyone kissed someone else, and the slowest one was *el burro* (the donkey), who must take a turn in the center.

Many of the dances had accompanying verses. So there was as much singing as dancing, by the middle of the evening. Hugo's fame as a song writer and translator had preceded him from Hermosillo. The company called on him again and again.

Between dances the ladies clustered together and were handed refreshments, while their partners went outside to smoke and talk, or back into the house where a table was prepared for them. A good deal of *aguardiente* was drunk, and at dawn the place was still crowded. The bridal couple had not left. They must dance this whole night and several more, for restful "honeymoons" were unheard of. It amused the *paisanos* to see them sleepy and impatient.

Doña Eulalia stole up behind Hugo, whom she now called her dear *yerno* (son-in-law). Crying *"Cascarones! Cascarones!"* she broke an egg over his head. Little pieces of gold and silver confetti showered down all over his face and clothes. It was the signal for pandemonium. The wedding guests had prepared *cascarones* and were ready, some with eggshells blown out and filled with confetti like Doña Eulalia's, and others with scented water or cologne. Friends became mock enemies, and soon the whole place was spangled and drenched. Enough damage done, a bedraggled lot took leave of Doña Eulalia, Don Hugo, and Doña Victoria— politely saying *"Hasta la vista"* and *"Viva usted mil años"* ("Till we meet again" and "May you live a thousand years").

The *caballeros* went gallantly home with their ladies, singing tender lyrics to the disappearing moon. This done, they changed character and rode into the streets, shouting ribald verses and joining in *la misa del gallo* (the Mass of the Rooster), heard at dawn. A few hilariously rushed out into the fields to *colear* (lasso by the tail) the drowsy cattle. The sun peered out in horror! When at last there was silence, the community slept a few hours till roused by the mission bells, tolling a summons to a noonday feast being given by Padre Tomás for the bride. Business was suspended in San Gabriel, and merrymaking went on for a week.

CHAPTER FOUR

The Indian Wife

As soon as San Gabriel quieted down after the wedding *fiesta,* Don Hugo commenced to build a home for his bride. While the work progressed, they lived on with Doña Eulalia. Since the old lady's position was unassailable, staying under her roof set the seal of respectability on a union which had caused a great deal of gossip. Reid's friends in far places may have continued to think of him as a "squaw man," traveling the road toward degradation, but in the vicinity of San Gabriel no doors were closed against the bridal couple. Even in the Pueblo all resentment, down to the deepest that lay buried under smooth Castilian courtesy, gradually subsided, leaving scarcely a trace.

Indeed, it soon became apparent that the Scotchman had benefited by the marriage, in more ways than one. Not only was Doña Victoria a delightful person, admired by all who knew her; but more, she brought her new husband a substantial dowry of land. Largely through the efforts of Doña Eulalia, she won back a portion of her heritage, becoming one of the few members of her race ever to hold land in Alta California under a Mexican grant. At this time she claimed title to two *ranchos,* the large and beautiful Santa Anita and La Huerta del Cuati, later known as Lake Vineyard.[1] Through his marriage to the Indian woman, Hugo Reid, so long a homeless wanderer, was able to realize his dream of becoming a *hacendado*—a man of property and enviable position in the community. Although neither of Doña Victoria's *ranchos* had been much developed, they yielded nonetheless an appreciable income from cattle, a few sheep, grapevines, and some "short crops kept by the Indians."

For the time being, Don Hugo decided to remain the absentee landlord of his wife's property, preferring the sociability of life in a community to isolation in the country. He acquired several acres in the vicinity of the mission as a site for their home. Later on, he intended to build a house at Santa Anita for his convenience when he should have to attend closely to the seasonal activities of ranching, such as *la siembra* (sowing) and *la cosecha* (harvesting).

The San Gabriel place, Hugo called Uva Espina (Gooseberry). He had ideas of his own and did not hesitate to depart from the conventional plan of a rambling, one-story building. He set Indians to work making *adobe* bricks and mixing mortar; but the Reid home was to be out of the ordinary: it would have two stories, topped by an attic, and the *adobe* construction would be strengthened by the use of clapboards and beams hauled all the way from the forests of the San Bernardino Mountains.

Since '33, Don Abel Stearns had been operating a *tienda* in Los Angeles in partnership with Don Juan Bandini. It was to Don Abel that Reid sent frequent orders for building materials and household supplies impossible to procure in San Gabriel. His account was carried in the Stearns-Bandini books, and a settlement made at intervals, partly in cash and partly in produce.

Hugo wrote and spoke Spanish as idiomatically as English. Even to Don Abel, the former Yankee, he lapsed frequently into Spanish. A typical *carta de orden,* written while Uva Espina was under construction, reads, in translation:

Uva Espina.
8 de Sept^{bre} 1838.

Mi estimado Amigo,

The boards turned out to be perfect, both in their number and in length, for which I thank you, and I feel very grateful to you for the favors which you are constantly doing me.

Besides the dollar I sent you yesterday, I enclose another so that you may send me its value in nails of two and a half inches. They are to be used for doors—you will know best.

You may send what I have just asked you for, with the bearer.

And will oblige,

PERFECTO HUGO REID.

Presently the day came when Uva Espina was completed, and the Reid family could move in. But to Hugo's dismay he found that his wife lived in daily fear of earthquakes. As a tiny child she had been terror stricken by the great earthquake which was felt from San Diego to Santa Bárbara, on December 14, 1812. Many smaller shocks had followed the first terrific one. Lives were lost, and buildings shaken down. The great bell tower at San Gabriel Mission fell like a playhouse of cards, striking terror into a child's soul. Victoria's family had told her that earthquakes were caused by the restless stirring of seven giants who held the world on their shoulders. Since then there had been other serious shocks and minor ones, so that her terror always remained intense. She absolutely refused to set foot on the stairs of the new house and said that she must live on the ground floor. A living room had to be redone into a bedroom for her and Hugo. The children and guests, who did not share her fear, would sleep upstairs.

Separation from her children had seemed unbearable to Doña Victoria, since it would mean committing them to a hard life in the mission *monjerio,* like her own unhappy childhood. With ready sympathy, Reid agreed to take the little Indians as his own—even to give them his name—and he grew very fond of them all. Felipe, the eldest, was a strong, handsome boy of fifteen, olive tinted like his mother and precociously showing the tastes of a gentleman in horses, cockfighting, and dress. Two years behind him followed José Dolores, seeming always the shadow of his brother. At nine, dark-eyed little María Ygnacia already promised unusual charm. Besides being pretty, she had an affectionate nature, and delighted in caring for the baby "Carlitos," still in the cooing stage.

Doña Victoria had many servants in Hugo's house, among them, Chona, the best washerwoman in San Gabriel, who would never wear shoes; Juan Juncas, the centenarian, who said he could remember when *la señora's* grandfather was the greatest chieftain in Alta California; and ugly little Pinacate, the Black Beetle, who played his flute and worked for the family, equally cheerfully, till he took too much *aguardiente* too many times and died a dreadful, drunkard's death.

Most of the servants assumed that they would stay with the Reids all their lives, working without wages. They lived in *jacales,* dome-shaped brush shelters erected on the willow-lined bank of El Río de los Temblores, as they all called the San Gabriel River. The young ones married and had children. The very old ones sat in the sun. None of them worked too hard, and Doña Victoria did for them what Doña Eulalia so long had done for the mission Indians; she fed, clothed, nursed, advised, and scolded them. It was a kindly, respectful relationship.

Living near the mission bells, the Reids obeyed the summons in their daily schedule. At daybreak came *desayuno,* of chocolate and bread. Doña Victoria taught her Indians to make bread out of wheat and corn, both grown on the place and made into flour at Bowman's mill. She flattened the dough, and cut it in circular shapes which she baked in fat over a slow fire, on a flat earthen pan, and called *tortillas de harina* or *de maíz.* While the Indians went to morning Mass, the family dressed at leisure and ate *almuerzo,* or breakfast, between half-past eight and nine o'clock. Dinner came at noon, a large meal served in several courses, with wine made by Hugo from Santa Anita grapes.

Toward sunset the women in the community would gather for *cha,* or tea; and the men, for a small glass of liqueur. No bells announced this social hour, the most delightful of the whole day. A light *cena* (supper) was served after dark, when the Indians came home from work in the fields, and then the whole household went to evening prayers at the mission, to a great tolling of bells. Later there might be music, Felipe and his father singing to a guitar perhaps, but no one stayed up very late except for a *fiesta.*

Doña Eulalia had given Victoria thorough training as a housekeeper; and the Indian wife embroidered and sewed until her linens were the finest in San Gabriel. Taking pride

in the legends of her people, she would sometimes depict
Indian symbols with incredibly fine beadwork, as decora-
tion on a dress, or the edging of a linen tablecover.

Soon after the wedding, two old friends of Hugo's came
to San Gabriel on business. Of course he asked them to stay
at his home. At first they demurred, imagining that Reid,
as a "squaw man," must live in a squalid *jacal*. But when they
finally consented, it was with astonishment that they found
him and Doña Victoria "living very happily together"; and
were "surprised and delighted with the excellence and neatness of the housekeeping of the Indian wife, which could
not have been excelled. The beds which were furnished us
to sleep upon were exquisitely neat, with coverlids of satin,
the sheets and pillow cases trimmed with lace and highly
ornamented."

Such praise from these visitors dispelled any lingering il-
lusions about Don Perfecto's married life, because both were
influential men. One of them, William Heath Davis, went
on to generalize that "the Indian women of California are
far better stock than those of Mexico, which accounts in a
measure for their finer children";[2] and that they "are sus-
ceptible of being trained and educated as keepers of homes.
There are similar instances of this kind with other Indian
wives I could mention, who had been tutored and reared by
Castilian [foster] mothers, who have left the seed of purity
for others to sow."

Davis' respectful attitude toward other members of her
race was gratifying to Doña Victoria. She herself always
commanded respect, but how often had she flinched at
thoughtless remarks about her people!

Among the prejudiced ones was Davis' companion, a Scotchman named James McKinley. Hugo admitted that "Jim and the Indians can't agree," but he enjoyed the visit because of mutual business interests and the fact that he and "Jim" came from the same village, Cardross in Renfrewshire. They both had attended the country school strictly kept by the Presbyterian minister, a friend of Hugo's father. To be sure, McKinley had run away from home at the tender age of eleven, to be cabin boy on a whaler; but he could remember making purchases in the shop owned by Hugo's father, and playing many times with Hugo himself in the shadow of Cardross Castle, a gray stone pile heaped high on a hill, where Robert Bruce had crept home to die, and Robert Burns had composed many a famous poem. The sharing of tradition and childhood memories seemed almost miraculous to both *paisanos*—so many years and so many miles from the Old Country.

After so fine a time, McKinley always planned to spend a few days with the Reids whenever he came south. Being the representative of Thomas O. Larkin's[3] interests in southern California, he made frequent trips. His admiration for Victoria as an individual increased with each visit, although their points of view remained diametrically opposed.

Hugo could find no fault with the way his house was run; so he turned his attention to another matter—the education of his wife and adopted children. Doña Victoria had learned to speak correctly and fluently in Spanish from Doña Eulalia, but no one had ever taught her to read and write. She was not anxious to learn, for she saw so much that interested her in housekeeping, in human relationships, and in nature, that there was no time to spare on mechanics of the primer. Besides, they bored her, and when the necessary housework was done, she wanted to be out of doors. Hugo contented himself with showing her how to form letters, to write and recognize them, without enforcing daily practice. With the children he resolved to start earlier and do more.

Schools were a farce in Old California. They had been started as far back as 1795, but had never flourished. The general attitude was one of indifference to them. Scholarship came low on the list of social requirements. In 1833, William Hartnell made an attempt at founding a select academy for boys in Monterey, but it lasted only a few years. Some men sent their sons to Boston or to Mexico City for an education, while the girls were left to learn what they could at home, from mothers who usually could neither read nor write.

At one time, several of Hugo's friends decided that a missionary school in the Sandwich Islands was the best place for their boys, and packed them off across the wide Pacific. In a little while the fathers received homesick letters, asking for horses and equipment as consolation for exile. The first Sunday after the horses reached them, the boys went out to amuse themselves. No cattle being at hand, they lassoed and nearly killed three Kanakas. They were arrested and put in jail, and the Mexican consul had to bail them out.

Hugo considered foreign schools inadvisable for a boy and impossible for a girl. The San Gabriel school existed for only three months of the year, the summer ones, and then in a mustard patch under a *tule*-roofed *ramada*. So he decided to teach the children himself, having had experience in Hermosillo.

There were daily lessons in French, English, Spanish, arithmetic, and geography. Hugo took keen pleasure in them,
for he was a good linguist, an excellent accountant, owing
to thorough training in his father's store; and the geography
lessons were little more than thrilling reviews of his own
adventures. They were an outlet for the wanderlust that had
been stemmed by marriage. Felipe and José Dolores and
even María Ygnacia listened, big eyed, and went at their
studies with fervor.

Hugo made them see the romance, the sesamic quality of
education, overlooking the necessary drudgery. He took
them up to the dusty twilight of the attic, where their
mother would never go, and showed them piles of books
and magazines. He told them that these contained more
thrilling adventures than one man could ever experience,
and more sublime thoughts. But the children knew that first
they must learn the hard words in their textbooks.

Doña Victoria used all her ingenuity to find distractions
for the young ones, for she feared that too close indoor application would ruin their health. Certainly her husband's
was impaired; possibly by early exposure to the hardships
of a sailor's life, although she considered it more probably
due to his scholarly habits. Recently he had developed what
threatened to be a chronic "complaint of the chest." It caused
him frequently to postpone trips into town and immediate
chores. *Mañana,* always *mañana,* he would perform these
uncongenial tasks. A slight rainfall might put him to bed
for a week with a cold; and the heat of the San Gabriel sun,
if he worked more than a few hours in the fields, would
bring on prostration.

Undoubtedly Hugo's inclination was toward a gentle-
manly life of leisure and reflection. A casual, typical note to
Don Abel, written in October, 1838, explained why he did
not show up for a business appointment in the Pueblo:

My dear Sir,

Ink, paper, and health are scarce commodities at the Uva Espina *por ahora*. The ink was taken from the mill pond fresh this
morning, being composed of three parts of water, two of mud,
and one of tadpoles well ground. I am glad to hear you are
"back" again; I would come in to see you but am convalescent at
present, having been *tapado⁴ otra vez,* a total, not a parcial eclipse.

Let me know what (k)news [*sic*] and what satisfaction the
northern gents gave you.

If you bring my papers, you may confide them to the bearer
who is Mr. Bowman's secretary, a goodly person, for being black,
he will keep everything dark.

Yours ever truly,
REID.

P.D. I think by Saturday I will be in town, God willing.

In return for the many favors which Don Abel did for
Don Perfecto, executing commissions and making excuses
for his friend, Reid often helped Stearns with the store accounts. And sometimes he was able to give Don Abel a tip
about a new account or an old debt. As in this note, translated from the Spanish:

Casa ni Mía ni Tuya
[Neither my house nor yours].
8 S^{bre} 1838.

My dear friend Don Abel,

As I am extremely busy today, it may happen that I shall not
be able to pass by your house today. However, I am enclosing a
draft of what, in my opinion, I consider sufficient to carry or,
more properly, to start the investigation of the claims you have

on José Pérez. Of course it is advisable that it should appear in your own hand. If you think it lacks the tact called for by this matter, you may be able to fix it by adding here or taking off there.

Reid's informal affiliation with the Stearns-Bandini firm became strengthened when Don Juan came to live in San Gabriel in the fall of '38. He had met with misfortune the previous year; hostile Indians had sacked his Rancho Tecate near San Diego, leaving nothing but a smoking ruin and the bloody carcasses of livestock which they could not take with them.

On September 28, Governor Alvarado granted to Bandini the Rancho Jurupa.[5] It was not many leagues from the San Gabriel Mission, where he left his terrified family while preparing their new home. The governor also appointed Don Juan secular administrator of the mission.

Though the circumstances of Bandini's move were unhappy, the results proved far reaching and favorable to Hugo and Victoria and Don Abel. Stearns, as a homeless bachelor, was provided with rooms in the Bandini home, which he retained until his marriage to Don Juan's daughter Arcadia, in '41. Both Don Perfecto and Don Abel stood as *padrinos* (godfathers) to children of Don Juan, thereby entering into a peculiarly intimate, purely Spanish relationship—that of *compadre* to the Bandinis. Doña Refugio, Don Juan's second wife, became devoted to Doña Victoria and always called her *comadre*. Indeed, the Reid-Bandini-Stearns clan seemed to an outsider as closely knit as though the ties had originally been of flesh and blood.

In '39 Don Perfecto was elected to his first public office,

that of *regidor del muy ilustre ayuntamiento de la Ciudad de Los Ángeles* (member of the city council). The *ayuntamiento* was composed of an *alcalde,* a *subalcalde,* six *regidores,* and a *síndico;* and election to these offices meant a great deal in prestige, although no salaries were attached. Only four years previously, Mexico had lifted Los Angeles officially from pueblodom and appointed her capital of California. Though too lazy to erect public buildings, *La Ciudad* began to feel extremely important. Decisions of the *ayuntamiento* were couched in a courtly style, and meetings were conducted with close attention to parliamentary procedure. Hugo Reid's facility of language and superior education made him invaluable to this august body, and his signature, always a complex *rúbrica,*° headed a number of petitions and regulations in the records.

The Pueblo archives, during the time of Reid's public service, abounded with interesting news items. For example, it was found necessary to fine all individuals serenading "promiscuously" around the streets at night without first having obtained permission from the *alcalde.* Offenders would be fined a dollar and a half for the first offense; three dollars for the second; and, for the third, would be punished "according to law." The punishment was not specified, because the lawmakers had an effective way of fitting the punishment to the offender. It has been said that "men's pleasures and vices paid the cost of governing" in those days. Property was not taxed. Only the tariff on imported goods; fines for drunkenness and other vices; and licenses for dances, stores, cockpits, bull rings, *et cetera* provided the necessary revenue for municipal expenses.

The Los Angeles *ayuntamiento* legislated not only for the Pueblo, but indeed for the whole countryside—from San Juan Capistrano north to San Fernando. Within this large area there was no resident lawyer, doctor, or schoolmaster; no resident priest in the Pueblo, only the mission padres who conducted occasional services in the Plaza church. Money was little used—horses and cattle being the circulating medium of large denomination; hides and produce, of small change. As yet, no hotel, no schoolhouse, no public buildings—save the church and jail—had been built in Los Angeles, the capital of Alta California, a territory larger than that occupied by the thirteen original colonies at the time of the American Revolution. Furthermore, there were no newspapers, few books, and mail arrived at irregular, long-spaced intervals, or not at all.[7]

To counterbalance the lack of "civilized" facilities, there was a conscientious regard for the opinion of the constituents. Whenever a deadlock occurred in the council—over a question of public welfare or a designing politician who wanted to sway an *ayuntamiento* decision for personal gain—the "public alarm" was sounded, and all citizens assembled at the council hall. The *alcalde* then spoke "in a loud voice," setting the question before the people.

Rivers of eloquence flowed. The question was decided by a show of hands, and everyone went home happy and glad to think the country was saved and they all had a part in it. The clang of bell and roll of drum that sounded the "public alarm" exorcised the malign influence . . . of the scheming politician.

Hugo Reid had to go to town twice a week, on Tuesdays and Thursdays, to attend sessions. Sometimes he went alone, on horseback, but more often his whole family piled into the *carreta* and followed him to Los Angeles. Since Doña Victoria feared horses almost as much as earthquakes, she preferred to take what to her husband was an interminable time on the road, riding behind the "safe," broad backs of an ox team. Only once did her *carreta* reach Los Angeles in record time. It happened to be a bright, sunny day. Suddenly the oxen felt spring in the air, kicked up their heels, and set out on a run, leaving the naked Indian driver sprawled in the dust!

Usually, Victoria and the children went straight to the *tienda* of Don Abel, because they enjoyed looking over new shipments while the two men attended sessions. In '36, Stearns had been elected *síndico* (lawyer and fiscal agent) of the *ayuntamiento,* and he still retained the office. Three years later, about the time that Hugo received notice of his own election, a committee was appointed by the *ayuntamiento* to draft a map of the city and its jurisdiction, and to mark off municipal lands. The versatile Stearns offered his services as surveyor.

Previously, in '37, the *ayuntamiento* had appointed a committee "to report a plan for repairing the monstrous irregularity of the streets brought about by ceding house lots and erecting houses in the city." However, no draftsman could be found "equal to formulating a plot of the city as it actually existed," and the matter drifted, as did all matters in the old pueblo, now a *ciudad* in name only. A decree of Spanish *regidores* was dug up to defend the narrowness of the streets. It proclaimed that "in cold countries streets should be wide, and in warm countries, narrow."

Early in May, '39, Hugo Reid petitioned the district prefect for a clear title to the Rancho Santa Anita. There were certain *vecinos* who had never considered Victoria, as an Indian, qualified to hold land in California. Even since her marriage to the Scotch *paisano,* two claims had been filed against the *rancho,* by *los señores* Tiburcio López and Vicente de la Osa. Both these men were sons-in-law of Doña Eulalia, and resented the old lady's constant championship of the Indian woman.

Intimidated by López and De la Osa, a committee appointed by the governor would not commit itself to Reid further than to say that, "since the petitioner's claim is strengthened by his family, it recognizes that he has some right in his favor." In disgust at such weak indecision, Don Perfecto wrote as follows to William P. Hartnell,[8] an influential friend living in Monterey:

Angeles.
Enero 27 de 1840.

W. E. P. Hartnell, Esqr.
Monterrey
My dear Sir,

Having ever in remembrance the good will and disposition shown by you toward me, without any merit whatever on my part to have given occasion for it; it being entirely the spontaneous production of your own natural good heart, I make the more bold in addressing you at present.

Bandini (through your kindness) having given me the necessary possession of Santa Anita, I immediately made corrals and a *jacal* for the present, until the rains are over. I have sown 10 *fanegas* of wheat—cleared ground to put in a vineyard of 10,000 vines and 1000 fruit trees. I have put on the farm a *manada con burro* consisting of 62 mares and in April intend putting on my stock of cattle.

This I consider doing more than the López family would do in fifty years, and notwithstanding I am told not content yet, your Uncle D. José Antonio Carrillo has made out new representations for them and intends pleading for them with the governor. This is for me a hard case. Castro gave them a house in the mission; they have let it go to wreck and ruin, and if it survives the present rainy season, it never will another. Now, since you were down, I have built a new house in the mission, flat roof'd and corridor'd [Uva Espina]. Certainly government will never be so blind to take away land from one anxious for the progress of the country, to give to another who has neither a just claim, means, or yet will to do anything.

As long as you have anything to do with missions, I am not afraid, and in the present case merely inform you so as to avert what Carrillo with his interest might do.

Excuse my confidence and the trouble I cause, receiving the best regards of the whole family to you, Mrs. Hartnell, and the children, believing me to be,

Yours ever sincerely,
PERFECTO HUGO REID.

Still the case dragged along, for more than a year, before Reid took drastic action—or so it could fairly be considered in the Land of *Poco Tiempo*—and wrote direct to Governor Alvarado (translation):

Monterey, April 13, 1841.

To His Excellency the Governor:

Perfecto Hugo Reid, naturalized Mexican, resident of the former Mission of San Gabriel and married to Victoria of the same [mission], declares, before the well-known justice of your Excellency, with due respect and through the customary procedure, that: In the year 1839, under date of May 6, I solicited from the prefect of the district at that time, for the benefit of my family, that piece of land known as Santa Anita, belonging to the former mission wherein I reside, and after my petition passed the customary procedure, it was placed before the Departmental Superior Government for a decision, which was an order directed to the then administrator, Don Juan Bandini, which stated that I was permitted to introduce in the land I solicited my farming goods until further disposition should be made.

With this permission from the Superior [Government], assuming the land to be mine, I introduced all my farming possessions; I planted a vineyard consisting of a considerable number of vines and built a house of stone where some person, assigned by me, would always stay to look after all that is there; and besides, I have incurred enormous expenses for its cultivation while awaiting the final decision; but since up to now none has been reached, owing perhaps to the manifold business of government, and not considering as secure my possessions on the above-mentioned land in the absence of a legal title to it, I find myself obliged to trouble your Excellency, entreating that, taking into consideration the labor and expense I have undertaken, as well as the fact of having a family who have a right to it, you may cause the respective title to the property to be issued to me, that I may live in security and work as I desire.

I assume that your Excellency must have my first solicitation and plan of Santa Anita which was attached to the papers with the necessary information, for which reason I deem it unnecessary to expatiate further on details which are in favor of my family, whom I am really representing, considering that what has preceded and the reasons I have hereby presented shall be considered as sufficient, so that if your Excellency is agreeable to it, you may give your consent to my request.

Therefore, I humbly ask of your Excellency that in all justice and for its due security I be granted the before-mentioned property title corresponding to the land I occupy, which shall be received by me as a token of grace coming from your benevolent hand; I swear that I am not guided by any malicious motive.

PERFECTO HUGO REID.

Governor Alvarado, knowing Reid and Bandini well, immediately replied to Reid's petition (translation):

Inasmuch as Don Perfecto Hugo Reid, a naturalized citizen married to a Mexican, has solicited for his personal benefit and that of his family the tract of land known as Santa Anita, having previously complied with the investigations and proceedings proper to the case as decreed by laws and regulations, I, making use of the rights and power conferred upon me, have granted, by decree of this date, the above-mentioned land, binding him to pay a fee that may be imposed on him, should it be found to belong to the proprietors of the establishment of San Gabriel when the general division of boundaries is finally made, and under the condition that he is not to deny the above-mentioned establishment the use of its water and timber, nor impair the pathways, roads, and rights of way.

In consequence of which, an entry must be made of this provisional grant in the proper book and the petitioner given [the papers] for his own safekeeping or for any other purposes.

JUAN B. ALVARADO.
Constitutional Governor of the
Department of the Californias.

At San Gabriel, the Padre Tomás Estenaga expressed approval of the governor's action, describing the grant to Reid as a "reward for services rendered for the benefit of this mission by his wife and her late husband Pablo, who did greatly contribute to the existence of said mission."[9]

It is notable that "Perfecto Hugo Reid" referred to himself as a "naturalized Mexican" in his letter to Alvarado. Having turned Catholic in order to marry Victoria, Hugo did not object to one more metamorphosis in order to secure her property. He was merely complying with the custom of the country. In a letter to Don Abel he alluded to yet another custom, which apparently had been observed by the governor (translation):

His Excellency has attended to the papers of my ranch in the same manner in which I would dispose of a dish of lima beans for breakfast—fattening myself in so doing!

Pride in possession stimulated Don Perfecto toward further improvements at Santa Anita. His "house of stone"—a slight exaggeration calculated to impress the governor; the greater part was common *adobe*—he had planned to have of only one story, out of consideration for Victoria's fear of earthquakes. He had also placed it on the site that she chose—at the edge of a lake, with stone steps leading down to a little boat landing.[10] It seemed miraculous, in a dry country, that there could be such a cool green spot.

The house stood on an eminence overlooking the entire San Gabriel Valley. It was shaded by cottonwoods and willow trees which grew to extraordinary height, standing near all-year water. The children, especially, loved Santa Anita, for there were fish in the lake and various birds hiding in the *tules* and water grasses.

Formerly, cattle had grazed all over the *rancho,* but Reid decided to diversify his products, as seldom was done in California. He planted fruit trees, a vegetable garden, grapevines, and grain, still keeping a great many head of cattle for indispensable hides and tallow. This entailed such seasonal activities as *siembra,* or the sowing of wheat and corn in December; harvest from July to September; irrigating and picking at different times; grape gathering and wine making—Hugo's main agricultural interest; then the great *rodeo,* or roundup of cattle in April, and smaller ones throughout the year for *la matanza* (slaughtering), doctoring, dehorning, or branding. Of course there were also intermittent activities like hide curing, garden fencing, whitewashing, and reroofing after a rain.

With so much to do at Santa Anita, and the whole family so fond of the place, the Reids soon found themselves spending more time at the ranch house than in San Gabriel, at Uva Espina. The next time Jim McKinley and William Heath Davis together paid them a long visit, they found the family living in lavish *hacendado* style at Santa Anita. Davis' description of meals—epicurean feasts, we would now call them—supervised by Doña Victoria would make anyone's mouth water:[11]

During our stay as guests at Santa Anita, we feasted daily on good food. For breakfast we had honey (the production of the land, and in fact everything we ate was), fresh eggs from the poultry yard, which was well stocked with chickens, ducks, geese, and turkeys; coffee, with rich cream; chocolate and tea; "chino beans" (curley beans), which looked like scramble eggs, especially for breakfast; *tortillas* made of flour or corn; but no butter, strange to say, with hundreds of cows on the place, but however this was characteristic of the *ranchos* at that season of the year. This composed the first meal of the day. The cloth was neat, and the furniture of the table was exquisitely clean.

As the house clock sounded the noon hour, the visitors were summoned by a maid servant to the dining room for a midday meal, which was a solid meal of beef steak with and without onions, broiled beef, stewed chickens, or hash made of *carne seca* (dried beef) with scramble eggs mixed, seasoned with onions, tomatoes, and a sprinkling of red pepper (this dish was very

HUGO REID AT THE RANCHO SANTA ANITA

palatable), beans prepared with plenty of gravy, the water from which it was boiled preparatory for the frying pan, and seasoning; homemade bread, California wine, and finished with black coffee. This noon repast could not be excelled in respect to neatness and in preparation of the food.

The dinner consisted of chicken soup, roast ducks, *guisado de carne* richly flavored, sweet potatoes grown on the land, *frijoles,* chicken salad, and lettuce. This fine dinner was served with old wine of the make of the Mission of San Gabriel, and custard and pies and coffee.

During our stay of nearly two months, we were well fed, the meals varying but little from day to day in the makeup of the viands. On Sundays for dinner a turkey this week, roast geese for the next, and for the third Sunday roast ducks, and so on to the end of our sojourn, and we regretted when the day of our departure had arrived, which was the day succeeding the festivals of Christmas, the birth of our Saviour.

These festivals were prepared in grand style, with all the nice things for the celebration of such happy occasion. . . . The turkeys had been fattened for more than a month previously, with [green] walnuts whole with the shells on pushed down the throats of the mutinous birds as part of their food, the flavor of which is still on my palate, or the remembrance of it. There were many invited guests who contributed largely to the enjoyment of the occasion, and dancing prevailed after the sun had appeared above the peaks of the lofty mountains; and from the gay hall McKinley and myself departed for Los Angeles, amid the greetings of the assemblage.

Both Reid and his wife are epicures, and they had everything (their own market place on the *hacienda*) to entertain visitors sumptuously. Doña Victoria had a fine Indian cook who had been educated in the art at the Mission of San Gabriel, though the lady herself superintended more or less in the preparation of our good living.

James McKinley and Reid our host were both from Scotland
and from the same town, and knew each other in the Old Country; hence the great kindness bestowed on the former, and to me
as his friend, by Don Hugo and Doña Victoria. Hugo Reid was
the grantee . . . of the Santa Anita *rancho* of about eight thousand acres. It was then the most picturesque spot of Southern
California, with mountains, valleys, springs, and running silvery
streams. You would observe in riding over the *rancho* its having
more than its *pro rata* of towering and overspreading liveoak
trees, *manzanita,* laurel, and other forest in comparison with
other *ranchos.*

Reid was a cultivated and educated man, a big-hearted man, a
thorough accountant, and bred as a merchant in his own country.... The hospitality shown to McKinley and myself, not only
by Reid himself but by his Indian wife, was sumptuous. A Castilian lady of standing could not have bestowed on us any greater
attention or graciousness than was extended to us as I have described at the "Santa Anita."

Besides living the life of a *hacendado* at Santa Anita, Don
Perfecto also managed La Huerta del Cuati, which Victoria
retained in her own name; and another *rancho,* Los Coyotes,
for an Italian land baron named Leandry. He kept very busy
with the necessary ranch work and attendance at *ayuntamiento* sessions. There was little time for writing and reflection, and Stearns he saw so often that their correspondence
became scarcely more than a series of often amusing, but not
significant, *cartas de orden,* and excuses for nonattendance
at sessions, such as:

Bandini promised to communicate my sickness. *Quién sabe*
if he did so or not.
I have just risen from bed, and have put myself at last under

a radical cure. I have left off so long doing so, but have confidence that with a rigorous vegetable diet with dilutary drinks, I can bring myself round.

You will oblige by sending me two pounds of rice and a little coffee.

By the bye, please loan me your little milk pot again. My godchild is coming to spend Holy Week with us, and we lack a suitable teapot.

On Monday I will be with you, God willing.

References to Victoria, the children, and intimates like the Bandinis, Jim McKinley, "Old Bowman," and others continually slipped into the correspondence.

In a *carta de orden* asking Don Abel to send out some plates, cups and saucers, teaspoons, *et cetera,* Hugo concluded:

I think with the above and what is already in the house that the King, Queen, and young Princess [María Ygnacia] will be able to make out.

Felipe and José Dolores delighted in occasional vacations from school, when they were allowed to help with the ranch work at Santa Anita. Hugo, writing on "a cold morning, something of December, 1839," reported:

Felipe came from the *rancho* last night and says that the wheat there will all be expended today. You are well aware that I want a large *siembra* and wheat all of one quality. (I can get 20 ps. if you wish it of Bandini.) So therefore please send me 8 ps. of your good. I am of opinion that the ground will take more, but enough for the present. On my coming to town (tomorrow if nothing prevents) we will bargain whether as a loan, purchase, or barter.

Poor José Dolores, always trying to keep up with his stronger, smarter, older brother, once asked to "help" in Don Abel's *tienda,* but the adventure ended sadly. His father explained:

As José Dolores has come to me crying, complaining that your man made use of an oath, stamping his foot at him, saying moreover he was shamming illness, I have thought it better to take him with me. Should you hereafter be in want of any, you can have him, or perhaps Felipe may then be unemployed.

Jim McKinley had fallen into the habit of bringing presents to the children whenever he appeared at the Reid home. Once, he delighted Hugo by outfitting the two older boys in real Scotch "kilties," having sent their measurements to the Old Country. A humorous note written by Hugo to Don Abel in January, 1840, referred to McKinley's keen interest in "what is being worn," and also to the difficulty of buying store stock in salable quantities:

Don Abel or Mr. Howard:[12]
Please let Jim have a monkey jacket before they go off—right weather for monkey jackets—and in return I hope we may have such dusty weather afterward so as to oblige people to purchase brooms.
I also require for Mr. Leandry a small piece of tin to make a bottom for a coffee pot, and a small piece of rosin.
Yours truly,
Sunday afternoon.   PERFECTO HUGO REID.

Don Perfecto touched on diverse subjects in these trivial notes. He was not above a flippant reference to his own "conversion" (without which he could not have married Victoria), knowing that Stearns would chuckle over it.

From the state of my pulse you will naturally draw the conclusion that I am *non compos mentis*. No such thing. Religion
has hurt my nerves, having been yesterday at church.

Hugo's sense of humor ran away with him when he
learned that Don Abel had actually made up his mind to
marry Arcadia Bandini. She, a fresh young girl of fourteen,
and he, a weatherbeaten bachelor of forty-three, older than
her own father!—Though he knew, of course, that Don Abel
had been encouraged in his romance by the examples of
several friends, no longer in their first youth, who had recently married young *hijas del país*.

Everyone had been astonished when the old bachelor
Nathaniel Pryor took to wife María Teresa Sepúlveda, at
a *paisano* wedding celebrated in San Gabriel, on February
15, 1838. Among his character witnesses were Don Juan
Temple and Perfecto Hugo Reid. Pryor had been baptized a
short time previously, Louis Vignes acting as *padrino* (godfather). Next came the marriage of Don Juan Leandry—
that wealthy and colorful native of Sardinia for whom
Hugo Reid managed the Rancho Los Coyotes—to María, the
eighteen-year-old daughter of Marcela Cota of Los Angeles.

Finally, "Handsome Dick" Laughlin, for a reason not
understood by his friends, had decided to legitimate a long-
standing relation with Lutgarda Rubio, a twenty-four-year-
old *paisana* without "parents (living), grandfather, or
guardian." The exhaustive "marriage investigations" which
always preceded a *paisano* wedding caused some embarrass-
ment to Don Ricardo. He had to comply with stringent
terms, sent down from the Father Superior at Santa Barbara,

before being permitted to become a benedick. The communication from Padre Durán, dated October 13, 1840, read as follows (translation):[18]

Having seen the preceding marriage investigation, it appears that none of the witnesses has known the suitor for more than fourteen years, in consequence of which the Reverend Father of San Gabriel must try to find someone who may furnish this information. In default of which he must ask the suitor to give a new declaration of his singleness and freedom to marry, and warn that he shall be duly punished should he ever be found to have perjured himself. And also must furnish proof of his being a Roman Catholic. And because it is known that he has lived for many years in an unholy state with the betrothed, the Reverend Father is to fine him according to his means, the fine to be used for works of piety. All this having been attended to, the marriage may then take place.

Fr[ay] NARCISO DURÁN.

Inured by this time to romantic vagaries in his circle of friends, Hugo at first wrote with restraint and consideration to Don Abel, congratulating him on his choice and concluding, quite tenderly:

Should there be anything which my family can do for you in household affairs in order to facilitate matrimonial matters, command with the necessary confidence of a friend, because as an old bachelor you may be at fault.

But when Don Abel lopped a few years off his age and tried to keep the banns from being published, "wishing to avoid ridicule which might arise among the idle young because of the disparity in years," this was too much for Don Perfecto. He wrote a coarsely humorous letter to Don Abel, advising him how to conduct himself on the wedding night.

Indeed, he invited his old friend to spend the night preceding the ceremony at the Reid home in San Gabriel, so that
he himself could give Don Abel "a breakfast suitable for
the occasion—one which will prevent fever—a water gruel
one." The coupling "concluded, you can return to town and
enter your house as you never have entered it yet—a *maid*
(made) man!"

In spite of natural irritation at such levity, Don Abel
asked Hugo to be one of his witnesses, and he married Doña
Arcadia on a cloudless June day (the twenty-second) in
1841. Padre Tomás Estenaga officiated, and members of the
Stearns-Bandini-Reid clan gathered from far and near for
a week of merrymaking. The bride looked ravishingly beautiful in contrast to her husband, whom the *paisanos* called
"Cara de Caballo" ("Horse Face"). Stearns's own *vaqueros*
composed a song for the occasion. Translated, this refrain
ended each verse:

> "Two little doves sang in a laurel,
> How lovely Doña Arcadia!
> How homely Don Abel!"

CHAPTER FIVE

Cargoes and Contraband

THE REIDS and their friends found many diversions in San Gabriel and the vicinity. There were frequent *meriendas* to Santa Anita, both to the lake and to the lovely glades kept green by mountain streams; excursions to San Pedro when a trading vessel was lying at anchor, filled with exciting cargo and young officers starved for the sight of a pretty girl after months at sea; and long rides home, ending under a moon or the more mysterious stars, when everybody sang, save an extraordinary young lady-killer from the north who once was heard to remark:

"*No puedo cantar, pero puedo encantar!*"

("I can't sing; but look out!")

Nearer home there were river bathing parties on lazy summer days, family *bailes* and *fandangos*, bull-and-bear baiting during *la matanza*, occasionally even a real bullfight, and frequent cockfights. Week ends were full of activity. At noon on Saturdays, soap was distributed, and according to Hugo, "all the world went a-washing of clothes and persons to make a decent appearance at church on Sunday." Saturday night was given over to playing the Indian game of *peón*, and "with few exceptions none slept, for whites and Indians, men, women, and children were generally present."

Sunday also was a day of revelry, starting with late rising and a race to church between families in overflowing *carretas*. Such a screeching as the oak wheels made; such shrieks from excited children, encouraging the apathetic oxen! Solemnity suddenly descended on everyone during Mass at the mission, but thoughts of the "idle young" darted to approaching pleasures: a delicious dinner at noon; then the whole afternoon and evening for sport; games and horse racing, dancing, singing, and guitar playing.

Felipe and his young friends bet the buttons off their trousers, on a favorite horse, while their fathers and uncles were exchanging silver dollars. After the races, accomplished *caballeros* would swoop down the main street in front of the mission, picking up stones, silver dollars, and lost buttons from the ground. Sometimes a live cock was buried up to the neck in the dirt of the road, and its tormentor, mounting his horse at a run, would lean over and catch it up, squawking and flapping.

Favorite games for Sabbath playing were football and a game called "shinty" by the Scotch and "bandy" by the English, one set being composed of all men and one of all women, "who seldom had less than half a dozen quarrels, in which hair flew by the handful." People came from the outlying country to see such sport, and heavy bets were made. Then, "the game being concluded, all went to prayers, and so ended the Sabbath."

If San Gabriel suddenly palled or seemed provincial, the Reids and Bandinis knew that they were welcome to visit the Stearns family in Los Angeles. Here they found the same amusements, in a fresh environment.

The match that everyone had ridiculed proved to be a singularly happy one. Obviously, Doña Arcadia considered her husband superior to other men, and her own smiling hospitality attracted interesting people as definitely as did Don Abel's brains and business interests. A young sister of Arcadia's, Doña Ysidora, *ahijada,* or godchild, to Hugo Reid, lived with the Stearnses until the time of her marriage with Cave Coutts. These Bandini sisters, appearing always together at *bailes* and *meriendas,* enjoyed an enviable reputation for feminine charm.

Don Abel had built a wonderful home to frame the beauty of his child bride. The *paisanos* always referred to it as El Palacio de Don Abel, and showed it to strangers as the most imposing structure in town. Set a little back from the Plaza and surrounded by young trees and shrubs, it resembled all the other Pueblo houses in being of one-story, *adobe* construction; but El Palacio was remarkable in extent of house and patio, and in the elegance and taste shown in its furnishing. Don Abel laid the choice selection of all his cargoes at the dainty feet of Doña Arcadia.

No news pleased everyone more than an announcement from Don Abel that a ship was arriving and he must go down to the warehouse at San Pedro. It happened, frequently, that his family and friends could go along and make an occasion of it. Doña Refugio Bandini once pithily expressed what a ship's arrival meant to the *señoritas:* "Silk! Officers! *Rebozos!* Music! Dancing! Frolic!"

Don Abel felt the fascination of these trading vessels no less keenly than did the *señoritas.* When a share in one was offered him, he jumped at the chance.

"Don Enrique" (Henry) Fitch from San Diego, a man whom Hugo Reid detested, had bought an eighty-five-ton schooner from Pierce and Brewer in the Sandwich Islands, changed the name from *Morse* to *Ninfa,* and sailed her back to California. In '41 he had her equipped for trading purposes and asked Stearns, Jim McKinley, Juan Temple, and Captain John Paty, of the *Don Quixote,* to join him in a trading venture to Mexican ports, notably Mazatlán. Reid warned his friends against Fitch, assuring them that he had good reason to distrust the fellow. When they disregarded his advice, he continued to rail against the partnership. During the whole year of '41 his correspondence with Don Abel was unduly taken up with Fitch.

Since Don Enrique was a man much respected in San Diego, Reid's complete condemnation of him cannot have been deserved—though Richard Dana also detested him, and the business association which he had formed with Stearns and the others later went on the rocks, just as Hugo had predicted.

Dana, in *Two Years Before the Mast,* referred to Don Enrique as "that big vulgar shopkeeper and trader." But Bancroft explained this spleen as originating in an incident when Dana, "a wild young sailor disposed to put on airs by reason of his education and high connections," was once thrown out of Don Enrique's house, being already drunk when he and some sailor companions applied for more "grog."

Questionable as was Don Enrique's reputation among men, he seemed inevitably attractive to women. His elopement with Josefa Carrillo had a romantic, epic quality. In

'29, when he was thirty years old and had been three years on the coast, he fell in love at first sight with the lovely dark-eyed daughter of Joaquín Carrillo.

He implored her to marry him, and she confessed to her diary that she had been "immediately won by the handsome person and dashing manners of the captain." (Fitch had come round the Horn as master of the Mexican trading vessel *María Ester,* and still remained in command.) Several objections of religion, nationality, and character were raised to their marriage, but finally they prevailed on Josefa's easy-going parents. The two were actually kneeling before the altar when the bride's uncle, Domingo Carrillo, refused to let the ceremony continue, saying that it would unite a faithful daughter of the Church to a foreigner and an infidel.

The padre's courage failed him at so violent a denunciation of the intended bridegroom, and he would not go on with the service. To Josefa's tears and Fitch's pleas he gave only the answer—poor comfort, then—that other states were not so particular in their matrimonial regulations. They must go elsewhere to be married.

"Why don't you carry me off, Don Enrique?" naïvely suggested Josefa.

Pío Pico, the bride's cousin, was as delighted as Fitch at this unmaidenly suggestion and agreed to help him follow it. Next night, Don Pío took Josefa up before him on his saddle and rode swiftly to a cove of San Diego Bay, where Don Enrique was waiting in the *María Ester*. By daylight the lovers were far offshore on their way down the coast. They were married at Valparaiso by Padre Orrego.

This elopement caused a terrific scandal the length and breadth of California. Rumors flew around that it was a forcible abduction, and ecclesiastical circles were horrified. When Fitch, changed to the command of the *Leonor,* returned a year later with his wife and infant son, he stopped first at San Pedro. There a warrant awaited him, and a trial in Los Angeles, on very serious charges. He produced his marriage certificate, but certain technicalities had not been observed; so he was thrown into jail.

During the period of Fitch's imprisonment, Doña Josefa and her baby were committed to the care of Señora Eulalia Pérez at San Gabriel. Perhaps it was Doña Eulalia, faithful friend of the padres, who poisoned Hugo Reid's mind against Don Enrique.

After a great deal of mental suffering and numerous court appearances, Doña Josefa and her husband were released on promising to do certain acts of penance and to give the church of Our Lady of the Angels, in the Plaza, a long-desired belfry and a fifty-pound bronze bell. Before leaving San Gabriel for the south, the couple received a solemn nuptial blessing, at Mass in the mission, on January 8, 1831.

The Fitch family went to live in San Diego, where Don Enrique quickly reëstablished himself in business. He even secured forgiveness from Tío Domingo, who was responsible for all their troubles. After buying land, building a store, making it pay large returns, and holding minor public offices, Don Enrique received, in 1840, the honor of being elected *juez de paz.* When his term expired, he went to the Islands as supercargo of the *California,* and there bought the *Ninfa.* Of Fitch's ensuing deals with Don Abel and the other partners, Reid made continuous, opprobrious remarks—the first in a letter from San Gabriel dated "1º de Marzo de 1841":

> By my cart please give me the name of the person suspected; between you and I it will remain. I wish to compare it with former notes or hints, and if corresponding, I shall write you immediately.
>
> I have put prices to Fitch's sales and footed them up; you will observe they amount to $35,894.50, but it is a moral impossibility to do anything more with them. To make out the account sales as it ought will require Fitch's return. To solve more than one difficulty and to form any idea of how the business stands is still more so, from the circumstances that he has no portage bill among his papers; and whatever he may think a day back, if it had been kept, would have been an assistance of no small matter. However, in a couple of days, you shall hear more on the subject.

Two days later, Hugo continued:

> After a close examination of Fitch's accounts, I have come to the conclusion that his soul originally occupied some Yaqui Indian's body.
>
> He has opened no account of the expendition. He may answer that merely as a supercargo he is acting; if only as a supercargo, why be at such trouble as to charge Stearns, Temple, and himself with their third part of duties? Such a way of proceeding is very pretty, when arithmetic is but little known to the parties concerned, but certainly it had been much better to have deducted it (or them) from the gross proceeds of sale, on the same principle he should proceed with other charges, *viz.*:
>
> August 15. Abel Stearns dr. to his third share of a penny loaf purchased this morning from O'Larkin, to breakfast upon, 1/3 cent.
>
> It was well enough with regard to the company's invoice, on account of your shares being different.

At present *no hay más remedio; asi q. venga métense* up to the head and ears, by getting things in proper order.

And in my opinion a separate account sale of such invoice is required. You must certainly concur with me in *lo espuesto*.

During the next three or four months, Reid's correspondence with Stearns was full of uncomplimentary remarks about Fitch, such as:

18, *creo, de Mayo,* 1841. *Qué hace* Fitch? Let me know if any news are current regarding him. No doubt he is becalmed in Josefa Bay [a nautical reference to Fitch's romance with Josefa Carrillo].

2 *de Junio.* Fitch had me down at the beach talking *lunar* [insanely]. Whenever I'm better—the jaunt did me no good—I'll be in.

San Gabriel, 26 *de Junio.* I am all alone by myself, all the rest of the family being at the *rancho* [Santa Anita] cutting wheat.

I have thought over well the affair of Fitch and made another *si* which you must insist on having added to the agreement and signed by each and every one.

Hugo's suspicion of Don Enrique finally forced him to draw up a tighter contract between the partners than was usual in those days, when a man's word often was accepted in business without anything at all in writing. He advised Stearns earnestly:

My friend, I have thought over well Fitch's proceedings, and under the present system of doing business you can never get along. He will eventually ruin you and enrich himself. Therefore, when he comes down, being all present, you must insist on having something of this sort attached to each of your contracts:

No one of the granting associates, while the firm lasts, shall be able to do any business or commercial transactions—it is understood maritime—or have private commissions except those stipulated. Everything must be done by unanimous consent and for the benefit of the company.

However, we shall talk it over.

Hugo's concern over Fitch's way of doing business brought him often to San Pedro, to keep one eye on the *Ninfa*'s cargo and both on the supercargo. The harbor presented a very different aspect now from that at Hugo's first landing, and Don Abel was solely responsible.

With permission granted from Governor Alvarado in 1821, two *extranjeros,* William Hartnell and Hugh McCulloch, had erected the first warehouse in San Pedro. This was the dirty, one-room *adobe* that Reid found after disembarking from the *Ayacucho* in the summer of '32. The builders had abandoned the project after a few years, and their permit was transferred to the padres at San Gabriel Mission.

Under the progressive rule of Padre Sánchez, the *adobe* was used both as a storeroom for hides and as a place to do business with supercargoes from the incoming ships. Padre Sánchez even directed the mission Indians in building at San Gabriel a large boat called the *Guadalupe,* which was hauled to San Pedro and launched from the harbor.[1]

In '34, shortly after the tragic death of Sánchez, Don Abel bought the warehouse site, along with the lot in Los Angeles where he later built El Palacio for Doña Arcadia. He at once enlarged the little old *adobe,* transforming it into a big quadrangular building with transverse wings. Hugo Reid spent several months in San Pedro, before his departure for Hermosillo in '36, aiding in the remodeling. They used the wings as storerooms, and the center as an office and comfortable accommodations for visitors. Stearns himself headed a subscription list for the making of a good road from the warehouse to the beach, and this was the first public improvement of Los Angeles harbor.[2]

Don Abel showed characteristic acumen in acquiring the only warehouse at San Pedro. He himself rapidly made a fortune out of the monopoly, and also did a service to *rancheros* in the vicinity. No longer need they fear missing a boat with a load of hides which there had been no place to store nearer the anchorage. They need not even trouble to come to San Pedro on the arrival of a ship. For a commission, usually paid in hides, Don Abel would do their trading for them and send the merchandise on his own carts to the very doors of the ranch houses. Or else the housewives could come into the Pueblo and select articles from the whole shipment cleverly displayed in Don Abel's *tienda*.

As soon as the *tienda* and warehouse were well established, Stearns started a lumber business. He had agents in the north who bought and shipped logs down to him at San Pedro. He in turn traded them to settlers in southern California for hides and tallow, some cash, or liquor. The lumber business flourished, in a comparatively treeless country.

Another successful venture of Don Abel's was the "hunting and taking of the Sea Otters and Fur Seals that may be found in the Waters on the Coast of Upper and Lower California including the Islands adjacent to said Coasts." An agreement drawn up between Stearns and Alpheus B. Thompson (September 22, 1831) and witnessed by James McKinley had stipulated that a party of thirty hunters should embark on a vessel owned by Thompson, set out "overseen by a Person appointed by the two parties," and spend a year in pursuit of these sea animals. At the close of the contract, the rich furs were divided between Stearns and Thompson, after the Mexican government had received ten per cent on the collection "for the privilege obtained for hunting"; the overseeing agent, five per cent; and the hunters, twenty per cent.

Trade between merchants along the coast was carried on by *cartas de orden,* often no more formal than Hugo Reid's frequent notes to Don Abel. One merchant would draw upon another for a certain amount of merchandise, which the other then paid out. Captains and supercargoes of the trading vessels transacted the business, serving as middlemen. Orders also were drawn upon each other for debts, if they could not be paid in cash.

Stearns gradually acquired the largest cash fortune in California, in the years before gold was discovered. Only a small amount of silver or gold changed hands in separate deals, but Don Abel had innumerable opportunities of adding to his hoard.

Since jealousy always dogs success, Don Abel's case was no exception to the rule. From '35 on, he was repeatedly accused of smuggling, although the practice was widespread and usually winked at by fellow *paisanos,* because of excessive Mexican duties. Bancroft said in Don Abel's defense: "He was perhaps not more addicted to contraband trade than Larkin, Fitch, Spence, and others, but he was less cautious and less fortunate in keeping on the right side of the [Mexican] authorities." There is evidence that during his

early years of trading along the coast Don Abel did engage
in contraband trade. But where is the large fortune whose
origins can bear too close scrutiny?

In March, 1835, came the first complaint of certain citizens to the governor of California, asking that Stearns's
project at San Pedro be suppressed. It just happened that
Figueroa, a friend of Don Abel's, was in office at the moment. He appointed an investigating committee, who reported to the *ayuntamiento* that Stearns had received due
permission from the *jefe político* and that he was complying
with all requirements of construction. The committee declared that it was conducive to community interests to encourage settlement on the beach at San Pedro, as thus traders
were provided with a living.

On May 16 of the same year, another complaint came before the *ayuntamiento*, signed by a prominent citizen, Ángel
Ramírez. It stated that Abel Stearns had built large warehouses on the beach at San Pedro, where he received goods
of all kinds. Only about ten or twelve miles offshore was his
island of Santa Catalina with a fine port, where foreign ships
could enter and lie in safety while they carried on contraband trade with the said Abel Stearns. By arriving at sunset,
they had time to unload a cargo before daylight and thereby
escape observation. Ramírez asked that steps be taken to
stop such a fraud against the government.

No action was taken by Figueroa.

On May 29 came another complaint signed by a long list
of names. It stated that no investigation had even been made
concerning whether Stearns's warehouse was built in con-
formity with marine ordinances and permission of the Su-

perior Government in regard to capacity of the building and safekeeping of goods against dampness, fire, insects, and animals. It further charged that persons secretly took hides to the warehouse of Don Abel Stearns; that he bought them at a low price and loaded them on outgoing ships without anyone's knowing where he got them and to whom they belonged. It was well known that Don Abel had no *rancho*. Whence came the many hides that he sold to passing vessels?

Stearns was accused outright of illicit deals with men who went out into the country and killed cattle, bringing the hides to him to trade for goods or cash, and storing them in the warehouse without anyone's seeing the brands. He was further accused, in the same complaint to the *ayuntamiento,* of establishing warehouses in solitary spots in order to carry on his infamous operations without official interference.

The signers petitioned for strict orders to be given *el capitán* of the port of San Pedro that he remove warehouses already there, and withhold permission for building anything in the future without proper safeguards. It was moved that the governor's committee reopen their investigation.

On September 29, the committee, composed of three prominent Mexicans, Romera, De la Osa, and Guirado, reported to the *ayuntamiento* that they found no grounds for despoiling a citizen of his legal property. None of the accusations against Stearns could be proved.

For the time being, Don Abel was free to carry on his business without official interference. But feeling ran high against him, flaring dangerously in the summer of '35, when he sold a barrel of wine to a hot-blooded fellow named William Day. Señor Day, eager to make trouble, complained

that the wine had turned to vinegar before he received it.
He loudly accused Don Abel of having substituted bad wine
for the good that he had bought.

Stearns angrily denied the charge and attempted to throw
the man out of his store. But Day drew a knife and stabbed
Don Abel three times, in the hand, shoulder, and mouth,
severely cutting his tongue and leaving scars and a speech
impediment for life. Don Abel's life was saved only by the
skill of Dr. William Keith, who had not yet returned to practice in Hermosillo.[3] Don Abel was not satisfied to see Day
arraigned and put in irons; he insisted on handcuffs, too,
and secured a sentence against his assailant of five years'
penal servitude at labor on public works.

Stearns always resented the intermittent attacks that were
made on him—the charges of smuggling,—holding that he
never did anything which was not common practice. The
government imposed fantastically high duties on foreign
goods, and he protested it was impossible to observe an or-
dinance issued by Governor Chico on October 11, 1836.

Chico's widely distributed *proclama de bando* on commercial topics prohibited the practice, long established in
California, of retail trade aboard foreign vessels. It required
all foreigners to land their cargoes at Monterey, and imposed
other harsh trade restrictions which remained more in accordance with Mexican law than with California custom.

From time to time between '35 and '40, Don Abel was
arraigned for smuggling, but invariably he escaped with a
verdict of "not proven." Not until the fall of 1840 could his
enemies produce evidence enough to convict him. One night
in October an unknown vessel landed goods mysteriously

at San Pedro. Next day a search was made of Stearns's warehouse. Valuable silks and liquors were found, and were condemned by a citizens' committee as contraband. Don Abel wrote violent letters to all his friends in high places, talked loudly of his innocence, and appealed for justice; meanwhile exerting himself, according to Bancroft, to make false invoices and otherwise get his accounts in order. Records fail to show how well he succeeded, but, in December, hides asserted to be contraband were found by a new search of his warehouse. Don Abel protested sorrowfully:

The said-to-be contraband goods have been *repartido* and myself published as a *contrabandista,* all without giving me notice or even saying to me, "You are condemned."

He found quick sympathy from his friend, Hugo Reid, who declared: "I feel truly the unjust loss you have sustained, but every dog has his day, as the vulgar say."

Don Abel's "day" was not long in coming. On June 12, 1841, Don Perfecto was able to write reassuringly that "according to a letter Argüello showed me yesterday your commission as customs administrator has been made out and is to be brought by Don Agustín Zamorano in the clear."

No charge of smuggling was ever again entered against Don Abel, and as customs administrator he showed great zeal in keeping others on the straight and narrow path. Even his loyal friend Reid was soon to receive a pious admonition against engaging in contraband trade.

Spending so much thought on maritime affairs, legal and illegal, had an upsetting effect on Don Perfecto. When Don Abel told him of a ninety-two-ton Mexican schooner, called the *Esmeralda,* which was for sale at a low price, Hugo resolved to launch a trading venture of his own. In spite of Victoria's pleas and the children's tears at losing their teacher, if only for a few months at a time, he bought the *Esmeralda* with the idea of himself acting as captain and supercargo. Frankly, he was tired of ranch life, and the old wanderlust was troubling him. To Don Abel he confided:

I shall be very glad to leave—go with me. The gentlemen say that the boat will be ready to sail on the twentieth [of October].

Reid's decision did not surprise Don Abel, because recent letters had shown a half-hidden dissatisfaction with his way of living. Domesticity was beginning to pall on a naturally restless spirit. A humorous letter, like the following, revealed more to his good friend Don Abel than Don Perfecto realized (translation):

Mi estimado Amigo,   San Gabriel, July 27, 1842.

I sent Güero with a flask so that you will do me the favor to fill it with whiskey.

When you have in your house, in proportion to its size, the children that I have in mind, you will often be annoyed.

What I told you about the Coyotes [*rancho*] soap came out true. There isn't any already cut, but as soon as Leandry comes, we shall cut it, because we have it all ready.

I have heard that Carrillo has returned. Please remember me to him, and if there are any letters for me in Los Angeles, do me the favor to send them with Güero. Tell me whether Carrillo's wife came out all right. I hope so, because he has suffered so much, and the devil is not as bad as they paint him.

I have grapes in the orchard already ripe, and those in the mission are still green.

Best wishes from Doña Refugio, Victoria, and María Ygnacia to you and the girls. The former says that she will go there [to El Palacio de Don Abel] in four weeks. When Don Juan gets there, he will tell you about it. One reason is that she is taking care of the vineyard until he returns; and the other, that she does not care for the town. And tell him, for my part, that he has to give me a dozen new chairs because his wife broke all those that I had in the house, with her weight.

Saludos to Doña Arcadia and Josefa. As ever your friend,

PERFECTO HUGO REID.

Two days later Hugo's annoyance with his family had become acute (translation):

They will end by driving me crazy. They had left me alone and with a great desire to do as you wish. And the worst is that having sent word this morning to ask Victoria when she expects to finish, she answers me the following: that it will take all of next week! I know the work well. It is hard because in some places they absolutely have to pick it by hand, and I have told them not to waste any. Nevertheless there are more ways to kill a dog, according to the proverb of those Gentiles called English.

The children might plague him, and for the moment Don Perfecto might rail at Doña Victoria, but it was usually with the greatest affection that he referred to his Indian wife and her children. He ended one of his last letters to Don Abel, before sailing away on the *Esmeralda,* with a poetic description of Victoria:

Hasta la tarde. Madame parece una rosa de Castilla, está sentada en frente y con sus ojos dice Salúdemelo. [Goodbye until this afternoon. Madame looks like a rose of Castile and is at this moment sitting in front of me and saying with her eyes, "Give him my love."]

Another day he gave the same message in blunt English: "The old woman sends her best respects."

One of the worst crosses that Reid, as a *hacendado,* had to bear was the country's custom of dispensing hospitality to unlimited numbers of people at any hour of the day or night. He once apologized to Stearns for sloppy bookkeeping, saying:

I enclose the notes, badly written because yesterday I was tormented with two *alcaldes,* their families, and a hundred more persons, and today I have here the family of our mutual friend Argüello. Please sign and return the notes of Leandry and Yorba. I shall take care of them.

Reid often retailed minor annoyances to Don Abel:

I am obliged to go to Santa Anita to inquire into the robbery of some of my wheat. . . .

Please send me a *fuste* [saddle tree], as one of the boys in running a bear broke his saddle from a fall. . . .

The *ardillas* [squirrels] are eating all my fences down, and since the commencement of this present year have destroyed upwards of thirty hides which might have gone into trade. . . .

The coyotes—an army of them—are destroying my vineyard, for which reason I shall be very obliged to you if you will get me four pounds of gunpowder and the ammunition that is available. . . .

Having to see Wilson fairly off, I can do nothing until he is O.P.H., as I am busily employed assisting him to sleep all day!

More than a minor annoyance was disturbing Hugo when he sat down to write to Don Abel on September 25, only a week before his departure:

Bowman [the mysterious old miller] made an attempt on his life by trying to bleed himself to death, but it was discovered in time. I never saw such a dreadful sight. All he could say when I went in was, "All is over." However, I believe he will get over it. He was in his sober senses when he did it.

Hugo did not leave San Gabriel until poor Bowman was out of danger, and Don Abel did not go with him. But there was another good friend taking a hand at the ropes as the *Esmeralda* put out to sea. William Keith came up from Hermosillo—leaving his patients to their own devices—and shipped as supercargo aboard Reid's boat. It seemed like old times.

Don Abel received only three notes during the whole six months of the *Esmeralda's* first voyage under Reid's command. The earliest came from San Diego, dated October 25, 1841. Hugo was in high spirits (translation):

Mi estimado Amigo,
Don Tomás Yorba gave me your letter from San Pedro with the rest of the mail.

We are ready to set sail, and I just write you in order to send my regards to you, your family, and all my friends.

Please tell Don Juan J. Warner⁴ that having no place to put my papers, I had to take his wallet, but that if God grants my safe return, I shall see him about it.

May God keep you in good health, and may he send you a baby soon, to wet your trousers when you are all dressed up, to remind you that you are the father of a family and that your friend esteems you.

The thought of Don Abel becoming a father always seemed to give Hugo peculiar pleasure. He mentioned it again in his next note, from Mazatlán, dated "Mayo 1° de 1842" (translation):

Give my best and kindest regards to Doña Arcadia. I wish that she may be with child as soon as possible. [The Stearnses never did have any children.] I long to embrace her and call her *comadre*. Not only that, but I have bought a dozen [bottles] of Château la Rosa Legítima, which I have put away for the event, and from now on I shall consider myself as the godfather of the boy or girl, be what it may. I even dare to christen four if need be.

I am now busily engaged in shipping you off three vessels of
soldiers with a general.[5] How grateful you Californians ought to
feel. . . .

I am getting under way for *quién sabe adónde* [who knows
where], somewhere down the coast. Ruinous business nowadays.
Nothing has been done in this or any other port for six months!
But I can only tell you month to month.

I am sick and tired of the coast, but God's will be done.

Hugo's wanderlust was wearing off, and he sent many
homesick messages to his family and friends, in the tenderer
Spanish. Then:

You must excuse me if I give you no news, for I am up to the
hatband in business, being now *capitán de buque Mexicano*.

Willis [is] well, Keith well, Paulding well, Dunn well, Day
[underlined twice] well. I weary to see you and have much to
say on my arrival.

At the end of the month, Reid put into San Pedro for re-
pairs and a brief glimpse of his familiars, but he had to go out
again in a few days and was not heard from until the middle
of July. Then from the fabled Sandwich Islands came an
uncommunicative, weary letter:

> *Buque Gobta* [*gobernata*, flagship] *Esmeralda*.
> Honolulu, Oahu, Sandwich Islands.
> Julio 19 de 1842.

Abel Stearns, Esq.

Angeles

My dear Sir,

Not lost up to this date, but I have been very near it. I merely
write to show I'm not dead yet and have not forgotten you.

Remember me kindly to Arcadia. Tired writing and hearing
caulking.

> Yours ever sincerely,
> PERFECTO HUGO REID.

In September, Hugo landed at Monterey, coming from Honolulu, and found that the duties which were levied against him more than exceeded the value of his cargo: cargo, $1167; duties, $1305.⁶ His adventure had been a costly one. But by the end of October he was back at Uva Espina, taking up his familiar tasks with a forgiving wife and children happy to have him home again.

He arrived home in time to hear reverberations from a startling event which had recently happened in Monterey, and which threatened to cause war right away between Mexico and the United States. Hugo wrote from San Gabriel on November 18, asking Don Abel to tell him all he knew about it, concluding:

> I wish to be informed if Commodore Jones has yet arrived [in Los Angeles] or when he is likely to do so. The state of this affair as it stands at present; and the items of the claims which the governor [Alvarado] intends making; moreover, your opinion as to what the probable result will be.

Reid referred to the unprovoked seizure of Monterey, a month previously, by an American naval officer, Commodore Ap Catesby Jones. Don Abel said that Jones had received orders from the United States government to stay in Monterey Bay ready to tear down the Mexican flag and hoist the American tricolor, if and when another country (meaning England) should attempt to claim California.⁷

On his way round the Horn to take up this position of watchful waiting, Commodore Jones ordered a stopover in Callao, Peru. His ship, the *Cyane,* happened to anchor near two British frigates, which were gone next morning. When Jones inquired their course, he was told that it lay in the

direction of Monterey. Leaping to the obvious conclusion,
considering his instructions, he quickly weighed anchor and
set out in pursuit of the "enemy" ships.

There was no sign of them either on the high seas or
in Monterey Bay; so the impulsive commodore, thinking
proudly that he had won the race, landed his marines, took
possession of the town, pulled down the Mexican flag, and
hoisted his own. While the residents of Monterey were recovering from the shock of such an unexpected attack, a
report came back that a ship to the windward had seen the
two frigates sailing peacefully on their way to China.

Commodore Jones at once realized his dreadful mistake;
he had violated neutrality and probably had started a war
with Mexico, prematurely. It would be months before instructions could come from Washington. Meanwhile, the
residents of Monterey were making him feel most uncomfortable, in spite of a profuse apology and the restoration of
their flag to its rightful position. Governor Alvarado, in particular, stressed the enormity of his crime against neutrality.

Finally the commodore could stand the strain no longer.
He sailed down the coast to San Pedro, in order to apologize
officially to the incoming Governor Micheltorena, who was
then making an official visit in Los Angeles on his way up
from Mexico.

Micheltorena was the same official whom Hugo Reid had
aided in preparing a fleet a few months previously. Writing
from Mazatlán on May 1, 1842, Don Perfecto had told Don
Abel that he was "busily engaged in shipping you off three
vessels of soldiers with a general who embraces the two com-
mands," and remarked, "How grateful you Californians

ought to feel." Señor Manuel Micheltorena's official title was *comandante general y jefe político de la Alta California.* He had made a name for himself in a celebrated campaign, fighting with Santa Ana against the "Texonians," and the Mexican government considered him capable of exercising the authority single handed which formerly had been divided between a governor and a general.

Commodore Jones enlisted the aid of Hugo Reid and Don Abel Stearns, having heard that Micheltorena might be influenced by them. At first he found Don Abel angry with Micheltorena and unwilling to speak to him because he had brought so many convict soldiers with him—*cholos* who were bound to be a harmful influence in California society. But Jones appealed to Don Abel's patriotism, striking deep. In spite of his opportune change in nationality, Stearns never forgot that he had been born in Massachusetts, and always remained American in his sympathies. He became greatly exercised and agreed to talk the situation over with the new governor.

A little later, Stearns reported that, "being a wise and charming gentleman," Micheltorena had been able to understand Jones's position, and was ready to give cordial welcome to all the officers from the *Cyane.* Realizing that the feelings of many remained ruffled, especially those of the sympathizers with the displaced Governor Alvarado, Don Abel had even persuaded Micheltorena to invite the Americans to a grand ball. Canny Stearns knew the childish Californians well enough to feel that the *fiesta* spirit might straighten out an international complication when all else had failed.

Doña Arcadia, loving any kind of party, was delighted at
her husband's suggestion that she invite the most beautiful
señoritas in town to come and dance with the American
officers. Conscious of the gravity of the situation and carrying Don Abel's confidence warm within her, she planned
a state dinner to take place in El Palacio. Later the guests
could step across the street to the ballroom at Doña Basilia's,
where large dances were always given.

The naval officers, not being horsemen, came up from San
Pedro in *carretas* provided by Don Abel a full week before
the ball, and were entertained all that time at El Palacio.
Finally the gala night arrived. The dinner, of course, was a
great success, attended by members of the Bandini, Reid,
and Argüello families, besides the town belles and their attentive escorts from the *Cyane*. The music could be heard
striking up across the street. But another, more dismal sound
was in the air. While the merrymakers were dining, it had
started to rain, to pour down in torrents from an ominous
sky. The street, where dust had lain several inches thick all
summer, quickly became a sea of mud.

Seeing the impossibility of wading across in party shoes
mostly made of fragile "chicken skin," and of exposing elaborate coiffures to the elements, Don Abel gallantly offered
his closed carriage—the only one in Los Angeles—to ferry
the guests over. They had a merry time, and each load lingered, laughing at the next, under the awning at Doña Basilia's. Unfortunately this awning, like the street, had not
been relieved of accumulated dust. Its slender *carrizo* (native
bamboo) supports snapped under the unaccustomed weight
of dust and water, and the whole structure collapsed. Only

a few toilettes escaped muddy desecration, and to make it worse, the horses were already on their way back to the stables a mile away.

The courtly governor, exclaiming that the ladies never should "soil their saintly little feet with the dust of Los Angeles," ordered his Mexican soldiers to draw the carriage across the street so that Don Abel's guests could change their clothes at El Palacio, returning as soon as possible.

Presently they all came back, dried and beautiful again, and the dancing lasted later than the dawn. None of the guests remembered the international complication, but by noon next day the whole town was placarded with *pronunciamentos*—fiery denunciations against the new governor, who, in the first place, had been too quick to accept the Americans' apology for their unforgivable act of pulling down the Mexican flag; then had given a *baile* for the invaders; and finally, unbelievably, had harnessed Mexican men of honor, like burros, to the carriages of the already overarrogant Commodore Jones and his officers. This was not to be borne, and the *pronunciamentos* called for an immediate revolution against the traitor, Micheltorena, and for the retention of Alvarado in office. Rage against their own governor deflected the Californians' thoughts from an immediate declaration of war against the United States.

It was only after the excitement of the Jones affair had somewhat subsided that Hugo Reid found time to tend his long-neglected *ranchos*. Life had pressed heavily on Doña Victoria when her husband had left her, with only the children to help her keep things going. She still felt deeply discouraged, in spite of her husband's reassuring words.

But the children forgot their resentment the moment
they saw wonderful presents emerging out of the depths of
Don Perfecto's trunk. From far corners of the world he had
brought gifts for his "rose of Castile" and the "little princess" María Ygnacia and his three boys. They were struck
dumb with amazement at the wonderful shells and pearls
that he had found in the South Sea; tapa cloth and strange
musical instruments from the Sandwich Islands; spices and
silks and strange weapons from they knew not where. *Quién
sabe adónde?* When Doña Victoria still showed, by her expression alone, that such presents did not wholly compen-
sate for months of hard work and worry, Hugo declared
that he knew a way of solving all the financial difficulties
that irresponsibility had brought upon his loved ones.

He proposed to exchange some of their outlying property
for land nearer Santa Anita. Then he could keep in intimate
touch with all his holdings and by concentration make up
for mismanagement and neglect. Perhaps they might even
live all the time at the *rancho* and dispose of their house near
the mission. Governor Alvarado, who was going into retire-
ment soon, owned some property suitable for exchange. Before approaching him, Reid, as was his custom, asked Don
Abel for advice:

There has been some talk of the general's [Alvarado] coming
here to live. I therefore beg your advice as to making him an
offer of my house here in the mission, for exchange of the pear
orchard and ground, squaring it with mine. Do you think I can
do anything with him, for although my house is worth more
and the pear garden nearly ruined, yet it is more advantageous
for me to have everything under my own eyes than *repartido*.
Do advise me.

The exchange with Alvarado fell through, and Hugo, having had great success with the wines maturing that year, decided to take a short trading trip on the *Esmeralda,* carrying a miscellaneous cargo partly composed of his own liquor casks. He wrote Don Abel just before departure, saying that he intended to be gone no more than a month, and only to the California ports of Santa Barbara, San Diego, and Monterey; concluding:

I cannot come in to see you until my unfortunate affair is finally settled, and my letters all written.

When do you think the *Chato* will leave?

I have five hundred Manila cigars for you, first chop, but you must come for them yourself, *asi q. haya lugar.*

As you are a widower [Arcadia being away on a visit to her family], there is no necessity of sending *saludos. . . .*

P.D. I have six barrels of *aguardiente* ready for Don Juan Everitt of the *Tasso,* to be deposited in your house at San Pedro. Have you casks there to put it into, because I shall want mine on delivery.

When Hugo returned, he found William Workman and John Rowland waiting to see him on business. Only the year previously the large La Puente *rancho* had been granted them by Governor Alvarado, and they now seemed anxious to add to their property by the purchase of Huerta del Cuati from Doña Victoria. To Don Abel, Reid wrote from the mission on February 24, 1843:

I will positively be in on Tuesday morning, nay, I should have been in now, but one of the Puente gentlemen made pretension of purchasing the ranch, and after three days spent in viewing, examining, etc., have come to nothing. Leandry sent for me four days ago, and I must go tomorrow.

The old woman is at the mill.

While Hugo was considering various ways of solving his
financial problems, he spent many hours in wine making
and ship gossip with congenial friends like Don Abel, Jim
McKinley, Pryor, Padre Tomás Estenaga, Don Benito Wilson, "Old Bowman," Laughlin, Warner, William Workman,
Bandini, Pío Pico, Louis Vignes, and William Wolfskill.

Among the events which entertained Don Perfecto that
spring, and which he found worth telling to Don Abel, were
that "a pear tree which to all appearances was dead during
the whole summer here at the house is now covered from
top to bottom with blossom!" and that the baby of the Reid
family, little Carlos, had passed his sixth birthday and now
was ready for confirmation. On March 24, Reid wrote to his
"estimado amigo":

> You will confer a particular favor by coming to the mission
> early on Tuesday morning and confirming Carlitos. My *coma-*
> *dre* is so slow about these things that I am obliged to use other
> measures to ascelerate [*sic*] our *compadrazco*. Your *comadre* that
> is to be [Victoria] sends you four *tortas de pan,* not because you
> stand in want of them, but merely to put you in mind of what
> bread we will eat some day on our own ranch of the *Alamitos.*[8]

Three days later (translation):

> The bishop says that my *comadre* and Doña Ysidora [Bandini]
> should come, that my *comadre* [Doña Arcadia] will be able to be
> godmother.
> Please send me ½ *arroba*[9] of sugar.

The hospitable Reid roof sheltered a large number of
house guests during the ceremonies of confirmation and the
fiesta that followed. Evidently Don Abel could not spare
the time from his business affairs to remain in San Gabriel

as long as his family did. On March 31, Don Perfecto wrote
from San Gabriel to Don Abel in Los Angeles, making the
first use of the title by which they would address each other
for the rest of their lives. Upon the day of Carlitos' confirmation, Reid and Stearns first called each other *compadre,* thus
showing that they had entered the intimate relationship of
parent with godparent (translation):

Mi estimado Compadre,
   Su *popa* [Don Juan Bandini] is here with his family. The
bishop and his *dependientes* [subordinates] have finished up my
sugar. So please send me an additional ½ *arroba.*
   Your affectionate *compadre* who is a bit pressed.
                                                     P. H. REID.

Always hospitable, even if "a bit pressed," Don Perfecto
finally wrote Don Abel, a few days later: "With some difficulty I got off your family, as we were disposed to keep them
ten or twelve days longer."

So extended a visit must have left the Reid family in a
weakened condition. To complete the damage, Felipe got
married, on August 18 of the same year, to María de la Re-
surección Ontiveros, daughter of Don Juan Pacífico Ontiveros and Doña Juana Martína Osuna. The wedding took
place at the mission in San Gabriel, the Padre Tomás Estenaga officiating. Witnesses were Perfecto Hugo Reid and
Don Juan Bandini, and the usual ceremonies were observed.

A letter from Hugo to Don Abel, following the wedding
fiesta, had a gloomy tone:

Mi estimado Compadre,
   I have been unable to keep my word, not from *grandes aten-
ciones* but from sickness in the familyia [*sic*]. Your *comadre* and

ahijado [Carlitos] are nearly blind with sore eyes, Dolores worse and María Ygnacia sick. Felipe's wife was unwell but now better. The moment I can leave, you shall have me with you. . . .

Dr. Den ought to be—(I would say d——d if I were not a magistrate) for going away.[10]

Reid came into the Pueblo only for *ayuntamiento* meetings, and between times carried on a frequent, casual correspondence with Don Abel—notes like the following:

Please tell Mr. Celis that the wine I have remaining is not so good as that I sold Padre Tomás, having like a jackass made *aguardiente* of all my good wine. That now on hand was manufactured at the mill by Old Bowman, and I would never think of poking it on a friend.

I consider myself a first-rate wine maker, and with my experience of this year will turn out better next.

At Hugo's suggestion, his *comadre* Doña Refugio had purchased a vineyard adjacent to the Jurupa *rancho* so that he could make wine for the Bandini family out of their own grapes. From his *vecino,* Don Luis del Aliso, Don Perfecto procured several age-old French recipes for vintage wines.

Besides cultivating carefully selected wine grapes, Don Luis, whom the *paisanos* called *"del Aliso"* because of his pride in a giant sycamore growing in his vineyard, had started an orange orchard on shares with William Wolfskill. They were first, save for the early padres who brought slips from Baja California, to try growing citrus fruits, and had been very successful. The *Southern Vineyard*[11] gave them full credit for valuable experimentation and for interesting others in scientific farming. Without difficulty the old Frenchman had persuaded Don Perfecto to try his hand at

various citrus fruits,[12] perhaps by such an inspiring statement
as he had made to William Heath Davis as far back as '33:

William, I only regret that I am not of your age. With my
knowledge of vine and orchard cultivation and of the soil and
climate of California, I foresee that these two are to have a great
future; this is just the place to grow them to perfection.[13]

Nine years later, in '42, Davis again paid him a visit,
and Don Luis asked if he remembered that conversation.
He then took Davis and a friend down into his cellar and
showed them the different vintages stored there. Bringing
out choice bottles, he told them that he had written home
to France, revealing the advantages of California for wine
making. As a result, several of his relations and other adventurous countrymen were coming to Los Angeles in the
very near future. Again he prophesied to the younger men
that the day would come when California would rival *la
belle France* in producing wines of all varieties, not alone in
quantity but in quality also, not even excepting champagne.

During casual meetings and regular *ayuntamiento* sessions, the whole talk in Reid's circle that year seemed to
center around wine making and trading ventures. Friends
would always ask each other, whether they had a financial
interest or not, about the charted courses of all the well-
known trading vessels. Some of Hugo's own questions to
Don Abel were:

When does the *Alert* leave the coast? Does she return to San
Pedro?
Has the *Tasso* gone or not?
What news of the *Chato?*
Don Juan tells me the *Llama* is in. Does she bring *alambiques
de venta?*

In April (1843) Hugo had fallen under a cloud, being accused of smuggling in some goods acquired on his January trip on the *Esmeralda*. False suspicion, perhaps; although his guilt is not improbable because of his experience the previous year when such heavy duties had been levied as to eat up all his profits and throw him into debt. As usual, Don Perfecto asked Don Abel for advice. But Stearns had become so straitlaced, since the early days when he himself was not above suspicion, that Hugo went in some trepidation and was not absolutely frank with him, giving an involved explanation:

My dear *Compadre,*

When I first arrived, I had so many spies on me, so many lies told about me, that Captain Phipps [of the *Alert*] offered to take on board two China trunks I brought on for my own use, containing partly sewing thread, cotton wick, and some of my own clothes. When I had the settlement with my owners, I gave in my list these two trunks and their contents. Phipps never returned to San Pedro, but I understand he put them on board of the *Barnstable* under care of Captain Hatch. Now, although already included in my list, yet you yourself too well know how suspicious some people are [underlined twice]. For which reason you will confer a most particular favor by procuring them from Captain Hatch, paying any charges on them, and bringing them to town. I have been so used up that I want no more disputes—whatever justice I may have on my side—and remain quiet.

Still, *compadre,* if you feel any compulsion as regards conscience's sake, I beg you will not do it, though I give you my word of honor that they contain not an iota more than I gave in, unless it be my own apparel and dirty clothes. . . .

Please send me what lead you can spare with some powder. Should any outbreak occur, an early advice would be most acceptable. . . .

P.D. Captain Noriega paid me a visit yesterday afternoon. He behaved himself and J. the same. [J. is Jim McKinley, who now had settled in the Pueblo as the proprietor of a small *tienda* and spent a great deal of time in San Gabriel, helping Hugo to make wine.] Still J. was the only member of the family he had the pleasure of seeing.

This visit seemed ominous, since Captain de la Guerra y Noriega was the most influential man in Santa Barbara, and always had been militant against smuggling. His daughter Teresa had been married to Hugo's firm friend and fellow "schoolmaster," W. P. Hartnell. This connection alone saved Don Perfecto from persecution, because he most probably was guilty. Obviously he did not expect a pleasant interview, taking care to be out when the captain came, and observing with surprise that he "behaved himself." It all subsided in more exciting news from the other side of the world. At *ayuntamiento* meetings Hugo was able to deflect interest from his own affairs by broadcasting the situation in the Orient:

Los papelos públicos [newspapers] that they send me from Sandwich, dated April [1843], contain *The Comet,* eight articles of treaty between China and England: twenty-one millions; five ports, *viz.,* Canton, Amoy, Foo-Chow-Foo, Ningpoo, and Shanghai, open to British commerce; the island of Hongkong ceded to H.B.M. [Her British Majesty, Victoria], her heirs and successors forever; all British subjects of every denomination confined in any part of China to be released immediately; regular duties at the above ports to be established, also transit duties. Everlasting peace and friendship between the two empires: an act of amnesty to be published by the Emperor under his Imperial Sign Manual and Seal to all Chinese subjects on account of their having held intercourse or resided under the British gov-

ernment; the islands of Chusan and Kulangsoo to be held by
the British until the money is paid. Dated on board the steam
frigate *Queen* in Yangtze-Kiang River off Nanking, the twenty-
sixth of August, 1842.

Sandwich Islands delivered to the English the twenty-fifth of
February, 1843, to Her Majesty's frigate *Marysford,* Right Honor-
able Lord George Paulet, captain. The United States ship of war
Boston at the islands.

At Otehaite [Tahiti] they are laying an English and French
man of war side to side, guns double shotted, quarreling as is
their use, and threatening to fire into each other with both flags
flying on shore.

Pretty *Comet, mis amigos.*

With such excitement in the Orient and too many difficulties at home, departure seemed inevitable for Hugo Reid.
Once again he sailed off in the *Esmeralda,* hoping that
shawls and a few pearls would make peace with Doña Victoria. Resolutely he pushed away the thought of ruin falling
on his untended *ranchos.*

CHAPTER SIX

Calamity at the Mission

S OON AFTER Hugo's return
from the Orient, he wrote confidentially to Don Abel that
he must sell his ranch or vineyard:

Uva Espina.
Mi estimado Compadre,   Junio 1, 1844.

As you are one of the very few persons with whom I can consult, or ask advice from, I shall at once go ahead. In debt as I am
at present, I find it necessary to dispose of either the *rancho* or
the vineyard; in fact, even were I not in debt, I would have to do
one or the other. Because the *rancho, por falta del amo* [through
the master's fault], does not go right. Having taken everything
into serious consideration, I am convinced that my interests will
be more advanced in retaining the farm. There I have a number
of horses and about four hundred head of cattle. Please therefore to give me your opinion of how much I ought to ask, remembering that I require part cash, part goods, and part hides
and tallow to pay debts or assumptions of them.

The vineyard is walled around. It contains vines totaling 22,730
and ground sufficient to make up the number of 40,000, besides
430 varieties of fruit trees: 20,500 *parras* [vines raised on stakes]
of *uba prieta* [dark grapes], 2,070 *uba blanca* [white grapes], 160
uba cimarrona [maroon grapes],[1] in all, 22,730 vines and ground
sufficient to make up the number of 40,000; 21 fig trees, 7 plums,
25 pears, 5 apples, 32 oranges, 40 *granadas* [pomegranates], 2
alvechegos [probably *arvejos,* or honey mesquite trees], 240 *du-
raznos* [peaches], 8 *capulines* [blood oranges], 3 *nogales* [wal-

nut trees], 7 *olivos* [olive trees], 40 *limones* [lemon trees], in all, 430 trees.

I don't include my *tuna* [cactus fruit] patch, as that must be a separate bargain.

Now after making your calculations, bearing in mind all its advantages, tell me who would be most probable to purchase.... I don't wish it noised abroad for many reasons. Therefore I count on your secrecy further than is indispensable.

Of course I am not going to make a sacrifice, and the vineyard will pay a most excellent interest on the purchaser's money. *Con dolor de corazón* I do it, for the situation is beautiful and the ground enjoyable.

I want your answer as soon as you can give it, because I must take prompt steps.

While this matter of selling Doña Victoria's dower was simmering, other troubles broke over Hugo's head, as the result of an honor paid him a few months previously. His neighbors in San Gabriel had elected him to their highest public office, that of *juez de paz*. He was sufficiently impressed with the necessity of being a good example to stop saying "damn." And his sense of responsibility extended even farther—to his wife's people, the lowly Indians, who were forgotten or abused by almost all his fellow office holders in California. As a result the Indians became devoted to him, and many women wanted Don Perfecto rather than the padre to baptize their children. Hugo wrote amusingly to Don Abel one busy day:

Juan Pacífico's wife and half a dozen more women took it into their heads to bring forth, and have given me a general power to make Christians of the produce. Now the Padre Blas, governed on the principles and by the same laws as comets are, is at present in this hemisphere where he remains some thirty hours, performing his evolutions every three hundred forty-two and a half hours. Besides I have taken it into my head that good luck will ensue.

In spite of Don Perfecto's just administration, the mission Indians, long restive under the abuse of others, now rebelled openly against the arrogance of the *gente de razón*. They started sporadic raids on outlying *ranchos,* and other outbreaks of a serious nature, after being roused by a careless statement of Don Juan Pérez. Unfortunately, Doña Eulalia's kindly attitude toward the neophytes was not shared by other members of the family, such as her cousin Juan. To intimidate the Indians completely and get them to work without recompense, he said that now, under the secular administration of mission property, they would be kept in more hopeless subjugation than ever before, when the padres were all-powerful; and never in all their future would they know freedom.

Reid heard of this threat. He at once made a report to the *ayuntamiento,* asking for permission to regulate Indian affairs more humanely than had been the custom for many years—since the death of the wise Padre Sánchez in '33. He also asked the present mission administrator, Manuel de Oliveira, to assure the frightened Indians that no one intended to keep them in slavery all their lives. But, wary after years of abuse, the Indians attached more significance to Juan Pérez' careless prophecy than to official protestations of kindheartedness and ineffectual blessings from the padre. They were ready to take their own stand for freedom and some measure of justice.

No one man, or even one party, can be blamed for de-
basing the California Indians. But the fact remains that
within sixty years a race of self-respecting people, whose
religion, legislature, and standard of living revealed a high
degree of civilization, had been transformed into helpless
slaves serving white masters without recompense and giving lip service to a religion which few of them understood.
From the first, the pageantry of Catholicism appealed to a
love of color and music in the aborigines, but most of them
continued secretly to live by age-old beliefs and customs of
Oriental origin.[2]

A great deal remains, of lasting beauty and significance,
from the untiring efforts of the Franciscans to start a missionary colonization in California. By appealing to the mys-
ticism buried deep in the Indian nature they persuaded some
of the proud red men to work for them, willingly enough
in the beginning. On Indian labor the padres superimposed
their own imagination and romantic love of beauty. The
twenty-one missions, which even now, in the years of decay,
are the most romantic spots in California, stand as monu-
ments to the imagination, the religious fervor, and, equally,
to the cruelty of those early padres, many of them men of
iron who drove "lazy" Indians before the lash in the service
of the white man's God, whom few Indians reverenced as
a Supreme Being like their own Giver of Life. The aborigines had no wicked spirit connected with their ancient creed,
and never heard of a "Devil" or "Hell" until the coming
of the Spaniards.

Spanish soldiers sent to "protect" the mission communities were of coarser fiber than the selfless Franciscans, and

from them the poor neophytes caught venereal and other diseases never suffered in the natural state, which took heavy toll among them.

There are two explanations for the fact that the California Indians submitted as passively as they did to the Spanish "conquest." Hugo Reid has given one, which he evolved out of conversations with intelligent members of the race:

The priest having "converted" some few by giving them cloth and ribbons, and taught them to say *Amar a Dios,* they were baptized and coöperated in the work before them.

Baptism as performed, and the recital of a few words not understood, can hardly be said to be a conversion; nevertheless, it was productive of great advantage to the missionaries, because once baptized, they lost "caste" with their people, and had, *nolens volens,* to stop with the oppressor. This, of course, was put down by the padre as a proof of the influence of religion on their minds, and the direct interposition of the Virgin Mary! Poor devils, they were the *Pariah* of the West! Not one word of Spanish did they understand—not one word of the Indian tongue did the priest know. They had no more idea that they were worshiping God than an unborn child has of astronomy. Numbers of old men and women have been gathered to the dust of their fathers—and a few still remain—whose whole stock of Spanish was contained in the never-failing address of *Amar a Dios!* And whose religion, as Catholics, consisted in being able to cross themselves, under an impression it was something connected with hard work and still harder blows. Baptism was called by them *soyna,* "being bathed," and strange to say, was looked upon, although such a simple ceremony, as being ignominious and degrading.

The second explanation is offered by Edwin F. Walker, writing on Indians of southern California:[3]

Peace is much talked of nowadays as a mark of civilization. Until the whites arrived, there probably had been almost no organized warfare for hundreds of years in most of southern California, where there were no war drums, no war chiefs, no well-defined tribal organization. In fact, "tribe" meant so little to these Indians that they could give the whites no definite idea of it; consequently most of them are referred to as Mission Indians, named after the Spanish missions established in their vicinity, as Gabrieleno from Mission San Gabriel and Juaneño from San Juan Capistrano. Many of these Indians belonged to the great Shoshonean family, who had penetrated the country unknown centuries ago, doubtless as conquerors; but once having secured a foothold, they seem to have settled down to enjoy in peace the climate and the abundant food supply. At the time of the discovery they probably were as inoffensive, contented, and happy as any Indians in all America.

But the white pioneer applied "Diggers" as a term of contempt to all tribes whose women carried sticks with which to dig up edible roots, just as a white gardener would use a spade to gather his potatoes—a food, by the way, which the world obtained from the Indians of Peru.

No one can justly cast aspersions on the padres' purity of purpose in trying to "convert" the Indians from their former way of life. It was proved beyond a doubt during the years of disintegration of the extensive mission system, following the Secularization Act of 1833. There were padres who endured starvation along with their Indian neophytes, remembering that it was absolutely forbidden in their order to have personal possessions. In the prosperous years they had lived well—very well,—but when the Church was poverty stricken, the padres often went hungry and dressed in rags.

It touched Don Perfecto and Doña Victoria to the heart to see Fray Tomás, who had married them, perform his spiritual duties sadly, without hope of a change while he was on earth. It hurt them also to see Indians, whom they both had known well, turn surly and desperate under unjust treatment. In every way Hugo and Victoria tried to lighten the load of the padre and his Indian *hijos* (children)—as the lonely man always referred to the neophytes. So many distressing incidents occurred that Don Perfecto in his capacity of *juez de paz* had his hands full, and Jim McKinley often relieved him of the management of his ranching business so that he could dispense justice. But in one letter to Don Abel, the first in which Hugo mentioned trouble with the Indians, he confessed:

Nothing new or strange. Merely Jim and the Indians can't agree, or I must settle affairs in my double capacity of master and magistrate.

Hugo found a more valuable aid than Jim in another old friend. Henry Dalton, his former partner, came up from Lima in '45, bought land at San Gabriel, and settled near the Reid home. He accepted the post of *mayordomo* (secular administrator) at the mission and tried, working with Hugo, to bring some order out of the chaos that had existed ever since the Order of Secularization. But their efforts did not meet with public approval. The majority of *paisanos,* having enriched themselves on mission property, had no intention of returning to the old order. A petition to Governor Pico, dated February 20, 1846, while Estenaga was padre and Henry Dalton and Mariano Roldán were *mayordomos,* showed dissatisfaction and a desire to do away entirely with ecclesiastical control. It was signed by one hundred and forty Gabrielenos.

After stating a number of grievances against the *padres administradores y mayordomos,* they asked that a pueblo

be made of the former mission, "since its present condition
was so bad." But on March 17 *la comisión de misiones* passed
a resolution not to allow the Mission of San Gabriel to become a pueblo, because of its heavy debt. This, it said, "will
be settled as the governor shall presently dictate."

Meanwhile, things had come to such a pass that several
rancheros had to leave their homes and gather at the mission for protection against renegade Indians. Hugo Reid,
having as much influence over the Indians as over the *gente
de razón,* was reappointed *juez de paz* and also an administrator of mission affairs. He expected an outbreak momently
and asked Don Abel to send him some soldiers to help keep
the peace. Acknowledging their arrival, he wrote:

I think it very probable that *next* week will find me in the
blessed city, and I think it would have been more than probable
you would have seen me *this,* but your kindness in dispatching
so many soldiers prevents it.

It is hard to tell just what motive inspired Hugo's next
step. On June 8, 1846, all San Gabriel was startled to hear
that the mission and what lands were left to the Church had
been sold, by order of Governor Pico, to Hugo Reid and
William Workman. At the same time, the governor appointed Reid and Antonio Cot to receive, audit, and adjust
outstanding claims against the mission.

Perhaps Don Perfecto imagined that he could manage the
mission affairs more effectually with the authority of ownership. Ambition may have played a large part in the transaction. At any rate, Reid and Workman promised to put up
$7000, pay the debts of the mission, and support the padre.
Where they expected to find the money is a mystery. Per-

haps it was fortunate that Colonel Frémont, acting for the United States government, came in and dispossessed them before the term of payment was over.

Don Perfecto had some cash in sight to make the first payment, because Henry Dalton wanted to buy Santa Anita. Seeing himself, theoretically, in possession of so much other land, Hugo decided to oblige his friend in spite of a firm resolve to sell the vineyard and not the *rancho*. Dalton paid $2700 for the most beautiful *rancho* in the valley.⁴

In the heat of his fever for land, Hugo had even considered a partnership with Don Abel in the Rancho Los Alamitos, but this idea passed out of his mind as the mission "ownership" began to give him trouble. Writing to Don Abel from Uva Espina, he confessed to his "dear *compadre*" (June 25, 1846):

The Gabrielenos are behaving very badly. Some remedy must be done to make them obey; if not now, at all events when the *gobierno* returns. I have taken notes of the whole. If said *gobierno* permits such blackguards still to remain in San Gabriel and its vicinity, God have mercy on us.

Yesterday everyone cleared out. Every door was shut with the exception of three persons. Those I ordered into town, under pain not only of chastisement but loss of lands. Last night on going to bed, about eight persons came on horseback wanting grog. I refused it them. They were pretty well drunk and would give no account of themselves. It being dark, the thing was done on purpose to *burlar* [as a hoax].

As a salutary measure, Reid tried recruiting the *gente mala* (bad people) as soldiers. He hoped that constant discipline would curb their lawless natures; but most of them ran away to the hills and hid. He sent Captain José Machado with

some troops out after them, and besides, rounded up all suspicious characters remaining in the *misión vieja*. After in-
terrogating them, he decided that "all people of the *misión
vieja* have good dispositions," and that the "invading Indians
are of the unruly Cahuila tribe and not peaceful Yutas."

Machado returned without having found the *ladrones;*
so Don Perfecto consulted with the governor upon the next
steps he should take. Pico suggested Don Benito Wilson as
a man capable of organizing a deadly serious manhunt. In
his diary Don Benito has left a full account of the affair,[5]
giving an excuse for his ruthlessness:

The Mojave and other Indians were constantly raiding upon
the ranches in this part of the country, and at the request of the
governor, Don Pío Pico, who had promised me a force of eighty
well-mounted men, well armed, I took command of an expedition to go in pursuit of the Indians.

I organized the expedition in San Bernardino, sent the pack
train and soldiers (less twenty-two which I retained with me)
through the Cajón Pass; myself and twenty-two went up the San
Bernardino River through the mountains, and crossed over to
what is now Bear Lake. Before arriving at the lake we captured
a village the people of which had all left, except two old women
and some children. On the evening of the second day we arrived
at the lake; the whole lake and swamp seemed alive with bear.

The twenty-two Californians went out in pairs, and each pair
lassoed one bear and brought the result to the camp, so that we
had at one and the same time eleven bears. This prompted me
to give the lake the name it now bears.

Pursued our course down the Mojave River, before we met the
balance of the command. Then all together marched down some
four days. I was in advance with one companion some two or
three miles, with a view of looking for signs of Indians.

I saw ahead of us four Indians on the path coming toward us;

noticing that they had not seen us, I went down into the river bed and continued on my course until a point was reached that I supposed was opposite to where they would be, and then went up on the bank again. My calculation was correct; the Indians were right opposite on the plain, and I rode toward them. I spoke to them, and they answered in a very friendly manner.

My object was not to kill them, but to take them prisoners that they might give me information on the points I desired.

The leading man of the four happened to be the very man of all others I was seeking for, *viz.*, the famous marauder Joaquín, who had been raised as a page of the church, in San Gabriel Mission, and for his depredations and outlawing, bore on his person the mark of the mission, that is, one of his ears cropped off and the iron brand on his lip. This is the only instance I ever saw or heard of this kind. That marking had not been done at the mission, but at one of its *ranchos* [El Chino] by the *mayordomo*.

I entered into conversation with Joaquín; the command was coming on, and he then became convinced that we were on a campaign against him and his people. It was evident before, that he had taken me for a traveler. Immediately that he discovered the true state of things, he whipped from his quiver an arrow, strung it on his bow, and left nothing for me to do but shoot him in self-defense; we both discharged our weapons at the same time. I had no chance to raise the gun to my shoulder, but fired it from my hand. His shot took effect in my right shoulder, and mine, in his heart.

The shock of his arrow in my shoulder caused me involuntarily to let my gun drop. My shot knocked him down disabled, but he discharged at me a tirade of abuse in the Spanish language such as I never had heard surpassed. I was on muleback, got down to pick up my gun; by this time my command arrived at the spot. The other three Indians were making off out over the plains. I ordered my men to capture them alive, but the Indians resisted stoutly, refused to the last to surrender, wounded several of our horses and two or three men, and had to be killed.

Those three men actually fought eighty men in open plain till they were put to death. During the fight Joaquín lay on the ground uttering curses and abuse against the Spanish race and people. I discovered that I was shot with a poisoned arrow, rode down some five hundred yards to the river, and some of my men, on returning and finding that Joaquín was not dead, finished him off. I had to proceed immediately to the care of my wound.

This was the first of three efficient campaigns which Don Benito directed against the Indians. His own men met defeat in the second, but fully redeemed themselves in the final attack. After his unexpected defeat, Don Benito at once wrote to "his old friend and companion," Don Enrique Avila, to ask him:

. . . if he would join me with ten picked men and renew our campaign down the River Mojave. He answered that he would do so, *con mucho gusto*. He came forthwith, and we started for the trip, twenty-one strong.

Some seven or eight days after we reached the field of operations, myself and Avila being in advance, we descried an Indian village. I at once directed my men to divide into two parties, to surround and attack the village. We did it successfully, but as on the former occasion, the men in the place would not surrender, and on my endeavoring to persuade them to give up, they shot one of my men, Evan Callaghan, in the back.

I thought he was mortally wounded, and commanded my men to fire. The fire was kept up until every Indian man was slain. We took the women and children prisoners.

Such unhappy scenes were more than old Padre Tomás could stand. He died in Christmas week, '46, and was succeeded by an equally ineffectual, less kindly priest named Ordaz. The poor Indians continued to find open rebellion more disastrous than cruel and monotonous servitude. But when Juan Pérez died, soon after Fray Tomás, they drew a long breath and hoped for better days. He had been their cruelest oppressor, in sharp contrast to their beloved Señora Eulalia Pérez, his cousin.

Hugo described the last hours of Don Juan, which he himself spent in trying to collect an amount of money long owed to Don Abel. As chief magistrate of San Gabriel, he sometimes was called upon to make wills in addition to his more usual duties. He wrote, on "Mayo 20 de 1847":

Mi estimado Compadre,
  Yesterday died Juan Pérez at a quarter from 9 a.m. On my first arrival here his will had already been made out, but not satisfying to any of the parties concerned. I was accordingly called in on the fourteenth to make it out anew, which I did not until the fifteenth, and observing that your name was not among the creditors, I immediately made the *reclamo.* Juan Pérez' answer was that he owed you nothing; on the contrary that you owed him besides ten dollars for oranges.
  I finished the will accordingly but put in of my own self a saving clause in favor of any creditors, etc., omitted; by which the *albaceas* [his two sons][8] are obliged to pay any debts of which *comprobantes* are produced.
  Yesterday morning early, Manuel the Portuguese informed me you had mentioned that the *finado* owed you five hundred dollars. I immediately sent for the *albaceas* and requested that their father should be again asked the question, which he was, about an hour before he expired.
  "Do you owe Don Abel anything?"
  "No! He still owes me about ten dollars."
  "You were formerly owing Don Abel a large amount. How or in what manner did you cancel the debt?"
  "In making him a *saca de agua,* and the goods taken up were for the purpose of paying his servants."

I put you in possession of this for your own government. I have made several remarks to the *albaceas* on the subject, but nothing glaring, as they might think I had sinister motives. However, I doubt not but the affair can easily be settled, particularly as they are bound to consult with me on everything and take no step without my approval. Be therefore cautious, and use my name sparingly in any interview, so as not to frighten them. I can serve you better as their *aconsejero*.

I wish you could get your *compañeros* to pass their opinions as commissioners on my claim [on the mission land] so as to send it to windward for approval, by Temple.[7]

Saludos from your *comadre,* María Ygnacia, and Carlos to my *comadre, ahijada,* and yourself.

The death of Juan Pérez did not benefit the Indians as they had hoped, for a few days afterward some renegades murdered a *vaquero* named Simón at Rancho Santa Anita, and Hugo had to call on the *ayuntamiento* for troops to pursue them. Colonel Stevenson arrived with his New York Volunteers and ordered everyone, not legally authorized to live in the mission, to clear out. He left some dragoons and told *el juez* (Hugo) to use them in protecting Manuel de Oliveira, while he carried out his duties.

Padre Ordaz had spiritual charge of the mission, but could do nothing to soften the spirit of the secular administrator. All during May and July the *paisanos* were continually protesting against the increasingly arbitrary acts of De Oliveira, and finally demanded his removal.

Under Padre Estenaga's kindly rule, mission Indians had often been allowed to retire from the community to their own *rancherías* and others. De Oliveira ordered them back to the mission grounds, under his eye. They were unwilling to submit to this, if he was to remain in office. Their pleas did not result in his dismissal, but the *mayordomo's* powers were diminished, and the padre's extended. Military rule had been proved too harsh for practicality, and the padre was once more allowed to combine temporal with spiritual power, in a travesty of the old days.

Unfortunately, the Indians had little respect for Padre Ordaz, since he was indecisive and weak. Depredations continued, and the situation grew more tense than ever before. At last, on February 24, 1848, a bombshell burst over the local Indians, in the form of an official communication from the *ayuntamiento* (translation):

To Stephen C. Foster
First *Alcalde* of the City of Los Angeles
Sir,
The public peace requires that the Indian *rancherías* in the vicinity of the Pueblo be broken up and removed to a greater distance from the town.
You are therefore requested to cause their removal, or breakage-up, on or before the night of the twenty-sixth inst. . . .

This was too harsh, since it gave the Indians only two days to break up their homes, and left them no place to call their own, where they could live free from persecution. More spirited than many of their brothers, the Gabrielenos refused to comply without force to so unjust an order. So San Gabriel became more of a hotbed than ever before. The *ayuntamiento* records and archives of the next few years teemed with references to its distressing state.

But Hugo Reid soon went out of office, and his family affairs, the Mexican War, and the Gold Rush, for several years, superseded his interest in the Indians. His last mention of them, before his widely read letters about Doña Victoria's people appeared in the *Los Angeles Star* during '52, occurred in a letter to Don Abel dated March 30, 1848:

They are at this minute burying Orosco, who was killed by the Indians. Dalton had a cow shot by arrows in his corral a few nights since, at Santa Anita. . . .

There is little doubt but that the Indians were in this mission last night. Three horses have been taken off, and some Indians here, on whose word I can depend, assert the fact. Please procure me some powder.

The points of the arrows used by the Indians who killed Orosco are of iron. What Indians are they? *Vale*.

CHAPTER SEVEN

War Clouds

"FROM WAR deliver us, Lord!" So prayed Hugo Reid in a letter written to Don Abel two years before the actual outbreak. Don Perfecto had seen war clouds forming at the time when Commodore Jones seized Monterey, by mistake; even earlier, for relations between Mexico and the United States had been increasingly strained ever since the separation of Texas from the Mexican Republic in March, '36. The Jones incident ended, after a period of resentment, in a revolution of the Californians against the *Americano*-loving governor, Manuel Micheltorena. Indeed it was on the very day of Hugo's prayerful letter to Don Abel, November 14, 1844, that the Californians started a serious revolt which resulted in Micheltorena's exile, following the bloodless battle of Cahuenga Pass near Los Angeles on February 20, 1845.

Don Pío Pico, as president of the *ayuntamiento,* became *ad interim* governor in Micheltorena's place, retaining headquarters in Los Angeles. On April 18, 1846, Pico was confirmed in office by the central government, making him California's third native governor, and the last under Mexican jurisdiction.

Don Pío, born in San Gabriel in 1801, had moved to San Diego not long after the death of his father in '19. There he opened a *tienda* and made many friends. Perhaps the most intimate, always, was Don Juan Bandini, then a youth his own age and later secretary of state to Pico's governorship. Don Pío first entered politics as a *vocal* (member) in the *diputación* at Mexico City in 1828. He played a prominent part in the revolution of '31, started by Don Juan and Don Abel Stearns against Governor Victoria.[1] His friends offered to elect him governor at that time; but foreseeing great opposition, especially in the north, he declined the office and continued to serve in lesser political capacities until the revolt against Micheltorena.

By Mexican grant, Don Pío received three large *ranchos:* Temecula, Santa Margarita, and Las Flores. He also happened to be serving on the *diputación* when the Secularization Act was passed in '33, and secured a profitable contract to slaughter cattle at San Gabriel Mission. Again, he benefited in many ways by being secular administrator of San Luis Rey from '34 to '40. As governor, his record seems smudged by the antedating of several land grants and the questionable distribution of mission property among his own friends.

Hugo Reid and William Workman received title to the San Gabriel Mission lands about the time other valuable church properties went to other intimate friends of Governor Pico's. San Juan Capistrano was sold to Juan Forster and Jim McKinley for $710; La Purísima Concepción to Juan Temple for $1110; and San Luis Obispo to Scott, Wilson, and McKinley for $510. The extensive Santa Barbara Mission lands were leased to Nicholas A. Den and Daniel Hill for $1200 a year, and those of San Fernando, to Andrés

Pico, Pío's brother, and Juan Manso for $1120 a year.[2] The kindest explanation of Don Pío's extensive land grants is probably the correct one. He saw the American invasion coming closer, and tried to save what he could for his friends and family. Of course he failed, for very few of these hasty "grants" were honored by the *Americanos*.

War clouds seemed to be forming black and menacing when on July 10, 1845, the Mexican minister of interior relations ordered Governor Pío Pico to prevent further immigration of Americans to California. But by September such worried onlookers as Don Perfecto and Don Abel were reassured by President Polk's appointment of John Slidell to act as secret agent to Mexico. His instructions were to secure a permanent boundary between the United States and Mexico, through the peaceful purchase of Alta California and New Mexico.

In October, Secretary of State James Buchanan secretly instructed Thomas O. Larkin, serving as United States consul in Monterey since the previous year, that he should encourage the Spanish-Californians to resist any French and English overtures they might receive. Buchanan intimated that the United States would render "kind offices" to California, should she decide to declare her independence from Mexico.

Larkin's policy, always, was to secure California for the United States by peaceful methods. To this end he appointed William A. Leidesdorff, living in Yerba Buena, to act as vice consul, and then approached three men prominent in the other most important communities who, he felt, would be loyal to the United States, whatever the turn of affairs. It happened that all three were naturalized Mexican citizens, but each responded, as the consul had expected, with the assurance of loyalty to his mother country.

On April 27, 1846, a few days after hostilities commenced along the Río Grande, Larkin sent out a secret circular letter to Jacob P. Leese, formerly of the firm of Reid, Keith, and Leese, and now living in Sonoma, to Abel Stearns in Los Angeles, and to Juan Warner in San Diego. It read in part:

Mr. Polk has taken a high stand respecting the Oregon question, from which he will not descend. Mr. Slidell's ministry has been refused by Mexico, and great political dissatisfaction has been caused in Mexico by the struggle between Herrera and Paredes. When the *Portsmouth* left Mazatlán [April 1], the *comandante general* of Mazatlán, before leaving for Rosario taking archives *et cetera,* published a *bando* informing the inhabitants that the commodore would on the morrow declare the port in a state of blockade, thereby giving the Americans *reason to suppose that there was war*. However, Sloat [Commodore John Drake Sloat] had no definite news of war, although he was expecting it.

No two adjacent nations can continue long as Mexico and the United States have been of late. War or better terms is the only alternative. Should the former now be the case, I believe that the Stars would shine over California before the Fourth of July, helping those who see them and their posterity after them! If peace should continue, and friendship between the two nations be established, some change in the near future is bound to occur. I am partial to the Californians and hope to see them profit by the change. There is much at stake in the coming events. Only better government by Mexico in California can keep the people here loyal to Mexico. They already begin to look abroad for help.

Some look to England, some to the United States, and a few to France; the last as a *dernier* resort. Those who look to Europe know nothing of the European colonist's life, or the heavy tax and imposition he suffers. The Californian should look only to the United States of America for assistance, as there only will he find a fellow feeling. Mr. Polk has reiterated the Monroe Doctrine and will make it good. The day that the European by purchase, or the European by war, places his foot on California soil, that day shall we see the hardy sons of the west come to the rescue!

I have given my opinion to you as a friend of California and wish no copies made of this letter. You will oblige me by carefully reading and with the same care giving me an answer, as I know you have always preferred excitement to indolence, and have been much in the political vortex of California. I must ask of you if you will inform me, by a safe conveyance from time to time, of any wish on the part of the people in your vicinity to change or to better their condition. Should circumstances require it, I shall visit the north and south this summer.

Warner and Leese both replied, after some delay, that they were favorable to the United States, but did not offer to take an active part in the coming events.

Stearns answered Larkin's interesting letter promptly and fully on May 14, being the only one of the three to plunge into the consul's campaign on behalf of the United States. He informed Larkin that an idea of independence had long been nourished in southern California, but that he, Don Abel, had opposed it, believing that there were neither means nor people to support a revolt from Mexican rule. Overtures had already been made by British agents, to the end that California declare herself independent of Mexico and under the protection of Great Britain. The people of the south desired to call a convention, toward the end of the month, and to send deputies to Mexico City protesting against misgovernment.

On May 23, Larkin appointed Stearns as the confidential
agent, in southern California, of the United States government. In asking him to accept, Larkin had written: "From
various circumstances I consider it of the greatest importance to me to have a confidential correspondent in your
place of residence, one with whom I can rely on the con-
ducting and negotiating of my business." Don Abel would
not receive a salary, but Larkin said that he believed Stearns
and his interests could "be advanced at some future day not
far distant; therefore, the end may justify the means, at least
in the result. You must only look for a recompense in an
extended knowledge of affairs." He told Don Abel not to let
anyone know, at present, of his position.

Indeed it seemed a delicate one. Not only was Don Abel
a naturalized citizen of Mexico at the time of his appointment as confidential agent of the United States, but he also
served, simultaneously, as subprefect of Los Angeles under
the Mexican government. Secrecy was more vital to him
than to Larkin, who always stood in the clear as United
States consul.

Don Abel performed an invaluable service for Larkin, aiding him greatly in ascertaining the true feelings of residents
in the south. The two men concurred heartily in the belief
that California's interests could best be served by peaceful
annexation by the United States.

On June 12, Don Abel wrote a letter to the consul, asking
a question which was troubling many of his friends, among
them Hugo Reid: "Would the United States give immediate
and permanent protection to California in case of a favorable declaration?"

Whether Don Perfecto actually had knowledge of Don Abel's affiliation with Larkin, or merely suspicions, during these months of suspense, he bombarded his *compadre* with such questions as:

What more news have you procured *via* the *Man of War* or other sources?

What is your opinion of things at present? Some *envido,* I am afraid, is going on.

The *envido* that troubled Don Abel most, at the moment, was the Macnamara affair, wherein lay the chief reason for Frémont's opening of hostilities a few months later.[4]

On June 14, a letter came to Don Abel from the United States consul, saying:

We have in Monterey the Rev. Mr. Macnamara, who arrived here from Mazatlán in H.R.M. ship *Juno.* The officers of the ship were by the captain prohibited from bringing letters. Mr. Macnamara is a Catholic priest, an Irishman; has been in the City of Mexico all 1844 with Herrera; almost concluded a negotiation for the London Emigration Society to land ten thousand Irish in California. Paredes refused to allow any emigrant whose native language was English, adding that the Irish in California would join the Yankees at once.

Mr. Macnamara dresses in citizen's clothes; has in my opinion full as much government and political information as theological. He and the captain of the *Juno* appear to be satisfied that no government course can prevent the destiny of California as it now appears to be going.

I have purchased a farm at Sonoma. I have repeatedly advised those in power at Monterey to ask for large tracts of land by which means they will become rich; as in a few years they may not stand as they do now, and all will find their level according to their merits. The *prefecto* of this district, I believe, does not

see affairs as I see them, and yet believes their usual fortune will
carry them through. The Oregon question to your knowledge
remains as it was; only the government at Washington has given,
I understand, the twelve months' notice to England. . . .

Mr. Macnamara has correspondence for the bishop; now goes
south; will call on the governor, I suppose. He brought to me
letters of recommendation from our consul in Mexico. He has
a very good appearance; his actual business, I presume to be
of a private nature, as agent of his company to find available
lands for the Irish. I should think his government had cognizance of the business; perhaps affords assistance. Will you inform me of his motives and movements, as far as they may come
to your knowledge. . . .

                                                              T. O. L.

Don Abel found Macnamara already in the good graces
of Governor Pico, who, besides being a Catholic, always favored Great Britain over the United States in the event of a
foreign invasion. Don Pío was inclined to give the priest as
much as he asked for—a large tract of land in the interior
and on the San Joaquín River, commencing at the Arroyo
Concomnes; extending south and southeast, and skirting
San Gabriel. Macnamara would obligate himself to bring
two thousand families, about ten thousand souls in all, to
settle the colony, which he prophesied would act as a buffer
between Protestant America and Catholic California.

Since it involved a very large grant of mission land, Governor Pico could do no more than recommend the proposition to the central *diputación* in Mexico City, adding his
own belief that it might serve to resist the dreaded encroach-
ment of *los Yanquis*.

Macnamara's colony of Irish Catholics seemed to many,
among them John Charles Frémont, an unmistakable at-

tempt on the part of England to gain some legal claim on
Alta California. Captain Frémont, just arrived on his second
exploration expedition to the Far West, immediately compre-
hended that if the grant once became legalized, England
would have a permanent stronghold in California. So while
the priest was down in Los Angeles obtaining the governor's
support to his project, Frémont erected a fort and raised his
own flag on Gavilán Peak. He prepared to resist orders of the
Mexican general, José Castro, requiring all *Americanos* to
clear out of California. Remaining only three days in his
own camp, Frémont decided to retreat during the night of
March 9 to the more impregnable Sutter's Fort. He always
contended that he had warded off a later, more serious war
with England by this prompt action.

Frémont also had a hand in instigating the Bear-Flag Revolt, by promising protection to the impetuous Californians
who raised their black-bear flag, standard of the "California
Republic," over the Plaza at Sonoma, following the capture
of General Mariano Guadalupe Vallejo, Lieutenant Colonel
Victor Prudon, and Captain Salvador Vallejo. Jacob Leese,
acting as interpreter, was imprisoned along with the Mexican officers, first at Captain Frémont's camp on the American River and then at Sutter's Fort. He wrote an interesting
eyewitness account[5] of the short-lived revolt, which ended
in Frémont's reorganization of the insurgents into the intrepid California Battalion, fighting for the United States.

A month preceding the bear-flag episode, the conflict so
long expected, and so dreaded, by men of peaceful nature
like Larkin, Abel Stearns, and Hugo Reid, turned into ac-
tuality. On May 13, 1846, President Polk publicly proclaimed

that "by the act of the Republic of Mexico, a state of war exists between that government and the United States." Shortly afterward, on June 3, Secretary of War William Marcy ordered Colonel Stephen W. Kearny to advance from Santa Fé and, as commander-in-chief of all military and naval forces of the United States on the Pacific slope, to take possession of Alta California.

The American advance was machinelike in its implacable thoroughness. Apparently the Californians were surprised in their sleep; and they offered little resistance during the first four months of "warfare." From fear of interception, the letters of Hugo Reid to Don Abel became sparse and cryptic at this time, and can no longer be deciphered—the key was lost too long ago. For instance, on July 15, '46, Don Perfecto wrote mysteriously from Uva Espina to his "dear *compadre*" in the Pueblo:

On arriving here yesterday afternoon a woman (one who can be believed) assured me of the same—you understand. Moreover that Mr. Flowers has given his word that whenever the people were handed over to him, he would—

Starting in the north, the *Americanos* advanced by land and by sea, occupying one California pueblo after another on their way south to Los Angeles and San Diego. It was on July 5 that Frémont assumed command over the insurgent forces in Sonoma, following the Bear-Flag Revolt. Two days later, Captain William Mervine, commander of the U.S.S. *Cyane* and the U.S.S. *Savannah,* acting under orders from Commodore John Drake Sloat, raised the American flag over the customhouse at Monterey, thus formally taking possession of California for the United States. July 9,

Captain John B. Montgomery, commanding the U.S.S.
Portsmouth, occupied Yerba Buena (soon to be called San
Francisco). The same day, on orders from Commodore
Sloat, the Stars and Stripes displaced the singular bear flag
in Sonoma, and thus sent into oblivion the short-lived "Re-
public of California."

Within a month, American forces had occupied the following pueblos, in the order named: Captain Sutter's New
Helvetia (usually known as Sutter's Fort), San José, San
Juan Bautista, San Diego, and Santa Bárbara. On August 6,
Commodore Robert F. Stockton, who recently (in the last
week in July) had replaced Commodore Sloat as "commander-in-chief of all forces and operations on land" and
also as admiral of the United States Pacific Squadron, took
possession of San Pedro. A week later, on August 13, United
States forces under joint command of Stockton and Frémont
seized Los Angeles and raised the Stars and Stripes on the
Plaza flagpole. On September 2, Commodore Stockton appointed Major Frémont as military governor of the "territory" of California—and the war seemed to be over.

Poor Pío Pico had fled before the invading forces, across
the line into Sonora. All was lost, he thought, until word
came that the Californians had awakened, perhaps in time
to save their country from Americanization.

First he heard of an outbreak in Los Angeles, started by
the chronic peace disturber, Sérbulo Varela, who led a mot-
ley company of Californians, many of them fortified by
aguardiente, to surprise Captain Archibald Gillespie's men.
They accomplished the first American defeat on September
23, 1846, about three weeks after the "fall" of Los Angeles.

Varela's victory encouraged a general insurrection, led by Captain José María Flores and participated in by three hundred Angelenos. In the course of the renewed hostilities, the first real battle was fought between the Americans and the Californians. It occurred on September 26 at the Chino *rancho* of Isaac Williams and resulted in another victory for the Californians. Only one of their men was killed, with three wounded, to three Americans wounded and fifteen captured.

The jubilant Californians returned to Los Angeles, and there, by the strategic use of the one cannon that the Pueblo boasted, they once again managed to rout their foe. The *Americanos,* hearing of this big gun, had tried to capture it. But an old Mexican woman[6] hid it in the *tules* until they stopped looking for it. Then the "old woman's gun" was dragged out from its hiding place and caused such havoc among the Americans that they retreated to San Pedro and took refuge on the U.S.S. *Vandalia.*

On October 8, some sailors under Captain William Mervine attacked Californian "insurgents" under command of Captain Flores on the Domínguez *rancho.* Six sailors were killed and six wounded in the skirmish. The Americans buried their dead on a lonely little island in San Pedro Bay which from then on was known as La Isla de los Muertos, or Dead Men's Island.

It was on October 31 that members of the Donner party, traveling overland with the idea of being pioneer settlers in the new United States "territory," were trapped by heavy snows in the Sierra Nevada and forced to camp for the winter in the vicinity of Lake Tahoe. While awaiting rescue by relief expeditions from Sutter's Fort, thirty-nine out of eighty-seven died from illness, cold, and starvation. Some of the survivors had sunk to eating the flesh of their companions before the last of them were carried out, more dead than alive, April 13, 1847.

Such reports as Pío Pico heard about American disasters seemed like music in his ears. He decided to return to his rightful position of authority. For a confidant and aide, he chose his friend Hugo Reid, remembering a conversation at the time of his deeding of the San Gabriel Mission lands to Reid and Workman.

Don Pío had confided to Don Perfecto that his main reason for selling the land was to obtain funds "for the common need in case of a foreign invasion which, according to credible information, is very close at hand." Hugo, not being an American by birth, had seemed sympathetic. He was also deeply indebted to Don Pío for his ultimate concession, and most conveniently seemed on excellent terms with Colonel Stevenson of the New York Volunteers, who had submitted Don Pío's governorship to unheard-of indignities. A retraction must be secured, in addition to safe passage back into California. Reid could help him in many ways, he decided.

While Don Pío was considering the form of his appeal to Don Perfecto, the last battles of the war were being fought. The winter had turned fearfully cold, and both sides suffered from unexpected snow and ice, even in southern California. On November 16, 1846, American forces under Captain Charles Burroughs of Frémont's California Battalion met with Californians under *Comandante* Manuel Castro, at Natividad, near San Juan Bautista. American casual-

ties amounted to some four or five killed and five or six
wounded. The losses of the Californians were about the
same, but the victory was an American one.

The bloodiest battle of the whole war occurred on December 6, when eighty Californians under the command of
Don Pío's brother, Andrés Pico, and one hundred and sixty
United States soldiers commanded by General Kearny, supplemented by forty of Captain Gillespie's men, engaged in
the battle of San Pascual, between Warner's *rancho* and San
Diego. Eighteen United States soldiers were killed and nineteen wounded. No Californians were killed, but twelve were
wounded. It was not decisive, for though the Californians
were first to leave the field, they continued to harass their
enemies seriously for days afterward. In spite of severe losses
and an unfamiliar type of guerrilla warfare, the United
States troops kept their morale and won a technical "victory."

The last fighting occurred in the first months of the new
year. On January 8, 1847, the battle of San Gabriel was
fought at Paso de Bartolo, on El Río de los Temblores. The
Californians were under the triple command of Andrés
Pico, General Flores, and José Antonio Carrillo. Stockton
and Kearny led the Americans. Casualties were two dead
and eight wounded, on each side, but the Californians took
flight after an intense, two-hour engagement. They lacked
the grim, bulldog determination of the invaders.

January 9: American forces won another skirmish at La
Mesa, in southeastern Los Angeles, and next day Stockton
and Kearny recaptured the Pueblo. Once again they raised
the Stars and Stripes, which had been torn down by Varela
and his men.

January 13: General Andrés Pico and Lieutenant Colonel Frémont signed articles of capitulation at Rancho Cahuenga, thus terminating, for good and all, hostilities between the Californians and the American forces.

January 19: Frémont assumed the office of first American civil governor of California, which he relinquished to General Kearny after only forty days. A serious charge of insubordination then led to his court-martial in Washington.

Pío Pico, in his retreat at Sonora, did not realize the decisiveness of his countrymen's defeat. Some baseless rumors gave him false hope, and he decided to cross the line without waiting for a passport, feeling that his country needed him now as never before.

He arrived at San Diego on July 6; reached his own *rancho,* Santa Margarita, a day or so later; then Workman's *rancho* at La Puente; and San Gabriel by July 17. Hugo Reid was surprised to find the former governor a guest in his home when he returned, toward evening, from the exercise of his magisterial duties. He was delighted to see such an old friend, until he heard that Don Pío had crossed the line without credentials and even now was being pursued by two searching parties composed of New York Volunteers. Colonel Stevenson had become alarmed by the rumor that Pico was returning to regain his governorship in spite of an earlier signed agreement that he would remain a private citizen. Stevenson had posted an order that Pío Pico present himself at once, if he did not wish to be treated as a traitor and a spy.

This was too high handed for the former governor. So far he had successfully evaded the searching parties, and he now prepared a plan of action which he retailed to Hugo Reid in language emphatic and pleading, about as follows:[7]

Don Perfecto, *you* go to Colonel Stevenson. Remind him that Pío Pico is a gentleman and has given his word to be a private citizen *now*. But, Don Perfecto, you also tell him that it would be for the glory of the *Americanos* and for the happiness of the Californians to restore Pío Pico to his rightful rank.

Hugo went, in sympathy and sincerity, on his quixotic errand. Like Don Pío, he could not believe that the old order had gone, never to return.

He obtained what might be construed as an apology for doubting the word of a gentleman, and an exceedingly courteous safe-conduct note from the colonel. In Spanish, it read to the effect that Don Pío Pico could go in peace to his own *rancho,* Santa Margarita, if he promised in no way to interrupt the tranquillity of the country or to interfere in civil or military matters till the pleasure of his excellency, Richard B. Mason—now governor, succeeding General Kearny—should be known. It concluded with instructions to treat the said Don Pío Pico with all the consideration to which his former position entitled him. But, alas, there was no intimation that his "former position" would ever be restored to him.

It was on May 31, 1847, that Colonel Mason, on the departure of General Kearny for the court-martial of Frémont and by order of President Polk, proclaimed his own assumption of the position of governor and commander-in-chief of the United States forces in California. He was fated to govern California during the most unsettled period in her history, the three years when she remained a territory without a clearly defined code of laws, before being admitted to statehood in '50. No one realized more clearly than Mason himself the dangerous activity of the volcano on which he was living.

On June 18, 1847, he made an official report to Washington, expressing his need of mounted troops for Indian service, giving attention to various "California claims," and concluding:

The country continues to be quiet, and I think will remain so, though the people dislike the change of flags, whatever may be said or written to the contrary, and in the southern part would rise immediately if it were possible for Mexico to send even a small force into the country. Nothing keeps them quiet but the want of a proper leader and a rallying point.

Neutral though Hugo Reid had been, keeping friends on both sides, he found himself as badly off as any of his *vecinos*. It became the American policy to regard as invalid Pico's hasty grants of the mission lands; and to demand "proof" of the possession of land granted by earlier Mexican governors. Back to the United States government went Hugo's title to the San Gabriel Mission.

Stripped of the lands he once had owned—besides the mission property, Santa Anita also was lost to him through the Dalton sale,—and so deep in debt that even Huerta del Cuati and Uva Espina itself could not be cared for properly, Hugo Reid was a desperate man. But it happened that, at this moment, he heard of gold in the north.

Talk of gold mines had been periodic in California since the first Spaniards came seeking the precious metal in the sixteenth century. Within the time of Hugo's own residence there, two discoveries had aroused more or less interest.

About 1832, David Douglas, the renowned Scotch bota-
nist, in preparing for shipment to Great Britain tiny speci-
mens of the firs that now bear his name, found enough gold
in the earth covering their roots to make himself a watch
case. Then again, ten years later, Abel Stearns sent gold to
be assayed at the Philadelphia mint. It had come from placer
mines discovered by Francisco López at San Francisquito,
about thirty-five miles northwest of Los Angeles. Don Abel
entrusted some twenty ounces of ore, California weight
(eighteen and three-quarters ounces, mint weight), to be
carried east by Don Alfredo Robinson. It was found to be
worth about nineteen dollars an ounce, and Stearns and
Robinson became greatly excited.

But their friend Reid had lived in the boom town of Hermosillo, and he had watched excitement die—there and in
the San Francisquito discovery, and in Mexican and South
American mines. Each time, as both ore and interest petered
out, Don Perfecto had become less of a romantic and more
of a skeptic. Now it was only the unbelievable, true story of
Sutter that drew him north to the new placer mines.

CHAPTER EIGHT

The Flower of San Gabriel

Before Hugo Reid started on the new, gold-mining venture which was to recoup his vanished fortune, he found time to attend to a few personal matters. There was his wine making, sadly neglected of late; and his reading to catch up on, notably a file of London newspapers from an old friend, Eustace Barron of Tepic, in which he found "nothing very interesting." He welcomed the arrival of his *compadre,* Henry Dalton, who wanted to be baptized, being in love and anxious to marry a *hija del país.* Don Perfecto obligingly performed the rite, but later confessed to Stearns that "Don Enrique was so d——d big that all sorts of calamities was the result!" Dalton selected, as baptismal names, those of his *padrino*—Reid,—calling himself Perfecto Hugo Dalton from then on. His ladylove was a daughter, named Guadalupe, of Don Agustín Vicente Zamorano, who lived in Monterey and won renown by being the first man to operate a printing press in California.

About this time, Don Perfecto Reid also stood as *padrino* to the first child of his stepson Felipe. He performed another, even more gratifying office for Felipe in relieving him of ranch work. The education that Victoria deplored had made her son discontented with farm life, rebellious and indifferent. He was continually begging Hugo to release

him from uncongenial tasks. Slightly more responsible than
the older man, he could not cut loose and leave his mother
with added worries until some provision was made for her.
Since the selling of Santa Anita, a long-awaited opportunity
seemed at hand.

Felipe asked Don Perfecto's advice about obtaining a cler-
ical position in the Pueblo. Hugo suggested his going in
with Jim McKinley, who had a small store in Los Angeles,
but the boy was keen and felt that Jim, though very likable,
was not much of a business man. He countered with the
suggestion that Don Abel's *tienda* would be a safer proposition. After some discussion, Felipe went with this letter:

Señor Don Abel Stearns
Mi estimado Compadre,

Your *comadre's* son Felipe is not fond of *rancho* business, by
any means, and seems inclined to think that a situation in a shop
would be more agreeable to him. He has spoken to me on the
subject, and I proposed his waiting till Mr. McKinley came back,
for the purpose of seeing whether he wanted anyone.

You may depend on Felipe's honesty, although not much
versed in accounts, that is to say, with regard to keeping them
in form. But he calculates in true Yankee style and is excessively
fond of letter writing.[1]

He himself proposed my speaking to you, as he says a situation under you would be more congenial than the other.

I am of the opinion that you might safely try him and see if
he would suit, *U. dirá.*

Your *comadre* sends *muchas saludos* and wishes to know when
her *comadre* Doña Refugio will start for San Diego, as she wishes
to come in with María Ygnacia a day or two before, so as to
despedir [say goodbye to] her.

Yours truly,
P. Hugo Reid.

In early February, '48, the rain poured down in torrents for a number of days. Don Perfecto relieved his feelings about such "unusual weather" in a note to Don Abel:

Mi estimado Compadre, Enero 14, 1848.

God be thanked I've got to live once more on an island! The old *bodega* [cellar] leaked so, that only one small dry spot is visible in the whole house, which from courtesy we have named Great Britain; Ireland remained alongside for many days, but is now drowned entirely, O'Connell and all. No more famine for them.

Your *comadre* wishes to know how María Ygnacia is. When will the rain cease? It is playing the devil with me; I can neither settle accounts nor prune.

Saludos from your *comadre* to you and all. The same from yours, P. HUGO REID.

Please procure for your *comadre* a piece of brown *manta* and a piece of prints for my Indians, to be paid next week.

In saying, "Your *comadre* wishes to know how María Ygnacia is," Don Perfecto referred to the fact that Victoria's daughter, now a young lady of seventeen, was making one of her frequent visits to El Palacio de Don Abel. Described by William Heath Davis as "a beautiful girl" seeming older than her years, María Ygnacia had lately discovered the delights of city life, and was becoming as discontented as her brother Felipe with the monotonous round of daily tasks in San Gabriel. It came to the point that Don Perfecto had to threaten and cajole his adopted daughter into coming home. Knowing that she still loved her garden, he wrote slyly to Don Abel, on March 17:

Sirvase U. avisar a [Do me the favor of informing] Doña María Ygnacia Reid that the flowers in her garden are all dried up,

having no one to water them, but it is still useful, as we are keeping there two pigs which were brought from San Juan [Capi-
strano]. On Monday your *comadre* will go for her.

On this occasion, María Ygnacia returned to find the quiet
mission community in an unusual state of excitement. The
raids of Indian *ladrones* had become increasingly frequent
while she was away, and her stepfather, who still retained
the responsible position of *juez de paz,* had been obliged to
call upon the militia to maintain order. From Los Angeles,
Colonel Stevenson sent a lieutenant from the New York Volunteers in command of twelve dragoons, with instructions
to bring back the culprits, alive or dead. The young officer's
name was John McHenry Hollingsworth, and he kept a
diary, recording of the expedition to San Gabriel:

The birds had flown, but I had an opportunity of seeing a very
beautiful part of the country, and we paid a long visit at Mr.
Reid's, who gave us a fine dinner, and I had an opportunity of
seeing the fair Doña María [Ygnacia]. She was very polite and
gave me a splendid orange. I tried hard to make friends with
them all, and I think my fine charger dressed off in dragoon
trappings and the military appearance of the rider made quite
an impression on the flower of San Gabriel.

What young girl could resist such resplendence? The dragoon uniform was very dashing, consisting of a blue coat
trimmed in scarlet, pantaloons of dark gray with a scarlet
stripe running up the leg, and a "new style of French hat,
very becoming." Hollingsworth had a fine figure and sat
his horse easily, pricking it surreptitiously with enormous
spurs to make it more mettlesome. Undoubtedly Don Juan
touched the girl's defenseless heart, as she had his.

María Ygnacia, at seventeen, was a miniature of her mother, somewhat shorter and smaller boned; even lovelier, for she was fragile looking and very feminine. She had the same clear, olive complexion and finely chiseled features. Every surviving mention of María Ygnacia is a tribute to her beauty and her charm.

When Don Juan Hollingsworth returned to the Pueblo, after an unsuccessful attempt to round up renegade Indians, he did not forget the pretty little "flower of San Gabriel." Indeed he made the trip many times from his post to her garden. She held him, with her extraordinary charm, as Doña Victoria had Hugo, against the loveliest ladies in Los Angeles.

Don Juan might go to a gorgeous ball, like Señora Mellus's, naïvely pleased to be invited where the hostess was "very particular in invitations." He might flirt with the famous beauty, Señora Arcadia Stearns; even tell her he had "many fears that were it not for her hateful encumbrance of a husband, he never should leave California." He always danced several times with her sister Ysidora Bandini, whom he found equally fascinating. Recalling one strikingly beautiful costume, he wrote in his diary:

"Doña Ysidora was dressed in a rich pink and gold silk, with a shawl on worth two hundred dollars."

Señora Enrique Dalton and Josefa Ontiveros, sister-in-law to Felipe Reid, also seemed most attractive and beautifully dressed, to this observing young man. But the day after every party in the Pueblo, Don Juan came back to his little Indian's gate, admitting that he spent the happiest hours in her company.

When Doña Arcadia learned of María Ygnacia's romance, she invited her to visit at El Palacio more frequently than ever before. This caused a number of discussions in the Reid home, because María Ygnacia hated to refuse an invitation, no matter what duties demanded her attention at Uva Espina. She was extremely popular at the dances she attended in Los Angeles, as Doña Arcadia's house guest, and the handsome young dragoon was always her most attentive swain.

When her friends from town knew that María Ygnacia must stay at home to tend her garden, they flocked to San Gabriel. Even the Padre Ordaz became suspicious when so many young people came to confession, strangely coinciding with María Ygnacia's own appearances. Don Perfecto sometimes found her loath to accompany him and her mother to the mission, and once confided to Don Abel that "María Ygnacia was hanging on to confess with the main body," a gay troupe from town including her Don Juan.

But like all happy times, the young girl's idyll was short lived. In August, '48, Hollingsworth received orders to leave Los Angeles for a post at Monterey. He wrote a touching farewell to Doña María, in his diary. It ended by calling her "*ángel del Pueblo,* whose sweet smile and laughing voice have aided me in passing more than a year pleasantly and happily."

Ángel del Pueblo—Juan unknowingly was writing an an epitaph for María Ygnacia. She died a few months after his departure, of the dread smallpox which had carried away her own father. Superior in many ways to her race, she was constitutionally similar: unable to withstand its scourge.

She dropped down with hundreds of her tribesmen who could not be saved from smallpox by the remedies used at that time.

Hugo had started north for the mines when she sickened; so poor Doña Victoria, alone and helpless, had to watch her exquisite daughter succumbing to the ravages of the disease. Don Abel received a letter from his *comadre,* one of the two that she wrote in a lifetime,[2] which revealed a stoicism typical of her Indian nature. It said (translation):

Mi querido Compadre,   May 30, 1849.
Saludos to you, my *compadre,* and all the rest of the family. *Compadre,* I must give you sad news. My daughter, María Ygnacia, is dying. She and I wish you and my *comadre* to come as quickly as possible and bring the coffin. She is nearly gone, and I think she will die before the sun sets. I expect this favor of your generous heart.

Please bring also six pounds of wax candles for the funeral, twelve yards of white satin, some colored ribbons that we can use, lace, and any other thing you think we may need, because María Ygnacia says that she wants you, *comadre,* to fix the coffin. She says that she wishes to wear her white net dress to the grave.

VICTORIA REID.

Transportation was so slow that Hugo arrived home too late for the funeral and soon had to leave again for the north. From Monterey, June 26, on the return trip, he wrote Don Abel, thanking him for "the many, many favors bestowed" on his *comadre* and *compadre,* both. He also said, "Don Benito Wilson has orders from McKinley to pay you the funeral expenses of poor María Ygnacia."

Doña Victoria felt doubly deserted when Hugo went away, unutterably lonely. It is quite possible that José Do-

lores died in the same epidemic, for the last mention of him
in what remains of his father's correspondence referred to
his illness, saying he seemed "worse." Felipe was no longer
at his mother's side. He lived with his family in Los Angeles,
since Don Abel had taken him into the Stearns *tienda*. With
only the child, Carlitos, to lighten her thoughts, Doña Victoria began to brood, trying to find an explanation for María
Ygnacia's death on the threshold of life. Her reason became
undermined, after hours of thinking such thoughts as:

Study has killed my daughter. It is a waste of life to learn from
books. My husband kept her too long indoors, to read in English and French and do silly sums. Away from the sun she grew
pale and weak, unable to fight the dreadful disease. It is because
of Don Perfecto and his learning that she died.

This idea, of Hugo's having "murdered" María Ygnacia,
remained in Victoria's mind and could not be eradicated.
Only an unforeseen event saved the poor woman from complete derangement.

On a cool evening in the fall of '49, old Chona and Juan
the centenarian were squatting on the hard ground of the
Reid patio, grinding corn. Their cracked voices, like crickets
chirruping, and the harsh scraping of their pestles against
limestone pots seemed the only familiar sounds in a world
grown suddenly mysterious over the sun's disappearance.
The old Indians had served Doña Victoria since she came
as a bride to Uva Espina, and they were discussing sadly the
change that they saw in her. Chona moved her pestle slowly,
meditatively. Finally she whispered:

"*La señora* never comes out any more, even to see the sun
set. What can we do, Juan, to make her happy again?"

"She is *alocada,* Chona," the old Indian answered, tapping significantly at his own brain. "She thinks that Don Perfecto killed Doña María."

Chona started and half turned, fearfully, toward the house. "What's that you say, Juan? Why, the *señorita* died of smallpox! It was an act of God."

"*La señora* thinks it was staying too long *en la casa,* to do lessons for Don Perfecto. Doña María grew weak and could not live through a little illness. No, Chona, *la señora* does not think that the smallpox alone killed her daughter." His cracked voice grew so faint that old Chona had to strain forward to hear the last words: "Old Juan has heard her cry out in the middle of the night, '*Asesino!* Murderer!' and to ask for news of Don Perfecto. There are devils in her sometimes."

"Pinacate! Pinacate!" called a musical voice from the house.

"Hold your tongue, Juan. It is *la señora* herself calling for that little Black Beetle who drinks too much *aguardiente.* This minute he is lying drunk in the field."

The Indian servants were grinding corn ferociously when Doña Victoria appeared at a doorway.

"*Buenas noches. Dónde está Pinacate?*" she asked unsmilingly, as always, standing there tall and still, and black gowned in grief.

An absolute unawareness of the early evening beauty was indicative of her attitude toward everything and everybody, since the death of her daughter. She was roused to emotion only by the thought of her husband whom she hated. This hatred absorbed all the qualities that formerly composed her fascination. Now, to old admirers, the woman in mourning seemed no more than the sepulcher of a dead personality.

Doña Victoria repeated: "Tell me, where is Pinacate?"

"We do not know, señora," answered Chona and Juan, like a chorus of crickets.

"Then you, Juan, bring in *manzanita* sticks for the fire. I am cold tonight."

Doña Victoria turned back into the house, while Juan, creaking and grumbling, got up from his hard seat on the ground and limped off to fetch firewood.

Chona, alone, lessened her activity. She moved her pestle so that it swirled the corn powder into senseless patterns. Every moment it was growing darker, and presently across the road the mission bells commenced to toll, calling all San Gabriel to evening prayers.

It was hard for Chona, too, to move her stiff old bones off the ground, but she reached the dimly lit church cloister before time to go in, and fell to gossiping with her cronies.

Latecomers were lucky this evening, being first to see and tell and retell the most thrilling thing that had happened for a long time in sleepy San Gabriel. Evening service was not yet over when two prairie schooners, drawn by tired oxen, stopped before the mission. They were dusty and blood stained, all that was left of a long train after a raid by Indians in the Texas desert.

Neophytes rushed to inform the padre, and he cut short the prayers, hurrying out ahead of his excited congregation. In the wagons they found seven weary travelers: John R. Evertson, a Virginia gentleman, his wife, three small children, and two terrified negro slaves.

Being a man of some worldly experience, Padre Ordaz did not show undue surprise at the appearance of the new-comers, but the Indians seemed astounded. Negroes and white children were seldom seen in California. The little girl[8] fascinated them most, with her unheard-of short skirts. Little girls in San Gabriel all dressed like their mothers, in skirts to the ground.

With ignorant sympathy, old Chona and her friends offered gifts of dried fruits and nuts, but soon found that these unexpected guests wanted only a place to sleep. They were too tired to eat. Terror had electrified them so that they could not sleep for days, crossing the desert after the merciless Apache attack. Padre Ordaz remembered some unused rooms behind Our Lady's Chapel, and offered the party a haven there for as long as they liked. Nourishing food would be served them, after a good night's rest.

"Now I shall have something that will interest *la señora*," whispered Chona to herself, as she hurried back to evening duties at Uva Espina.

At first her mistress scarcely listened to the thrilling tale, but for days the Indian servants talked of nothing but the strangers, of their hair-raising escape from "bad Indians," and mostly of the little short-skirted girl; Lalita they called her, "little Laura," wonderfully white and small to have lived through that long dangerous journey.

La señora was roused from her melancholia sufficiently to express a wish to see this strange child. Faithful old Chona, overjoyed, went to Mrs. Evertson; in broken English, managed to tell her of the other mother's distraction; and asked if she might take the child across the road for a few minutes' visit at the Reid home. Mrs. Evertson allowed Lalita to go. Her own recent suffering made her deeply sympathetic with the sorrow of others. Losing one's reason from grief was well within her comprehension, now.

Chona's plan succeeded beyond her fondest hopes. Doña Victoria thought she saw in Lalita the reincarnation of her own little daughter, María Ygnacia. Gradually she grew happy and aware again of what went on around her. Emotions recently poured together into a crazy hatred for her husband started to flow again into safe channels, through yet another illusion.

Every day she would send a *criada* for Lalita, who delighted in coming to Uva Espina because, in spite of its timeliness, the Evertsons' new home was uncomfortable and overrun with fleas and black beetles. More than any other place, the child loved Hugo's attic, where red peppers were strung from the rafters, and dried fruits, herbs, and spices hung in baskets.

Here Don Perfecto still kept many of his books, old newspapers, and magazines sent by far-away friends. Lalita would spend long afternoons seated on the hard, dusty floor, with the sun slanting in on her through narrow dormer windows. She devoured everything—from Shakespeare to London *Punch,* from Byron to newspapers from the Sandwich Islands. Doña Victoria, seeing the intense pleasure she took in them, overcame a fanatic hatred of books; but, for all that, could never leave Lalita long uninterrupted. To distract her little friend, she would call up the spiral staircase:

"Lalita! Come down from among the spiders and sup with me."

Lalita, obediently descending, usually found *la señora* seated before a small fire in the patio, helping the *criadas* to prepare the evening meal. She might give the child a lesson in Indian epicurism and etiquette, while the flames danced in reflection on her glossy black hair and black satin gown.

Often Doña Victoria would tell Lalita legends; of why she feared earthquakes, believing them to be the stirring of seven giants who held up the earth; of seven sisters who became seven stars, the Pleiades; of the coyote who tried to race with the river. She might tell true stories too: about her own ancestors who once had ruled as powerful chieftains in California; and of the first, disastrous arrival of white men in Indian country.

Doña Victoria forgave her husband for his imagined part in María Ygnacia's death, now that she seemed to have her daughter back. She would talk for hours of Hugo's adventures in China, the Sandwich Isles, and South America. She even showed Lalita gifts that he had brought back after each long voyage in the *Esmeralda:* strings of pearls and other jewelry, silks, embroidered shawls, shells, and spices from foreign lands.

The child listened and gazed, entranced. What romantic beings they seemed to her, these Reids.

Doña Victoria wanted to shower presents on Lalita, articles of clothing and jewelry that had belonged to her real daughter, but Mrs. Evertson refused most of them, not knowing how to repay such generosity. Finally she allowed Lalita to accept a little brooch of exquisite design. When it was jolted loose and lost in the *carreta* on their way to a *gesta de San Juan* at Don Miguel Blanco's house, the little girl felt close to tears all day long. Afraid of being called *descuidada,* she said nothing until, on the way home, Doña Victoria asked gently:

"*Qué te pasa, mi querida?*"

("What is the matter, my dear?")

Lalita could not control herself. She burst into tears; but did not receive the scolding she dreaded: only these reassuring words:

"Do not cry. I will give you another—a prettier pin."

When Hugo Reid came down from the north next time, he found, in the beautiful dark eyes that were raised to his, all he had hoped to find. Of course Chona and old Juan would always enliven their tasks with mysterious whispered conversations, but no longer did they have their mistress' madness as a subject of delicious terror.

CHAPTER NINE

Gold and Dross

JOHANN AUGUST SUTTER dreamed of a New Helvetia for twenty years before he built it. He searched for a site in Switzerland, in France, in New York, in Missouri, and in New Mexico, taking any job to keep himself alive, because his schemes were always far beyond his means. It was in Taos that he met a traveler who told him of California, clearly "challenging a conqueror" with her natural riches and lackadaisical rulers. Here at last could he establish his utopia, with land to be had for the asking and virgin forests and rushing rivers at hand for the building.

Displaying energy surprising in such a dreamer, Captain Sutter—he had once served in the Swiss army—made his way west; by land until Apaches on the warpath repulsed him; then north and by boat from Fort Vancouver to the Sandwich Islands; and back again to Sitka, the picturesque Russian colony in Alaska. Here this man, who had started life selling newspapers, had the honor of dancing with a born princess, the governor's wife. And everywhere he went, Sutter seemed to kindle the imagination of others with the flint of his own enthusiasm.

By the time he reached Monterey, he had laid solid foundations for the utopian dream. The Californians were like wax in his hands, too indolent themselves to fear an empire builder, or even to take him seriously. Governor Alvarado granted him many leagues of fertile land on the American River where it runs through the Sacramento Valley.

Sutter arrived in the wilderness with a few white men to form the Pacific Trade Company; a shipload of Kanakas whose interest had been aroused during the captain's stopover in the Islands; and some cheaply bought stores and domestic animals. The enterprise took root and grew ever more rapidly.

By the time of the Mexican War, New Helvetia, more commonly called Sutter's Fort, was the most formidable settlement in California. A great wall, twelve feet high and five feet thick, surrounded it, and inside was an immense activity embracing almost every trade. Captain Sutter had learned discipline in the Swiss army, and he imposed it on his subjects. He had a strong garrison to scare the Indians, and two armed sloops in the bay. His "empire" produced more than enough for its own needs, and soon was trading with Sitka, Vancouver, the Sandwich Islands, Mazatlán, and other ports in Mexico and South America. Sutter preserved neutrality throughout the innumerable revolutions of California, and was respected by Mexican and American alike. Well might he sit back with an agreeable consciousness of power.

Perhaps this is what he was doing on the day in January, 1848, when his friend, James Marshall, appeared in his office, incoherent from excitement. Superintending some alterations in a near-by water mill, he had made a discovery.[1] Such a discovery! One that would bring them millions and millions of dollars, with little work.

"I frankly own," said Sutter later, "that when I heard this, I thought something had touched Marshall's brain, when suddenly all misgivings were put to an end by his flinging on the table a handful of scales of pure virgin gold. I was fairly thunderstruck."

When Marshall could make proper explanation, he said that his men had thrown up some sand and gravel in widening the water channel, and there, glittering in a mound, he saw what he thought at first was an opal, actually a scale of pure gold. Thinking it might be part of a small treasure buried by Indian thieves, he searched quite carefully in the gravel mounds and found them rich with gold. He leaped upon his horse, to tell Johann before anyone else.

They agreed to keep it a secret until Sutter could get the new American governor, Mason, to confirm the old Mexican grant, and doubly secure his title to the rich land. However, they could not resist revisiting the lode, and were too obviously excited to escape notice. A Kentucky laborer sneaked along after them, to see what they were stooping over. He spread a report, and when the two conspirators returned to the mill, a crowd met them, "holding out flakes of gold and shouting with joy." Marshall tried to laugh them out of the idea, and pretended that the metal was only mica. But an Indian who had once worked in a gold mine cried, "Oro! Oro!" and all were convinced because they wanted to be.

There was no stopping the rumor, now. It flew down to Monterey and Los Angeles, to Sitka, Sandwich, and Mazatlán. It sped round the Horn to Boston, and back again over the land route. Soon the whole world knew of gold in California, and this knowledge pounded at men's imaginations till it started a steady onrush of fortune hunters, streaming ever toward the mines.

Hugo Reid had been borne along with the others, and he shared in the common experience of disillusionment. Writing to Don Abel from Monterey on April 22, 1849, he warned his *estimado compadre:*

Don't go to the mines on any account. They are full of goods, and a rush of cattle streaming likewise to every digging. The mines are, moreover, loaded to the muzzle with vagabonds from every quarter of the globe, scoundrels from nowhere, rascals from Oregon, pickpockets from New York, accomplished gentlemen from Europe, interlopers from Lima and Chile, Mexican thieves, gamblers of no particular spot, and assassins manufactured in Hell for the express purpose of converting highways and byways into theaters of blood; then last, but not least, Judge Lynch with his thousand arms, thousand sightless eyes, and five hundred lying tongues, ready under the banner of justice to hang, half, and quarter any individual who may meet his disapprobation, either because said individual wears his hair cropped instead of a wig, as the afore-mentioned judge does, or that his waistcoat a'n't doublebreasted, or some other serious grievance and eyesore to the respectable jurist.

By the bye, *compadre,* I am not *merecedor* [deserving] of the blowing up you gave me respecting not writing, having done so the beginning of October last past from Dry Creek Diggings, just before starting for the Dry Diggings. If I recollect aright, a Sonoreño took the same.

You may depend on there being more truth than poetry in the following observations made by experience, which I have never made to anyone, for the simple reason that no one would believe me. You, *compadre,* may give them credence.

The placer, and its inexhaustible resources, is a complete humbug. It is overrated in the proportion of 1 to 500.

M·D
1931

FORTUNE HUNTERS STREAMING TOWARD THE MINES

If one-quarter part of the immigration reported as coming in the present year do arrive, starvation and crime which no country ever before witnessed to the same extent must ensue, unless they come provided with means, for the mines next year will not maintain them.

No one must think of making money by taking persons to work on shares or wages; it will not hold good, Andrés Pico's case being a solitary exception, only half carried out as yet.

Provisions from the lower country, even if stolen there, will not pay, unless shipped at a low rate for San Francisco, where a person will have to go in person to superintend, for no one will do it for you.

Flour is worth $15 per barrel in San Francisco, plus freight to Stockton and along the San Joaquín to the Estanislado, or up the Sacramento River. Length of passage, 8, 10, and sometimes 15 days land freight to mines, at $6 per cwt.; $35 and $40 per cwt. after water carriage. Passage money to either place $30 and not found in anything but water, kicks, and elbowings.

Stock to kill will not pay expenses, with the solitary exception of sheep. Working oxen will fetch a high price, say $150 to $200 a yoke. Mules are good articles, commanding from $200 to $300 a head if gentle; horses a capricious sale. At times you may buy a pocketful for $25 each, and occasionally you may sell one for $100, losing $10 more in taking care of him.

No single individual going to work must think of taking *bastamiento* [a supply of provisions]. He can board himself cheaper at any of the mines and live better at $16 a week, with three meals daily.

The grass was reported as having been all burnt up before we arrived, but I could see no indications of there ever having been what would be denominated grass or of there ever being.

The north and middle forks will be sicklier, the Estanislado probably healthier, than any other diggings.

The middle and north forks require a large crowbar to turn

over rocks of giant workmanship, from four and a half to five feet long and thirty to thirty-five pounds weight.

A knowledge of monte and poker is requisite to be admitted into good society. Nothing shorter horse, as we civilized mountain freebooters say.

All diseases in the mountains arise and emanate from an active accumulation of bile. The diseases may be reckoned as three in number, syphilis not being counted: first, mountain fever, or ague, without the presence of miasma as a cause. The chill, however, in general is slight, carried out with great lassitude and dreadful stretching of the limbs. Second, a bastard pleurisy, with the pain toward the region of the liver instead of left side; terminating often fatally in a few hours. Even in this disease the increase of bile is astonishing, and active emetics must be given, together with bleeding and blistering. Third, a compound patent nameless galvanic bilious fever, defying description; doing just as it pleases; in fact, a true republican democratic sickness, as stubborn as a mule and which kicks like a *macho*. The first and last diseases mentioned are those which the Old Gentleman will commence putting into operation from June until September. The middle disease and bastard pleurisy he reserves until the *fines de Octubre*.

People will have to go south for stock very soon, the consumption being far ahead of the increase.

The present discoveries are well turned up already; they will, however, for the present year give a fortune to some—comparatively speaking of what their circumstances have been—and subsistence to the rest. After this, mines not yet discovered, but bound to be, will fill the hands of a few and wind up the general matter, although I entertain no doubt but what the diggings will keep working south, but only to meet the fate of their predecessors. We have mines close on us now here in Monterey, only two and half days' travel—five days with carts—and anyone going to the mines had much better provision themselves here and save

horseflesh. Price of flour from $24 to $30 for a bag of 200 pounds.
Sugar $6 a pound; coffee $5 a pound; tea, best quality black, $1;
brandy and gin, lots of it, wine also; besides crowbars at $5 each,
and cooking utensils of all sizes; goods and clothing cheap. Recommend as having the largest assortment in Monterey, $100,000
worth of goods, and for cheapness, Messrs. James McKinley and
Company. [Jim McKinley had closed his Los Angeles *tienda* a
short time previously, and opened a new, general store in Monterey, hoping by being on the spot to benefit by the rush of inadequately equipped "miners" to the northern mines; just as
Hugo had done in Hermosillo almost twenty-five years before.]

Compadre, I should like to have an hour's more talk with you,
but must defer it until the fifth of next month, having a great
deal on my shoulders at present to do. However, by post I will
give you an idea of life in the mines and how our American back-
woods women smoke pipes! I saw one old lady there who had
sucked all the teeth out of her head smoking, and left the most
curious animal tubes remaining you ever saw. It was a carnivo-
rous pandoric flute, and the old woman on sighing produced a
sound like a harmonica.

Compadre, as you are ever kind, I want to trouble you a little,
viz.: The mines I could not stand, but came out on foot to the
Fort [Sutter's]. San Francisco nearly killed me with a complaint
of the chest from which I am only now recovering, being still
very hoarse but much better of the cough. There I could procure
no passage by water and no horses; so after remaining six weeks,
I started, sick as I was, on foot with my *compadre,*[2] Felipe, and
walked down here in five days, although the exertion at times
would bring on fits of coughing which nearly killed me. McKinley, having no great assistant and doing all the business of the
place, made me an offer better than gold digging. I have accepted
the same, and am now the Co. of the house. Such being the case,
Mr. Teschemacher[3] is now about advertising Uva Espina, to let
or lease. I have had applications already, and some will be on

your way in June to see and judge for themselves. By post you will therefore receive a power of attorney to let or lease said Uva Espina. You can do so to anyone, for I myself merely give a letter of introduction, but make no bargain. In which case I want the family up here, but the devil is to procure a conveyance. However, on this I will treat more fully.

I left some things for your *comadre* in San Francisco to be shipped in the *Olga* and some other things to be shipped here. I find, however, the following mistakes. They have sent me here a box of loaf sugar intended for San Pedro, and have sent a box of paper cigars to your *comadre* in its place; as likewise shipped a nest of Canton camphor chests to your port and sent the key to me.

In San Francisco I picked out, at Mr. Teschemacher's request, three dresses which you had encharged. I hope they meet your approval. I consider them as being the colors which my *comadre* would like best.

You will give my *comadre, ahijada* [Ysidora Bandini], and *compadre* Don Juan a thousand kind regards, and may God bless them all.

"Oh, carry me back to old Virginny."

There is no place like the Angeles yet, but circumstances oblige *me* to remain here. I suppose a couple of years will either make a spoon or spoil a horn. I have through my own good and proper management spoiled a tarnation lot of horns; so I am held in hopes of spooning it this time.

I had actually no idea of writing so long a letter, and must conclude, putting myself at your orders.

Your affo. compadre,
P. Hugo Reid.

He wrote again in a little while (May 22, 1849), answering a letter from *hacendado* Stearns about the market for dried beef, lard, and tallow in the north. Like McKinley and every other business man in California, Don Abel was anxious to profit by the influx of people to the northern mines:

Estimado Compadre:

On due reflection, I beg to give the following idea or hints on the subject on which you consult me.

Suppose you can kill a thousand head of cattle. . . . Allow me first to make the following remarks. All the dried beef of yours purchased by Teschemacher was sold in my presence at $5 per cwt., and T. blamed by others on the *qui vive* for selling it too cheap. There are no *matanzas* [slaughtering of cattle] to be made here this year. *Manteca* [lard] is now at $6 here; $9 or $10 in San Francisco. Not a candle procurable in all Monterey. Stinking mould Yankee candles, so soft you cannot handle them at thirty cents per pound in the Yerba Buena at wholesale. . . .

I think prices next October or November will be considerably more. Could you not kill a thousand head for a dollar apiece? If you can do it and write me to that effect, I think I could charter a vessel for you at the proper time for $2000, when you might send *aguardiente* and anything else beside.

In closing, Hugo referred to a charter before the legislature, increasing the "number of lay days at Monterey, to make sales here." Already, under the American influence, life was being speeded up in California. Yankee traders had no patience for the *fiestas* which, before their arrival, had celebrated frequent saints' days.

"Nothing more, *compadre*."

More about the mines, on July 14:

Estimado Compadre,

I sincerely hope that you and my *comadre* are enjoying good health. Numbers are now leaving the placer, to avoid the sickly season; and a great many Americans of the better disposed and orderly class left the mines and came down here previous to the Fourth of July, being fearful of an outbreak on that occasion. We have up to this date no certain news as to how things passed off on the day indicated, but our advices from the Estanislado on the second say: "Weather extremely hot, and an outbreak very shortly unavoidable." The bearer of this tells cock and bull stories as usual. He has been in the eleventh heaven and not in the diggings. His calculations are philosophical but confoundedly nonsensical. A great many are clearing out for the north fork; in fact, the whole of the diggings, from the numbers and continual movement, is well represented by an ants' nest. Only the latter possess order and morality, which are sadly lacking among the former. Cattle are now worth $15 or $16 a head here. The butcher has contracted for 400 at the first price and 250 at the second, deliverable in *partidas* of 50 at a time.

Goods in San Francisco keep falling, with the sole exception of flour, which from $6 has risen to $10. Still the cheapness is merely to be found in auction sales; when disposed of and stored, the prices are not so *very low*. The auction sales, however, are ruinous. Think of the following sales made June 26: English prints which cost 20 cents in Lima sold for $1 apiece duty paid, the duty being 62½ cents. Silk handkerchiefs, 12½ cents each. Thread 18 cents per pound. Cognac brandy, which paid $5.75 per gallon duty, sold for $12 a gallon. Gin at $1 per dozen. A Bremen ship, with a cargo of $62,000 cost in Europe, was offered only 30 for her cargo landed. The landing alone would have cost $5000. Freight is now cheap; from Weaver's Landing to the Estanislado, the Sonoreños doing it on mules for $6 per cwt., a ninth part of what it was. Goods in this place are most abundant and daily arriving. What a ruinous concern! Three bales of Mexican grapes were shipped the other day for Mazatlán, having been brought from there two months previous; no doubt to be again purchased and sent back!

The following are part of the new cities under weigh:

Sutter's Fort and Embarcadero make	Sacramento City
3 miles farther down	Sutterville
25 miles farther down	Webster
At mouth of Sacramento River .	Montezuma
At mouth of San Joaquín River .	New York of the Pacific
On the San Joaquín River . . .	Stockton
At the Pass of San Joaquín . . .	San Joaquín
At the mouth of Estanislado . .	Stanislaus
On the Tuolumne	El Dorado
On the Ubo River	New Mechlenberg
At mouth of American Fork . .	Grimes Town, or Boston
On Sacramento at mouth of Capay	Victoria Town

Besides some six or seven more, whose exact localities I cannot state. Another called the Town of San Pablo is on the San Pablo *rancho* laid out by Alvarado.

I enclose an order . . . They are paying three or four per cent a month in San Francisco. The highest rate here is two.

Mr. Palmer came down here the other day to trade for the Vineyard. He is new from New York, and his partner's name is Wright. Being recommended by Moss, Benton, and Company, of San Francisco. He returned immediately with a letter of introduction from me to you as a proper person to treat with. His intention is to start for Santa Barbara by the first *vapor* [steamship][4] to visit you. He wishes to purchase, rather than lease. Be it so, if he is willing to give you from forty to fifty thousand dollars for the Vineyard and premises, but not to include the house in the mission. By and by, *compadre,* please purchase for me from De la Osa his piece of ground adjoining the house in San Gabriel.

With regard to your *comadre*'s coming up here, I have at all events come to the following conclusion, *viz.;* I see no prospect of a speedy water conveyance. The grape season is close at hand. I will therefore wait and see how my gold-hunting party get on and how commerce is going to stand out. If everything goes right, I will bring her up; if not, only stop till my year is finished, which will be April 1, and turn clodhopper again.

I have already mentioned our having letters from the Estanislado to the second inst. The same makes no mention of it, but common report here states that on that very day the Sonoreño Camp took fire and destroyed from one to three millions of property. You can take your change out of the rumor. If such be the case, I think from one to three million lice more probable as having been destroyed.

The steamer due on the first and advertised to leave San Francisco on the fifteenth has not made her appearance. . . . José María Flores is president of Mexico.

The government do things so sly that I was not aware of their mail leaving until too late, or you would have received the governor's *proclama* by it. Better late than never, however. There it goes. The following little anecdote will give you an idea of your governor. A senator, the Hon. Thomas Butler King, came by the last steamer, God knows what to do—nothing, I presume, as all our great men bind themselves to do. Be that as it may, he notified his arrival to Governor Riley[5] and requested an interview. A very modest request, considering old Riley had only fifty leagues to go to see him.

Now for the story: "D——n my precious eyes," says the old man, speaking through his nose to his secretary. "Who the H——l is this Hon. Thomas Butler King? Is he a military man?"

"I believe not," rejoined his clerk.

"Aye," says the governor. "The b–gg–r's got three names. I remember very well, when I was a young man, of *my* general's saying to me one day, 'Riley,' says he, 'whenever you see a man with three names and he writes them all in full, depend on it he's a d——n chit.' Now look here," says the governor, "this King writes *his* name in full, and I believe him to be a d——n chit as my Old Man told me."

They are disputing, like the devil at home, about California, etc. One of the senators, on remarking that California never could or would support a large population, was answered by another to this effect: "What the honorable member has just stated is true only in part, for with such long periods of rain at a time, being nine months in the year, the country of course is inundated, but drain the country from the surplus water, and *then* you will find country enough to cultivate and maintain people." *Compadre,* if Lawyer Botts had not shown me a newspaper containing this debate and many others of a similar nature, I would not have believed it.

You will please remember me kindly to my *comadre,* and with the expectation of hearing from you soon, I remain,

Yours ever truly,
P. Hugo Reid.

From Monterey:

Estimado Compadre,   Julio 18 de 1849.

I had put up a couple of *rebozos* for your *comadre,* to go by Money,[6] but he has proved so careless that my *paisano* McKinley has advised me to retain them until a more fitting occasion presents. He says right; therefore tell your *comadre* that I send nothing until more sure.

The *cohete* [skyrocket] has at length burst. This afternoon arrived Mr. Smith (an Englishman and partner of Mr. Probst) from San Francisco, who states as follows: The north forkers ordered all foreigners out of the mines on the Fourth. They obeyed. The same was done on the American fork, when an American citizen from Barron and Forbes, of Tepic, protested against the measure. He had, however, to take possession of Sutter's Mill and defend himself and working hands [Mexicans] from the crowd. The crowd, however, was afraid to attack them, but commenced operations on other parties. A number were killed defending their property, and among them some French. Said property was taken and immediately sold among themselves at public auction. Further results were not known, but upward of one thousand persons came down last week to San Francisco and embarked, chiefly Chileños, and some are of the opinion that a massacre of Americans in Chile will probably be the result. General Smith is blamed by everyone as the sole cause of the outrage. He never has proceeded up the Sacrament—having previously sent cannon to Stockton before the Fourth—and hurries on to Stockton where Governor Riley joins him from there. Their intended measures we know not, but a vague rumor has been floating about town all the afternoon among the country people that all is not right on the Estanislado.

With outbreaks all over his "empire," and his "subjects" swallowed up in an unruly, self-seeking mob, what had become of Johann August Sutter? Of course his dream was shattered and his life ruined. Who cared about old land grants which could no longer be enforced? What law was there but that of Judge Lynch?

Captain Sutter lost his mind pondering on the injustice of his lot. To be the "richest man in the world," by right, and yet practically a pauper! He started a gigantic lawsuit against the United States and such individuals as he could name who had taken his right from him. For thirty years he battered against the indifference of Congress, and finally died, demented and poor.

CHAPTER TEN

"Old Reid"

WITH THE DISCOVERY of gold at Sutter's Mill, the world's interest in California increased alarmingly, shifting suddenly from the south to the north. Until then, the vicinity of San Gabriel Mission and Los Angeles had been the wealthiest, most populated center of activity, since the earliest arrival of Spanish colonists. After Spain lost California to Mexico in 1822, a Mexican decree had elevated the Pueblo of Los Angeles to be the capital of Alta California. And all the while that the drastic Secularization Act of '33 was destroying the power and prestige of the San Gabriel Mission community, the Pueblo's importance was steadily increasing—until its culmination in the Mexican War, in which Los Angeles played the undisputed lead. Fully two years after the American conquest, the American governor, Richard B. Mason, still regarded the southerners as dangerous. He reported to Washington that only the lack of a leader kept them from open revolt. For many years they refused to adopt *gringo* ways. The Spanish influence and the spirit of *poco tiempo* died hard in southern California.

But Yerba Buena, known as San Francisco only since '47, completely lost her identity as a pueblo. Overnight she became a crude American city, seeming powerless to resist the horde of "argonauts" who hastened by land and by sea to wrest a fortune out of the rich northern lodes. The original, compact community of *adobe* houses, centering around the Plaza, was quickly absorbed into a sprawling, noisy city of frame and canvas shacks. These were filled for the most part with men obsessed by violent desires: for gold, difficult to find; for women, scarce in such a setting; and for land, to be had only at the expense of *hacendados* and the Church. Such lusts, fanned by frequent disappointments, led to acts of vandalism committed by lawless men. It is a fact that six disastrous fires supposedly of incendiary origin occurred in the flimsy city between Christmas Eve, 1849, and June 22, 1851.

The shacks were easily rebuilt, but the early settlers, the *paisanos* who still lived in fireproof *adobes,* were filled with fears for their families far worse than any ever caused by hostile Indians. Robbery, murder, and rape—such specters almost daily stalked the streets of this strange new San Francisco. The *paisanos* wondered sadly, in bewilderment, what had become of their long-loved little Yerba Buena and their former way of living, leisurely and with grace. They had lived to the strumming of guitars; to the evening sound of violin and harp, at family *bailes*. Now music seemed transformed to noise, in songs like the *Americanos'* boisterous *O Susanna*.

The newcomers seldom brought families, and there were too many to assimilate, as had been possible in the past when the few foreign residents had found it to their advantage to adopt the country's customs. The tempo of life in California accelerated with the advent of so many gold-hunting *gringos*. Most of them seemed hopelessly uncouth to the *paisanos,* who watched them gobble down carelessly prepared meals, refuse to take *siestas,* and overlook saints' days— being so eager to make a fortune.

But insidiously the competitive spirit entered even into the *adobes,* crowding nostalgia out of the *paisanos'* minds, temporarily. Other pueblos besides Yerba Buena caught the gold fever, and, being farther away from the mines, quickly became depopulated, while rents in San Francisco went sky high. Hugo Reid, a little out of things in Monterey, wrote enviously to Don Abel Stearns (July 18, 1849):

Leidesdorff's property in San Francisco was rented the month last past for sixty-two thousand dollars per annum. The Parker House [Hotel] rents for eighty-five thousand per annum.

Only a few weeks previously, Reid's friend, Robert Semple, had become greatly exercised over this general exodus to the north. As editor of the *Californian,* the first California newspaper,[1] he issued an "extra," May 29, 1849, deploring the situation and taking drastic action:

To our readers: With this slip ceases for the present the publication of the *Californian.* . . . The majority of our subscribers and many of our advertising patrons have closed their doors and places of business and left town, and we have received one order after another, conveying the pleasant request that "the printer will please stop my paper" or "my advertisement, as I am about leaving for Sacramento." . . . The whole country from San Francisco to Los Angeles and from the sea shore to the base of the Sierra Nevada, resounds with the sordid cry of "Gold! Gold!! GOLD!!!" while the field is left half planted, the house half built, and everything neglected but the manufacture of shovels and pickaxes.

McKinley's store in Monterey was well stocked with shovels and pickaxes, and suddenly Hugo Reid, after a run of bad luck and recent disillusionment in the gold mines, found himself making a fortune in an unexpected manner. Don Perfecto, as Jim's partner, sold all sorts of supplies to optimistic "miners," and received a substantial share in the profits. He was able to keep the long-suffering Doña Victoria in unlooked-for luxury, and even to pay off some old debts incurred in the days when he had dreamed of becoming a great *hacendado,* like his *compadre* Don Abel.

In spite of a rush of business and many miles separating him from the center of activity, Reid continued to be a thoughtful observer of life in the mines and in transitional San Francisco. Realizing that it was the most exciting show on earth, he preferred watching it from a distance to acting in it, because his vitality was at low ebb. His old "complaint of the chest" had been aggravated by hardships suffered in the mines, and the long walk with Felipe from San Francisco to McKinley's home in Monterey did him no good.

Being a sea captain, Hugo was intensely interested to hear that even the clipper ships, which for so long had leisurely sailed the Pacific Ocean engaging in exploration and trade— even the clipper ships seemed to be responding to the fierce competitive spirit pervading the New World. Each voyage seemed shorter than the last, until, on August 31, 1851, the *Flying Cloud,* built by Donald McKay and commanded by Captain Josiah Creesy, blew in through the Golden Gate, having come from New York *via* Cape Horn in eighty-one days and twenty-one hours,—an all-time record for sailing ships.

Four years earlier, on November 15, 1847, *paisanos* living in Yerba Buena had been startled to see a steamship on the Bay. It was the *Sitka,* a sidewheel, thirty-seven-foot vessel built by an American at Sitka, Alaska, as a pleasure cruiser for several Russian officers and their families. Bought by one of the most progressive spirits in northern California, William Leidesdorff, it was making a trial run, chugging in and out among the Bay islands. A great herd of elk, still living on wooded Mare Island, seemed as surprised as the *paisanos* on shore to see such an apparition heralding the Machine Age.

From that day on, with astounding frequency, a miscellany of "firsts" sprang up in San Francisco, like exotic jungle growths. The *California Star,* first newspaper to be sold in the streets of San Francisco;[2] city mail service and a trial telegraph; the first public school in California; the first theater and the first bank; the first iron safe; ice; the first Methodist who preached his faith; the first Odd Fellow, Democrat, Mason—all these appeared in the north in the three years when California remained a territory, between the close of the Mexican War and her admission as a state into the American Union.

Hugo Reid himself became a pioneer, in the literal sense, as a member of the first constitutional convention. His *vecinos* in San Gabriel had unanimously elected Don Perfecto to represent them—a high honor, for only four other members of this unique body were from the vicinity: Abel Stearns, José Antonio Carrillo, and Stephen C. Foster, all from Los Angeles; and Manuel Domínguez, from San Pedro.

This so-called constitutional convention met without authorization of the United States government. For California's new masters showed more indifference than the old toward what she claimed were her "rights." Certainly they seemed in no hurry to admit her as a new state into the Union. Such a *laissez-faire* policy had not proved disastrous in the days before the Gold Rush, but now some sort of law and order emanating from an unquestioned source was vital to California's future.

Vigilance committees were forming in various localities to suppress lawless elements like the mysterious "Hounds," who roved the streets of San Francisco at night, plundering and molesting as the spirit moved. But the Vigilantes, though effective, themselves were acting outside the law. To thoughtful citizens, it seemed a vicious circle.

Most of California's *paisanos* tried to live in the past, considering themselves proud champions, to the last, of a lost cause. Only a handful, like Don Perfecto and Don Abel, made any attempt to bring order out of deplorable chaos. These men felt more keenly than anything else the necessity of drawing up a code of laws acceptable to the more reputable inhabitants, whether early or late comers, and of urging action on the part of the United States. Full protection, as a state, had been promised to California in the event of her separation from Mexico.

Governor Mason, keenly aware of the intolerable situation, went as far as he could, working with the few far-sighted *paisanos*. He recognized the international law that an occupying force should observe the laws of the occupied territory so far as they are just and equitable according to accepted ideas. But many difficulties interfered with observing this practice in California. The laws were in a foreign tongue and had never been duly disseminated among the people. The oligarchial system, of electing one man in each community to a many-term office of *alcalde* or *juez de paz* and letting him worry about the interpretation of laws, had worked well enough in the former pastoral scheme of life in California. But the incoming Americans, after their own hard-fought battle for representation in government, showed a contempt of the Mexican law, clamoring for legislative checks and trials by jury.

Mason had gone so far as to draw up a compromise code which should be in effect during the period of occupation. But it returned too late from the printer's[3] and was never used.

Although the Mexican War actually came to an end on January 13, 1847—with the signing of articles of capitulation by Andrés Pico and Frémont at Rancho Cahuenga—more than a year passed before the Treaty of Guadalupe Hidalgo, formally ending the war, was signed at Guadalupe Hidalgo, Mexico, on February 2, 1848, by representatives of the United States and Mexico. New Mexico, California, Nevada, Utah, most of Arizona, and part of Colorado were ceded by Mexico on the payment of $15,000,000 by the United States and the assumption of a debt of approximately $3,250,000, representing claims of American citizens against Mexico. The line made on the map by the Río Grande, continued west to the Pacific just south of San Diego, was accepted as the boundary between the two republics.

The first meeting of the commissioners appointed by the United States and Mexico to fix the southern boundary was held at San Diego on July 6, 1849. There were many dis-

agreements and several changes of personnel, with John R.
Bartlett distinguishing himself above his countrymen as a
diplomat and fearless surveyor of the rough, wild Southwest.
The work of the commissioners was not concluded until
September, 1851. Meanwhile, on August 29, 1849, the first
accurate map of Los Angeles was completed and filed, after
surveys made by Lieutenant E. O. C. Ord, of the United
States Army. In a few days this efficient engineer completed
a project that had been planned ten years previously by the
easygoing *ayuntamiento!*

Early in September, 1849, the First California Guard, nu-
cleus of the National Guard, received official sanction when
Governor Bennett Riley,[4] who had been appointed by President Polk, in April, to succeed Mason, commissioned Henry
M. Naglee as captain and swore in her other able officers.
They first saw service, acting as a governmental force, in
quelling the notorious squatters' riots which occurred during the summer of 1850, climaxing a long and bitter contest
between *Americanos,* mainly from Missouri, who had seized
land belonging to Captain Sutter, under the pretext that his
title, originating in a Mexican grant, was invalid.[5] Defying
court orders for eviction, armed civilians clashed with the
militia in what has come to be known as the Sacramento
Squatters' Riots, with a loss of four killed and five wounded.
Death of the squatters' leader temporarily ended the conflict. But it broke out again in various localities over a period
of years, wherever and whenever there was challenging by
unscrupulous Americans of Mexican land grants.

It was in response to a fiery proclamation by Governor
Riley that members of California's constitutional conven-

tion assembled in Monterey. In his call to action, the brusque
soldier-governor used plain language,[6] saying:

As Congress has failed to organize a new territorial government, it becomes our imperative duty to take some active measures to provide for the existing wants of the country.

A spirit of energetic idealism characterized the group of
men who met together for the first time on Saturday, September 1, 1849, in Colton Hall, for the avowed purpose of
"forming a state constitution for California." A message
from the governor, read by his able "brevet captain and secretary of state," H. W. Halleck, opened the session with these
stirring words:

You have an important work before you—the laying of the
cornerstone of the state structure; and the stability of the edifice
will depend upon the character of the foundation which you may
establish. Your materials are good; let it never be said that the
builders lacked skill in putting them together!

Hugo Reid did not happen to be present at that first meeting, but appearing a few days later,[7] he was greeted by a
number of old friends. Besides his fellow representatives
from the south, there was young John McHenry Hollingsworth, whom he had not seen since the death of María
Ygnacia. Hollingsworth was representing the district of San
Joaquín. From Sacramento had come Captain Sutter; from
Monterey, Thomas Larkin and Robert Semple; and from
Santa Bárbara, Pablo de la Guerra.

Immediately upon his appearance at the convention, Reid
was appointed to two important committees. The task of
one, consisting of Messrs. Moore, Sutter, Hill, Ord, and
Reid, was "to report . . . at as early a day as practicable, a

plan for taking the enumeration of the inhabitants of the
state of California." The second committee was asked by the
president to determine "what, in their opinion, should constitute the boundary of the state of California." Besides Reid,
Messrs. Hastings, Sutter, De la Guerra, and Rodríguez composed the boundary commission.

The forty-eight men[8] of varied nationality, age, religion,
occupation, and political conviction who were crowded into
the modest *adobe* called Colton Hall "disputed like the devil
at home"—to quote Hugo Reid's expression—about such
endlessly controversial subjects as the rights of women and
Indians and negroes. But they accomplished their purpose
in six weeks of hard work.

Aside from establishing the boundaries of the state, de-
fining a mode of election of executive, legislative, and judi-
cial officers, making the usual provisions for the protection
of life and property, and devising a system of taxation, they
also ordered the foundation of a state-wide public school
system, and they outlawed slavery. A constitution, patterned
mainly after those of Iowa and New York, was signed by all
the delegates on October 13.

The convention adjourned, on that last day, and "proceeded in a body" to Governor Riley's house. The "old man"
seemed pleased with his fellow patriots and spoke a few
words to them from the veranda of his home:

Gentlemen, this is a prouder day to me than that on which my
soldiers cheered me on the field of Contreras. I thank you all
from my heart. I am satisfied now that the people have done
right in selecting delegates to form a constitution. They have
chosen a body of men upon whom our country may look with

pride . . . and I have no fear for California while her people choose their representatives so wisely. Gentlemen, I congratulate you upon the successful conclusion of your arduous labors; and I wish you all happiness and prosperity.

General Riley was interrupted by three cheers from the crowd, as "governor of California," and three more as "a gallant soldier." Then they all started home, glowing with the consciousness of a hard task done to the best of their ability.

Exactly a month later, by a count of 12,064 to 811, voters in the wide territory of California ratified their "state" constitution, drawn up and adopted at Monterey by the convention. At the same time they elected Peter H. Burnett⁹ as first constitutional governor, and Edward Gilbert and George W. Wright as their representatives in Congress. Returning to the past for inspiration, they chose San José as capital of the new "state." San José had been established first of all the Spanish pueblos, on November 29, 1777, by Governor Felipe de Neve, and named in honor of St. Joseph, patron saint of the sacred expedition of 1769 headed by Gaspar de Portolá and Padre Junípero Serra.

On December 17, 1849, the first constitutional legislature of California convened at San José. It consisted of sixteen senators and thirty-six assemblymen. E. Kirby Chamberlain was elected president *pro tempore* of the senate and Thomas J. White speaker of the assembly. John C. Frémont and William M. Gwin were asked to serve as senators in Washington, as soon as recognition of California's statehood should be secured. Before adjourning on April 22, 1850, the legislature adopted a code of laws providing among other things for the creation of twenty-seven counties.

On the last day of the first session, and chiefly on account of Hugo Reid's insistence, a law was defined to deal with the increasingly difficult Indian problem. It went farther in an attempt at protection of the aborigines than any earlier law, under Mexican and Spanish rule. But still they were not accorded all the rights due adult human beings, including the vote. The law confirmed them in the possession of their villages, permitted them to contract for labor, but provided that in criminal cases no white man could be convicted on an Indian's testimony. This left a large loophole for abuse, which discouraged Reid, the Indians' constant champion.

The constitutional convention and the legislature acted entirely on their own initiative. The first encouraging sign of interest on the part of the United States in the development of California did not appear until September 20, 1850, when Congress appropriated $90,000 for the construction of lighthouses in California. After a survey by government engineers, six were planned, to be placed on Alcatraz Island, at the entrance of San Francisco Bay, on the rocky Farallones, at Monterey, Point Conception above Santa Barbara, and San Diego. San Pedro was overlooked, in spite of the importance of this "harbor" and its early development by Stearns and Reid.

Finally there came the long-awaited news of the admission of California as a state into the Union. It reached San Francisco on October 18, 1850, by the mail steamer *Oregon*. Overjoyed, the *Americanos* engaged in an impromptu celebration. Business was suspended, and it seemed even to the *paisanos* that *fiesta* days might be coming in again with the new régime. Formal celebration of admission occurred on

October 29, when a bright new star was added to the American flag flying from the Plaza pole. Truly Thomas Larkin's words had been prophetic when he had told Don Abel Stearns that the Stars and Stripes would one day prove a blessing to California.

Even if the Mexicans, rather than the Americans, had won the war, it is certain that the Mexican law as practiced in California could never have checked the depredations of the lawless element that arrived in '49, with the Gold Rush. The strength of the United States was vital then to the enforcement of law and order in California. The old *alcalde,* or oligarchial, system could never have prevailed against the hordes of rough "miners" of every nationality, who cared nothing for tradition and seemed to feel only contempt for "greaser" ways.

At the moment of triumph for the *paisanos* who had prepared California for statehood, one of the most prominent, Hugo Reid, encountered a personal disaster. His son Felipe's opinion of Jim McKinley as an unreliable business man soon became justified. Solely through mismanagement, McKinley, Reid, and Company began to lose money. This seems strange, when the year had opened so auspiciously, but probably it can be accounted for by the fact that Reid gave almost all his time in the fall of '49 and spring of '50 to state politics, and McKinley lacked the bookkeeping ability of his fellow countryman. As Monterey became deserted, not only by her inhabitants heading for the mines, but also by legislators moving to San José, the new capital, Reid woke up to the fact that most of the *tienda* profits had been spent and there was little left in reserve for the proverbial "rainy day."

Since the partners' private resources were not adequate to carry the business until conditions returned to "normal," it became necessary to liquidate the firm of McKinley and Reid, at the close of '50. This set Don Perfecto, several years older and in much worse health, back where he had started, before the Gold Rush. The haunting fear that he had confided to Don Abel—of being forced to leave Monterey at the end of a trial year, without having "made a spoon"—was realized. Once again he seemed to have "spoiled a horn," although, this time, the fault may have been another's.

Hugo Reid returned to the south, a man grizzled by sickness and worry. Though he had passed out of his thirties only a few months previously, the *vecinos* remaining in San Gabriel commenced referring to him as "old Reid." With Doña Victoria he took up life again at Uva Espina, but instead of the green-vined acres and golden fields of wheat that had belonged to them in the past, there was only a mean patch left for the house to stand on, and a few acres of farming land saved from devastating sales and losses. The house and the neglected garden surrounding it stood forlornly on the dusty road across from the mission, now also in want.

Had Hugo been well or exceedingly industrious, he could still have made a living out of the farming land that was left, estimated at 188 acres, the land valued at $1000 and improvements at $9000 in the Los Angeles County assessment roll for 1850. But as an old-time *hacendado,* once owner of thousands of acres, thousands of cattle, grapevines, and *arrobas* of wheat, he thought too expansively for his changed condition, and felt a profound disinclination toward petty truck farming. He also had other matters on his mind.

A strange thing happened to Hugo and Victoria in these last, lean years. Life would have seemed drab and uneventful without an absorbing interest. Fortunately the man's mind went back over the years to the time when he was a schoolboy in Scotland and had shown unusual literary ability; also to a promise made when he was courting Doña Victoria, that some day he would vindicate her people by the use of his pen. Recent discussions in Colton Hall had revealed the lawmakers' abysmal ignorance of the Indian nature. Even members of the *gente de razón,* who had lived all their lives in California, joined the *Americanos* in forcing the red men to remain at the very bottom of the social scale, indeed refusing them some of the fundamental rights of human beings as defined in the Constitution of the United States. Hugo's sense of justice had been outraged again and again, and now, having leisure, he resolved to keep that promise made in his youth to the woman who had given him so much and asked so little.

Vivider pursuits could no longer distract him—like young love, sailing to far places, and mining for gold—and he had acquired a deep understanding of the Indian nature after living so long, in rare companionship, with an intelligent member of the race. Victoria agreed to help him in every way possible; in searching her own mind and memory, and in gaining the complete confidence of her people. With this encouragement, "old Reid" started work on the Indian essays—finally, a series of twenty-two "letters"—that were to constitute his most lasting claim to fame.[10]

While the Reids were planning necessary interviews among the few Indians who could remember the ancient

"court language" and generally forgotten customs and beliefs, the Dalton family paid them a visit to welcome Hugo
home, stopping on their way out from Los Angeles to Rancho Santa Anita, which had been the Dalton home for
several years past. Fourteen of them—two entire families
belonging to Hugo's *compadre* Henry and his brother
George—had made a midmorning start from Don Enrique's
town house.

They traveled in two *carretas,* and the oxen were leisurely
in pace; so lunchtime overtook them not many miles from
the center of town at Rosa de Castilla,[11] where there were
shade trees and water. They had a delicious *bastamiento* of
fourteen squab chickens with old-time trimmings, followed
by a *siesta.* The sun had set before they reached San Gabriel,
but the Reids seemed pleased to put them up for the night.

A little boy named Charlie Jenkins, stepson to George
Dalton, rode in one of the wagons. As an old man he still
remembers vividly that delightful visit at Uva Espina with
Don Perfecto and his Indian wife.[12] To him, Doña Victoria
seemed a fine-looking, very dignified woman. She was tall
and unlike many Indian women, who are willowy in extreme youth but commence to grow squat at sixteen or so.
Victoria never lost her grace.

Felipe he remembers as an attractive young fellow of
splendid physique, Spanish in appearance and so well
dressed as to seem a trifle foppish. He looked twenty-four
or twenty-five years old and was more interested in horse
racing than anything else in life. His horse, wearing a silver-
studded bridle and elaborate saddle ending in long *tapaderas,* appeared as showy as himself. Poor Felipe always was

overfond of pleasure and never distinguished himself in business or in politics. Indeed, he is said to have fallen into bad company and actually to have become a member of the notorious Murieta gang.[18] Perhaps it is fortunate that Felipe died of smallpox while still in his youth.

Charlie Jenkins liked the looks of Don Perfecto. He found him no less striking in appearance than Felipe and Doña Victoria, but would have judged him fifty-five rather than his correct age. Reid, too, was tall and well built, with a luxuriant graying beard giving him dignity to offset a pair of twinkling blue eyes. A faint Sotch burr had never been lost in the daily use of other languages—Spanish, English, Indian, and even French, with his *vecino,* Louis Vignes.

Evening saw a merry company gathered under the Reid roof. A rare feast was spread, of old-time lavishness, including roast turkey, *tortillas, enchiladas, dulces,* fruit, and Hugo's own wine. Presently mission bells called everyone to prayers across the way; then home under the pepper trees to talk and sing Mexican love songs. The timbre of Hugo's flexible voice and the tinkling of Felipe's guitar carried each tune over passages that were unfamiliar to the English guests. Soon everyone was singing and dancing with complete lack of self-consciousness.

There was little excitement at such a family *baile,* not a great deal of drinking; only ungrudging hospitality, and a childlike happiness that is gone from life in California.

Next morning the Daltons all piled into their *carretas* and creaked on up the dusty road to their home by the cool green lake at Santa Anita. But they continued to keep in friendly touch with the Reids. When the grapes were ripe at the *rancho,* Hugo helped his *compadre* Henry prepare them for shipment to San Francisco. Working as a neighbor only, on the land that he had once owned, must have caused Don Perfecto *dolor de corazón.* But he never allowed such feelings to show on the surface. He always had something funny to say to little Charlie, who was underfoot most of the time. Jenkins remembers that Hugo and Uncle Henry Dalton originated the system, still in use, of packing grapes with redwood sawdust.

Since hard ranch work had never appealed to Don Perfecto, he did not long play the rôle of helpful neighbor. For a time after leaving Dalton to his own devices, he occupied himself gathering subject-matter for the long-planned Indian essays. Then suddenly he vanished from San Gabriel. Neither his family nor Henry Dalton nor Abel Stearns had the slightest idea where he had gone. In May, 1851, Stearns received this letter, containing a question which he could not answer (translation):

Para Señor Don Abel Stearns
Mi querido Compadre,

I take the liberty of writing and troubling you in order to ask whether you have seen your *compadre* Reid in San Francisco, or had any news from him.

We have not heard from him and are very much surprised that he has not written a single letter since he left, and for that reason I beg you to let me know whether you have heard from him and where he is.

Remember me to my *comadre* Arcadia, when you see her. Begging you to excuse this imposition, I am,

Yours respectfully,
VICTORIA REID.

The uncertainty of her husband's whereabouts, combined with an ever-present fear for his health, must have sent Doña Victoria almost out of her wits again. Only when driven by real emotion or necessity would she touch a pen, considering it a symbol of tragedy-dealing education. She wrote but two letters in her life, and both were prompted by deep unhappiness—first over María Ygnacia's death, and now this last disappearance of Hugo.

For several months there was no news of Don Perfecto, and then one day he reappeared, saying quietly, in a way that brooked no questioning, that he had been in retreat this time and not off sailing in the *Esmeralda* or prospecting in the northern lodes. In spite of serious ill health, he had completed the Indian essays, and they were now ready for publication.

William Rand, editor of the new *Los Angeles Star*,[14] accepted them without hesitation. Furthermore, he engaged Reid as San Gabriel correspondent for that paper, offering him a fair salary. A little paragraph in the issue of February 21, 1852, announced that the editor had received "a series of articles upon the manners, customs, *et cetera,* of the Indians, from the pen of Hugo Reid, Esq., a gentleman well conversant with the subject with which he treats." On another page of the same paper appeared the first of the series. Every Saturday morning, from then on, the *Star* came out with a new letter from Don Perfecto.

Reid started with a description of the Indians' language, customs, religion, and legends. Then, having understandingly shown their original state of contentment and true "civilization," he went on to tell of the Spaniards' arrival and

cruel treatment of the aborigines, of the padres' attempt at
bettering the Indians' lot, and of their complete failure, due
to circumstances outside their control. He concluded with
a poignant account of current conditions and a plea to end
"legislative oppression." These letters, being informal, dra-
matic, and devoid of unnecessary dates or statistics, were
read with a great deal of interest, and even with some effect
where effect was most needed.

Besides arousing a surprising amount of local interest,
they attained national significance in serving as the basis for
Don Benito Wilson's humane report dispatched to Washington within the year of their publication, while he was acting as United States Indian agent in the territory.

Encouraged by gratifying, and increasing, appreciation of
his essays, Don Perfecto tapped the brain of his much endur-
ing, but still admiring, wife for more information. He then
commenced another long-cherished project, that of compil-
ing a vocabulary and complete language manual, Indian-
English, for the southern California tribes, that they might
understand their new masters better than the old, and, he
hoped, fare more happily under them. But before finishing
the congenial task, Hugo fell sick again.

This illness was fatal, and Doña Victoria once again had
to watch a loved one die, without being able to help in any
way. Undoubtedly, her husband had suffered for many years
from tuberculosis, and his condition was aggravated, dangerously, by the hardships, physical and mental, that he had
experienced recently in northern California. No doctor
could have aided him in his last extremity, but he was denied the solace of his family physician's presence in the sick-

room. Dr. William Keith himself had succumbed to the hardships of life in the northern mines, not long before.

Hugo Reid followed his friend in death, on December 12, 1852. Many people attended the funeral ceremonies—as many Indians as members of the *gente de razón,*—starting from the town house of Henry Dalton, and proceeding to the Plaza church. Intimates of the Reid family each received an invitation like the following, printed by William Rand and delivered on the morning of December 14:[15]

Señor Don Ygnacio del Valle.

Suplicamos á U. tenga á bien asistir á las tres de la tarde de hoy al entierro del cuerpo de Don Perfecto Reid (Q.E.P.D.), y así mismo mañana á las nueve, concurrir á la Yglesia de esta Ciudad, á las exequias que se le deverán hacer.

La comitiva saldrá esta tarde de la casa de Don Enrique Dalton.

H. Dalton	Abel Stearns
A. Olvera	B. D. Wilson
Julian Workman	D. W. Alexander
John A. Lewis	J. B. Wilson
Wm. H. Rand	

The earthly remains of Hugo Reid found a resting place in the Pueblo's old Catholic cemetery. And over the new grave were read the beautiful words of the burial service, in Spanish, by a sorrowing padre[16] who had come in from San Gabriel Mission to do honor to "a great-hearted man."

Victoria was desolate, although friends flocked around her and tried to lighten her burden of grief and loneliness. The newspapers made an extraordinary effort to give Don Perfecto's personality, intellect, and influence their due. Mr. Rand and the other *Star* editors, of course, showed the deepest sorrow at the combined loss of a friend and important regular contributor. But even northern papers, which usually had little room for news items from the south, mentioned him honorably.

In part they quoted from the long *Star* obituary, published the day after his death and giving details of Hugo Reid's life and literary achievements; then each added a personal word of respect. John Nugent, himself a world traveler, adventurer, writer, duelist, and, at the moment, editor of the *San Francisco Herald,* praised Don Perfecto's rare scholarly type of mind beyond any actual accomplishments. He acknowledged the man's late finding of himself, and deeply regretted that his last, humanitarian project remained incomplete.

Nugent shared the general opinion that Reid's knowledge and humanity, given such lucid expression as he had shown himself capable of, would have been of inestimable value to California in helping her through a long, chaotic period of transition. Nugent's tribute ended with these words:

Of a good education, a fine mind, and a most remarkable memory, Hugo Reid possessed a fund of information concerning the history of California surpassing that of almost any other man in the state. No man certainly had an equal acquaintance with the history of the Indians.

There were few possessions for Reid to will away. His library alone proved of value. Doña Victoria gave a Bible, a letter of Byron to his publisher, and a Shakespeare, with "María Ygnacia" written childishly on the flyleaf, to "Lalita" Evertson King, once more her comforter. Since Victoria herself despised all books, the rest of Hugo's went to

J. Lancaster Brent, a well-informed lawyer who had helped him secure his title to the wide mission lands of San Gabriel in his old ambitious days. The volumes were scattered, like everything else, when Brent moved to Louisiana. He took some of them with him, but sold or gave away the greater number.

Harder days than she had yet experienced fell upon Doña Victoria, left alone for the last time. According to Lalita, "the guardian Reid had selected for his wife proved dishonest, and she was robbed of her small fortune." To ease her financial difficulties, Don Benito Wilson had bought the Lake Vineyard property from Victoria during Hugo's last illness. And Henry Dalton tried repeatedly to collect her interest in land deeded to the Reids by Alvarado and Pico, in the 'forties, but his efforts were unavailing. The United States Land Commission refused to confirm these Mexican grants, even to the small plot in San Gabriel[17] on which stood the house so carefully constructed by Don Perfecto at the time of his marriage to the Indian woman.

Misfortunes avalanched upon Doña Victoria. Three years after Hugo's death, one of her worst fears was realized. Uva Espina—in spite of its stout, beamed construction and 'dobe walls, four feet thick—fell down in an earthquake. Victoria had to sell even her personal ornaments, to live. Lalita saw her for the last time in 1863 when she came to call on her adopted daughter, attended by one faithful servant. Instead of the satins and silks that the little girl had so often admired, Doña Victoria was dressed in a common Indian print, and a quilt covered her shoulders in place of the familiar crêpe shawl. But the grown Lalita tearfully told her husband,

Judge King, that her foster mother was "the same grand, proud, cheerful woman. She would accept no favors; only wanted to see and embrace me once more."

Doña Victoria died at San Gabriel on December 23, 1868, and was buried on Christmas Eve by Padre Pedro Verdaguer in the mission cemetery. Like all her children and their father—the shadowy Pablo, whose identity has long been lost—she finally sank under the special scourge of Indians, for which they knew no cure. Only by a miracle had she lived through the most fearful epidemic of all, occurring in '62. And six years later, when smallpox struck the fatal blow at Victoria Reid, she was the last surviving member of a family unique in itself, yet always an integral part of the gracious life that the *paisanos* were leading when California could truly be called the Land of *Poco Tiempo*.

APPENDIX A

Register of British and American Residents in California Prior to 1840

NAMES OF THE British Subjects and Citizens of the United States who resided in Alta California, prior to 1840, with their place of residence, profession, and the year of their arrival as far as can now be ascertained. During this period, there were living in California, a few French, Germans, Portuguese and It[alians] (not forty) and 30 to 40 Natives of the Sandwich Islands and Foreigners of Color. Subjects of Spain and Citizens of the South American Republics were not classed as Foreigners. In 1840, Alta California, from the District of San Diego to the Districts of Sonoma and Sacramento, contained about [?]ooo People, with a revenue from Imports averaging 85,000$ per annum.

[Name and Chief Place of Residence]	What Na-tion	Year of Arrival	Trade or Occupation	†
Allen George *Monterey*	I	1822	Writer & School Master	M.D.
Anderson William *Santa Cruz*	E		Lumberman	M.L.
Alexander David *Los Angeles*		1842	Merchant	L.
Alexander Cyrus		1833		
Burke James *Santa Barbara*	I	1824	Sea Otter Hunter	M.L.

† Married in Cal. marked M. Now living marked L. Dead marked D. Absent part of the time marked A. [Gone marked G.]

[Name and Chief Place of Residence]	What Na-tion	Year of Arrival	Trade or Occupation	†
Burton John *San Jose*	A	1828	Town Officer & Retailer	M.D.
Brown Charles *San Francisco*	A	1829	Lumberman	M.L.
Burton Luis T. *Santa Barbara*	A	1831		M.L.
Branch Ziba *Santa Barbara*	A	1831	Farmer	M.L.
Burrough James	A			
Berry James *San Francisco*	E		Officer Mexican Army	D.
Bowls Joseph *Monterey*	A		Retailer	M.L.
Barker Robert S. *Monterey*	A		Carpenter	G.
Breck William *San Luis*	A		Gunsmith	D.
Bale Edward T. *Napa*	E	1839	Physician & Ranchero	M.D.
Bourn Thomas G. *San Jose*	A		Retailer	M.D.
Bell Alexander *Los Angeles*			Merchant	M.L.
Black James *Pajaro*	E		Lumberman & Ran[chero]	M.L.
Banks Archabald *Monterey*	S		Carpenter	G.
Byrns Edward *Monterey*	E		Teamster	
Byrns John *Monterey*	E			
Bee Henry *Monterey*	E		Teamster	M.L.
Burton Joseph *Monterey*			Laborer	
Bennet Gerald	A			
Brown John	A			
Burroughs Wm.	A			

[Name and Chief Place of Residence]	What Nation	Year of Arrival	Trade or Occupation	†
Brander William	E		Lumberman	
Monterey				
Bennet William	A			
Burns John	I	1823	Laborer	D.
San Luis Obispo				
Bullon Joseph				
Burton Herald				
Chapman George or	E	1818	Carpenter	M.D.
Joseph				
Santa Barbara				
Cooper John B. R.	A	1823	Sea Capt & Ranchero	M.L.
Monterey				
Cooper John	E	28	Soldier Mexican A	M.L.
Monterey				
Call Daniel	A			
Carpenter Samuel	A	1832	Farmer	L.
Los Angeles				
Coppenger John	I		Lumberman	M.D.
Las Pulgas				
Cooper	A		Sea Otter hunter. Showman	D.
Santa Barbara				
Cooper David	E		Retailer	D.
San Francisco				
Coulter			Naturalist	G.
Traveling [sic]				
Chards William	A	36	Lumberman & Trader	M.L.
Santa Cruz				
Carmichial Laurence	S		Retailer	D.
Monterey				
Cole Thomas	E		Teamster	M.L.
Monterey				
Chappel George	E		Lumberman	M.D.
Santa Cruz				
Clar John	A	3	Engineer	L.
San Francisco				
Collens Peter	A			
Cooke James	E			
Campbell Colin	A			

[Name and Chief Place of Residence]	What Na- tion	Year of Arrival	Trade or Occupation	†
Campbell Samuel				
Chamberlain John *Monterey*	A		Blacksmith	L.
Cooper Martin				
Doak Thomas *Monterey*	A	1818	Carpenter	M.L.
Duckworth Walter *Monterey*	E	1822	Teamster & Gardner	M.D.
Dana William G. *Santa Barbara*	A	1824	Merchant & Ran[chero]	M.L.
Douglas David *Traveling [sic]*	S	1831	Botanist	D.
Dye Job F. *Monterey*	A		Merchant & Ranch[er]o	M.L.
Day Benjamin *Monterey*	A		Hatter	G.D.
Day William *Los Angeles*	A		Hatter	G.
Davis John *San Francisco*	E		Ship Wright & trading	M.D.
Davis John Mrs. *San Francisco*	A			M.D.
Dickey William *Sacramento*	I	26	Disteller	G.
Den Nicholas A. *Santa Barbara*	I		Physician & Ranchero	M.L.
Daly Nathan *Monterey*	A		Disteller	D.
Daylor William	A			
Domingo John *Los Angeles*				D.
Dolieron Manuel				
Elwell Robert *Santa Barbara*	A	1824	Merchant	M.L.
Ebbets John *Monterey*	A	1832	Importer	L.G.

[Name and Chief Place of Residence]	What Nation	Year of Arrival	Trade or Occupation	†
Everett John	A	32	Supercargo	L.G.
Los Angeles				
Estabrock Ethan	A			L.
Monterey				
Edmands Nathan	A			
Fuller John	E	1823	Butcher & Lighterman	M.D.
San [sic]				
Fitch Henry D.	A		Sea Capt. Merchant	M.D.
San Diego				
Foster John	E		Merchant & Ranchero	M.L.
Los Angeles				
Fling Guy T.	A	1831	Blacksmith	L.
Monterey				
Fravel Ephraim	A	34	Tailor	L.
San Jose				
Frazer George	A		Trapper	L.
Sacramento				
Foxen Benjaman	E	24	Shoemaker	
Santa Barbara				
Furginson Daniel	E		Laborer	M.D.
Monterey				
Farnham	A			
Santa Cruz				
Farginson Jesse	A	1828	Trapper	D.
Los Angeles				
Faxon William T.	A		Storekeeper	D.
Monterey				
Foster Charles	A			
Forbes James			Merchant & Ranchero	M.L.
San Jose				
Flemming James	E		Teamster	
Monterey				
Fuller Asiel				
Fippard Charles	A		Lumberman	
Forsyth James				
Monterey				
Gilroy John	E	1814	Miller & Soap maker	M.L.
Gilroy				

[Name and Chief Place of Residence]	What Na-tion	Year of Arrival	Trade or Occupation	†
Gale William A. *Santa Barbara*	A	24	Supercargo. Imp[orter]	M.D.
Garner Wᵐ. R. *Monterey*	E	24	Lumberman	M.D.
Gulnac William *San Jose*	A	32	Blacksmith	M.D.
Graham Isaac *Monterey*	A	36	Disteller	L.
Greybatch Wᵐ.	E		soap maker	D.
Gilbreth Isaac *Los Angeles*			Blacksmith	D.
German John *Monterey*	I		Adobee maker	
Gardner Whyman *Monterey*	A	1839	Laborer	L.
Goddard Samuel				
Hill Daniel *Santa Barbara*	A	1823	Merchant & Ranchero	M.
Hartnell Wᵐ. E. P. *Monterey*	E	22	Ranchero & Gov't Employee	M.D.
Charles Hall [*sic*] *Santa Barbara*	A	31	Store keeper	D.
Hall James *San Francisco*	A	34	Sea Captain	Gone
Hitchcock Isaac *Traveling* [*sic*]	A	32	Trapping & Trading	G.
Hope Gerald *Monterey*	I		Hatter	G.
Hope John *Monterey*	A			
Hays Elias *Monterey*	A		Shingle Maker	G.
Higgens John *Santa Cruz*	A		Lumberman	D.
Howard William D. M. *San Francisco*	A		Supercargo	D.
Humphy Hatherway *Monterey*	A	39	Carpenter	G.

[Name and Chief Place of Residence]	What Nation	Year of Arrival	Trade or Occupation	†
Hughes William O. *Monterey*	A		Blacksmith	G.
Hewett George	A			
Hemstead Sidney	A			
Hinckley W^m. H. *San Francisco*	A		Town officer & Merchant	M.D.
House Thomas *Sonoma*	I	1817	Mason	L.
Hill Leas *Santa Barbara*	A	23	Ranchero	D.
Jones Jerimiah *Sonoma*	E	1822	Mason	D.
Johnstone James *Los Angeles*	E		Merchant & Ranchero	M.D.
Jones John C. *Santa Barbara*	A		Ship owner & Importer	M.L.G.
Jones Peter	A			
Jackson Edward	A			
Kenlock George *Monterey*	S	1829	Cabinet Maker	M.L.
Kenlock George Mrs. *Monterey*	S	29		M.D.
Kerith [Keith] William M. *Los Angeles*	A		Physician	D.
King Robert *Santa Barbara*	E		Lumberman	M.D.
Kennedy James	I			
Kelly Henry	A			
Littlejohn David *Monterey*	S	23	Dairy-man & Gardner	M.D.
Livermore Robert *San Joaquin*	E	23	Ranchero	M.L.
Lodge Michial *Santa Cruz*	I		Miller & Shingle maker	M.D.

[Name and Chief Place of Residence]	What Na-tion	Year of Arrival	Trade or Occupation	†
Larkin Thomas O. *Monterey*	A	32	Merchant	M.L.
Larkin Thos. O. Mrs. *Monterey*	A	32		M.L.
Leese Jacob T. *Sonoma*	A		Town Officer & Ranchero	M.L.
Laughlin R.				
Love James		34		
Lawson Peter *Sacramento*	A		Ranchero	L.
Leighton John B.				
Loring Samuel				
Lewis Thomas	A			
Libbey Elliot *San Luis*	A	39	Sea Captain	D.
Lucas John	E			D.
McKinley James *Monterey*	S	24	Merchant	M.L.
McAllester Michial *Monterey*	S	26	Blacksmith	D.
Martin John *Santa Clara*	E	25	Carpinter	
Martin John *San Raphael*	E		Ranchero	L.
Mulligan John *Monterey*	I	14	Ranchero	D.
Murphy Timothy *San Raphael*	I	29	Ranchero	D.
Mervett Ezekial *Sacramento*	A		Trapper	D.
Macondray John O. E. *Monterey*	A	32	Retailer	D.
Majors Joseph L. *Santo Cruz*	A		Lumberman	M.L.
Mellus Henry *Los Angeles*	A	35	Supercargo	M.L.G.
Marsh John *San Joaquin*	A	35	Physician & R[anchero]	L.

[Name and Chief Place of Residence]	What Na-tion	Year of Arrival	Trade or Occupation	†
McVickers Henry	A	36	Carpenter	L.
Monterey				
Mervett Joseph	A	32	Trapper	D.
Sacramento				
McIntosh Edward	S		Lumberman	L.
Monterey				
McFarland Wm.				
Mervett S.	A		Trapper	D.
McCoon Perry				
Meadows James	E		Lumberman	L.
Monterey				
McCarthy William	E		Teamster	
Monterey				
Mills John	E		Lumberman	
Monterey				
Mathus William	E			
Monterey				
McPherson James				
Miller Daniel				M.L.
McLean George				
Mellus Francis	A		Supercargo	M.L.
Los Angeles				
Matthus John	E		Soap maker	L.
Gilroy				
Mellish				
Niderer [Nidever] George	A		Sea Otter hunter	L.
Santa Barbara				
Niele Henry	A	1836	Disteller	D.
Monterey				
Nye Gorham H.	A	29	Sea Captain	L.
San Francisco				
Oliver John	E		Lumberman	G.
Pajaro				
Owens Charles	A			
O'Brien John	I		Lumberman	
O'Brien James				

[Name and Chief Place of Residence]	What Na-tion	Year of Arrival	Trade or Occupation	†
Prentis Samuel *Santa Barbara*	A		Sea Otter hunter	D.
Paty Henry *Monterey*	A	1833	Ship owner & Imp[orter]	D.
Park Thomas B. *Santa Barbara*	A		Supercargo	D.
Price John *San Jose*	A	32	Retailor	D.
Price John *Santa Cruz*	E		Lumberman	M.L.
Plummer Henry	A			
Paty John *San Francisco*	A	37	Ship owner & Importer	L.G.
Pickernell John	A			
Richardson Wᵐ. A. *San Francisco*	E	22	Port officer & Ranchero	M.D.
Rice George *Los Angeles*	A	25	Merchant	M.L.G.
Read John *San Raphael*		27	Ranchero	M.D.
Reid Hugh *Los Angeles*			Writer & vinyard	M.D.
Rhea John *Los Angeles*	A		Merchant	G.
Runnals Stephen *Gilroy*	E		Soap Maker	
Robbins Thos. M. *Santa Barbara*	A	23	Sea Capt. & Merchant	M.D.
Rainsford John *San Francisco*	E		Lighterman	D.
Rodgers James *Monterey*	E		Teamster	M.D.
Roe Charles *Monterey*	A			
Richardson Wᵐ. *Monterey*	I		Tailor	
Rollens John *Pajaro*	I		Hewer	

[Name and Chief Place of Residence]	What Nation	Year of Arrival	Trade or Occupation	†
Rice Isaac B. *Pajaro*	A		Lumberman	
Ridley Robt. T. *San Francisco*	E		Town officer & Ranchero	M.D.
Rightinson Thos. *Monterey*	A			
Rurnrill Geo W. *Monterey*	A		Blacksmith	G.
Robinson Alfred *Santa Barbara*	A	28	Supercargo &	M.L.G.
Spear Nathan *San Francisco*	A	1823	Importer	D.
Spence David *Monterey*	S	1824	Merchant	M.L.
Stearns Abel *Los Angeles*	A	1829	Merchant	L.
Scott James *Santa Barbara*	E		Ship owner & Importer	D.
Stone Daniel	A	1832		
Sinclair Prumet *Santa Barbara*	A	1832	Sea Otter hunter	D.
Smith Jedidiah *Traveling [sic]*	A	1829	Trapper & Trading	
Sill Daniel *San Francisco*	A	1831	Millwright	L.
Smith Charles *Santa Barbara*	A	1831	Store Keeper	D.
Stokes James *Monterey*	E	1833	Merchant	M.L.
Sparks Isaac *Santa Barbara*	A		Sea Otter Hunter	M.L.
Snooks Joseph *San Diego*	E		Sea Captain	M.D.
Stevens Capt. *San Diego*	A		Sea Otter Hunter	L.
Stevens Mrs. *San Diego*	A			L.

[Name and Chief Place of Residence]	What Nation	Year of Arrival	Trade or Occupation	†
Smith John *Monterey*	E		Carpenter	L.
Scott James *Monterey*	E		Lumberman	
Smith Capt. *Sonoma*			Sea Captain	D.
Simmons Stephen *Santa Barbara*	A		Sea Otter hunter	
Smith William	A			
Southard Eli *San Francisco*	A		Carpenter	L.
Shields Samuel	A			D.
Stetson Edward L. *Monterey*	A	1839	Writer	L.
Spaulding Joseph *Monterey*	A			
Slade Oliver *Monterey*	A		Carpenter	Gone
Stevens John				
Thompson William *Santa Cruz*	E	1822	Lumberman	M.L.
Thompson Samuel *Santa Cruz*	E	1822	Lumberman	M.L.
Thompson *Santa Barbara*	S	1824		
Temple John *Los Angeles*	A	1825	Merchant	M.L.
Thompson A. B. *Santa Barbara*	A		Ship owner & Importer	M.L.
Tevy *Monterey*	S	1826	Butcher & Packer	Gone
Tomlinson Thomas A *Monterey*	A		Hatter	M.D.
Thomas Thomas	E	1838		
Thompson Thomas	A			
Trask George				
Thompson Joseph P. *San Francisco*	A	1829	Supercargo	L.

[Name and Chief Place of Residence]	What Na-tion	Year of Arrival	Trade or Occupation	†
Trevethan William *Monterey*	E		Lumberman	L.
Young Levy *Traveling [sic]*	A	1833	Trapping & Trading	Dead
Yount George *Napa*	A	1831	Miller & Ranchero	Living
Young Francis *Santa Cruz*	E		Lumberman	M.L.
Vincent George W.				
William Wilson [sic] *San Jose*	A	1821	Laborer	D.
Watson James *Monterey*	E	1824	Merchant	M.L.
Welsh William *San Joaquin*	S	1824	Ranchero	M.D.
Wilson John *Santa Barbara*	S	1826	Ship owner & Importer	M.L.
Weeks James *San Jose*	E		Town officer & Retailer	M.L.
West William M. *Monterey*	E	1829	Carpenter	M.D.
Warner John T. *Los Angeles*	A	1831	Merchant & Ranchero	M.L.
Wolfskill William *Los Angeles*	A	1828	Vinyard & orchards	M.L.
Wolfskill John *Los Angeles*	A			L.
Ware William *Santa Cruz*	I	1832	Lumberman	L.
Williams Isaac *Los Angeles*	A	1833	Merchant & Ranchero	D.
Walker Joseph *Traveling [sic]*	A	1833	Trapper & Trading	L.
Watson Edward *Monterey*	E		Retailer	M.L.

[Name and Chief Place of Residence]	What Na-tion	Year of Arrival	Trade or Occupation	†
Webb William *Monterey*	A		Carpenter	Gone
Warren William R. *Monterey*	A		Store Keeper	Dead
White Michial				
Whitmarsh *Sonoma*	A	1836		
Williams Benjamin				
Watson Andrew *Monterey*	E		Carpenter	M.L.
Wood Henry *Traveling [sic]*			Mountain guide	L.
Wilson Alvin *Monterey*	A		Laborer	
Whitten Ezekial *Monterey*	A		Laborer	
Whitton Jedidiah *Monterey*	A		Laborer	
Warren Henry	A			
Woodworth John	A			
Warren Cornelius	A			
Williams George	E			

Hugo Reid's "Letters on the Los Angeles County Indians"

H<small>UGO</small> <small>REID</small>'s informal Indian essays, published as *Letters* to the *Los Angeles Star* during the year 1852, were widely read and discussed. Several of Reid's friends became sufficiently moved by his depiction of the Indians' sad plight to contribute toward the printing, in the same year, of Don Benito Wilson's humane and constructive report as United States Indian agent in the Southwest. Wilson admitted collaboration with Reid in the preparation of this report; and it was planned that Don Benito himself should journey to Washington, D.C., with the idea of interesting the President of the United States in the long-needed regulation of Indian affairs. Only a few months before his death, Don Hugo sent out from San Gabriel a statement of what he had done toward raising money, which he addressed as follows:

Marzo 29 de 1852 á los Señores Comisionados, para el arreglo de representación y á Su Ex^cia el Presidente de los Estados Unidos.

Translated, it continued:

In accordance with the commission entrusted to me, I have succeeded in collecting some amounts for the subscription; but because I find myself quite ill, I have been unable to interview some of the people appearing in the list. However, as soon as I feel better, I shall take care of that.

Don Daniel Sexton has not wanted to give anything because the envoy to Washington is not agreeable to him.

Don Juan Roland claims having already given five dollars to Don Abel Stearns.

Don Fran[cis]co Temple did not wish to contribute as belonging to the second class, but to the third [on a list, which has been lost].

The following amounts have been received:

From Don Julian Workman	$20
Juan Roland	15
Fran[cis]co Temple	8
Andrés Duarte	8
Andrés Courtner	4
Doña Victoria Reid	8
	$63

Which sum of sixty-three *pesos* I am remitting through Don Guill[er]mo H. Rand.

I remain, dear sirs,   Yours truly,
                                                                  HUGO REID.

To the Commissioners
  D. Abel Stearns
  Ant[oni]o José Cot
  A. F. Coronel
  Enrique Dalton

It is noteworthy that one of the four "commissioners" to whom Reid sent this statement was the same Don Antonio Coronel who later became the source of much of Helen Hunt Jackson's material on the California Indians which she used with telling effect in *Ramona*. Such an incident as the breaking up of Alessandro's village on impossibly short notice had precedent in San Gabriel in Hugo Reid's and Don Antonio's lifetime; and the death, from heart-

break, of Padre Salvierderra was painfully like the last days
of Padre Tomás Estenaga, who had married Don Hugo
and Doña Victoria at a gay *paisano* wedding in 1837. Don
Benito's well-planned report never reached a receptive au-
dience, but the pathos of Ramona's romance penetrated into
thousands of spirits and aroused almost as much sympathy
for the abused red race as *Uncle Tom's Cabin* did for the
black.

Obviously, Hugo Reid's letters about his wife's people
reached much farther and deeper than he ever dreamed they
would. Even within the few months of life that were left to
him, after their publication, he saw gratifying evidence of
interest in the Indians, aroused by his own pen.

For instance, John Russell Bartlett, the most active and
effective member of the United States and Mexican Boundary Commission from '50 to '53, came to Los Angeles in
the course of his western travels, in April, 1852. His first act,
after registering at the "very indifferent" Bella Union Hotel,
was to call at the office of the *Los Angeles Star* for the purpose of obtaining "a file of the paper which contains a
series of articles on the California Indians." Already the
fame of Reid's articles had reached San Francisco and San
Diego, where Bartlett had been stopping. The commissioner
reported:

Mr. Rand, one of the editors, cheerfully complied with my
request and gave me the papers I desired. I also met Mr. Hayes
here, a gentleman connected with the bar, who with Mr. Rand
manifested much interest in the objects of my inquiry; and Mr.
Hayes kindly offered to accompany me to the Mission of San
Gabriel, twelve miles distant, where resided Mr. Hugo Reid, the

author of these papers. These gentlemen informed me that Mr.
Reid was better acquainted with the Indians of that portion of
the state than any other person. With the hope, therefore, of obtaining more information on this subject, I gladly accepted the
proposal of Mr. Hayes; and we agreed to set off for the mission
as soon as horses could be procured.

Unfortunately none could be procured that afternoon, and
they decided to go "*mañana*." As it happened, this trip never
materialized, but Bartlett had several interesting communications with Hugo's publishers. They assured him that the
weekly letters were provoking continuous discussion and
interest among the *Star* readers.

A few months later, on August 14, the *Star* came out
with an article on California Indians by a writer who called
himself Philo. It was a direct offshoot of Reid's letters and
proposed constructive measures for bettering the Indians'
condition. The opening paragraph illustrates its tone:

The light that has been thrown upon the history of the Indians
of Los Angeles County in the interesting letters published in a
series in the *Star* must have a practicable tendency to ameliorate
their condition. No doubt every philanthropist, upon the perusal of those letters, has asked if nothing can be done for the
prospective and permanent welfare of this unfortunate race. In
taking up this subject, I hope to suggest such measures as will
secure the prospective goal of the Indians of this southern part
of California.

I regard the policy pursued by agents of the general government toward our Indians as being at war with the interests of the
people and of the Indians themselves.

Philo went on to detail his objections to government treatment of the Indians, before suggesting some splendid prac-

tical reforms. Hugo Reid accomplished a great deal merely in being the inspiration for so well-thought-out an article.

The first twelve of Reid's *letters* to the *Star* readers are preserved in manuscript form in the Antonio Coronel Collection of Californiana. Several times they have been reproduced, in county histories and elsewhere. But the last ten letters vanished from sight, after the first publication in '52. Not until 1926 was there a reprint of the original series of twenty-two letters, and then in an edition of only two hundred copies privately printed by Arthur M. Ellis, in Los Angeles. Gregg Layne declares that because "the last ten dealt with the mistreatment of the Indians by the mission padres, they had been rigidly suppressed." And Father Engelhardt, indefatigable chronicler of mission affairs, referred to Reid as "that embittered Scotchman," and honestly believed that he "lied about religious matters."

In order that those who have become interested in the characters of Hugo and Victoria Reid may judge for themselves the worth and truth of their observations, the *Letters on the Los Angeles County Indians* are reproduced here as they appeared in the *Los Angeles Star,* commencing on Saturday, February 21, 1852, and continuing weekly thereafter. The Bancroft Library possesses clippings of all the letters, from which they have been copied for the present purpose. For the reader's sake, spellings are normalized to accord with present-day usage, and Reid's peculiarities of punctuation are somewhat modified.

LOS ANGELES COUNTY INDIANS

[Letter No. 1]

Lodges

Before the Indians belonging to the greater part of this country were known to the whites, they comprised as it were one great family under distinct chiefs. They spoke nearly the same language, with the exception of a few words; and were more to be distinguished by a local intonation of the voice than anything else.

Being related by blood and marriage, war was never carried on between them. When war was consequently waged against neighboring tribes of no affinity, it was a common cause. The following are the principal lodges or *rancherías,* with their corresponding present local names:

Yang-na	Los Angeles
Sibag-na	San Gabriel
Isanthcag-na	Misión Vieja
Sisitcanog-na	Pear Orchard
Sonag-na	Mr. White's Farm
Acurag-na	The Presa
Asucsag-na	Azusa
Cucamog-na	Cucamonga Farm
Pasinog-na	Rancho del Chino
Awig-na	La Puente
Chokishg-na	The Jabonería
Nacaug-na	Carpenter's Farm
Pineug-na	Santa Catalina Island
Pimocag-na	Rancho de los Ybarras
Toybipet	San José

Hutucg-na	Santa Ana [Yorbas]
Aleupkig-na	Santa Anita
Maug-na	Rancho de los Felis
Hahamog-na	Rancho de los Verdugos
Cahueg-na	Cahuenga
Pasecg-na	San Fernando
Houtg-na	Ranchito de Lugo
Suang-na	Suanga
Pubug-na	Alamitos
Tibahag-na	Cerritos
Chowig-na	Palos Verdes
Kinkipar	San Clemente Island
Harasg-na	

There were a great many more villages than the above, probably some forty; but these are a fair sample of their names, in which it will be observed that, with the exception of two, they all terminate in *gna* or *na*.

Jurupa, San Bernardino, etc., belonged to another distinct tribe possessing a language not at all understood by the above lodges; and, although reduced by the Spanish missionaries to the same religion and labor, they never mixed their blood, they being considered much inferior, and called *Serranos* or *Mountaineers*. They look upon them to this day, with great disdain.

That these names formerly had a signification there can be no doubt of. But even the oldest now alive confess themselves ignorant of their meaning.

The chief of each lodge took its name followed by *ie,* with sometimes the alteration of one or more final letters. For instance, the chief of *Asucsagna* was called *Asucsagnie.* That of *Sibagna, Sibavie.*

The title of a chief's eldest son was *Tomear*. Of his eldest daughter, *Manisar*.

Their huts were made of sticks, covered in around with flag mats worked or platted, and each village generally contained from 500 to 1500 huts. Suanga was the largest and most populous village, being of great extent.

It probably may not be out of place here to remark, that this tribe had no distinguishing appellation. And it is almost certain that many other tribes are similarly situated; for the so-called *Cahuillas* have been named by Spanish missionaries through the mistake of taking the word to designate the people. Whereas *Cahuilla* signifies nothing more than *master*.

[LETTER No. 2]

Language

IT IS NOT the intention here, either to compose a vocabulary of their words, nor yet a grammar to their language. Yet probably an insight to a few terms, and their formation, may not be uninteresting to some.

They have a great many liquid sounds, and their gutturals are so softened down as to become quite agreeable to the ear. In the following examples, *i* has the sound of *ee*, *u* of *oo*, *e* of *a* as in *fare*, *a* of *a* as in *father*, *ay* of *i* as in *ire*, and *gn* is sounded as in French.

1	*Pucú*
2	*Wehé*
3	*Páhe*
4	*Watzá*
5	*Mahár*

6	*Pabáhe*
7	*Watzá caviá*
8	*Wehés watzá*
9	*Mahár caviá*
10	*Wehés mahár*
11	*Wehés mahár coy pucú*
12	*Wehés mahár coy wehé*
Once	*Pucushe*
Twice	*Wehés*
3 times	*Páhes*
4 times	*Watzáhes*
5 times	*Maháres*
10 times	*Wehés maháres*
20	*Wehés wehés mahár*
30	*Páhes wehés mahár*
40	*Watzáhes wehés mahár*
50	*Maháres wehés mahár*
100	*Wehés wehés maháres wehés mahár*
There is	*Woni*
There is not . . .	*Yahay*
Yes	*Ehé*
No	*Hay*
I	*Nóma*
Thou	*Oma*
He or she	*Mane*
Man	*Woróyt*
Woman	*Tocór*
Boy	*Quiti*
Black	*Yupiha*
White	*Arawatay*
Red	*Quaóha*
Blue	*Sacasca*
Yellow	*Payuhuwi*
Green	*Tacape*
The sun	*Tamit*

The moon	*Moar*
The stars	*Zoót*
Dog	*Woze*
Coyote	*Ytur*
Bear	*Hunar*
Deer	*Zucat*
And	*Coy*

Two examples of their verbs, in the present, past, and future tenses, will suffice to show their formation.

I hear	*Non im nahacua*
Thou hearest	*O-a nahacua*
He hears	*Mane nahacua*
I heard	*Non him nahacua*
Thou heardest	*O-a him nahacua*
He heard	*Mane him nahacua*
I shall hear	*Nop uom nahacua*
Thou shalt hear	*O-pam nahacua*
He shall hear	*Mane pam nahacua*
I speak	*Nou im sirauaj*
Thou speakest	*O-a sirauaj*
He speaks	*Mane sirauaj*
I spoke	*Non him sirauaj*
Thou spokest	*O-a him sirauaj*
He spoke	*Mane him sirauaj*
I will speak	*Nop uom sirauaj*
Thou wilt speak	*O-pam sirauaj*
He will speak	*Mane pam sirauaj*

It will be perceived that neither the person or tense alter the verb, but the pronoun preceding it.

Their language is simple, rich, and abounding in compound expressive terms. Although they have words denoting *to desire, to like, to possess, to regard, to have an affection for,* and *to esteem;* yet they have no word to express *love.* At the same time they have many phrases to which we have no equivalent.

Their innumerable stories are all legends, and more than half believed; being of incredible length and containing more metamorphoses than Ovid could have engendered in his brain had he lived a thousand years. Everything is Oriental, even to the language.—Their fables are few and short. We may perhaps be tempted on some future occasion to give a couple of their traditions, one of their legends and a fable, as an example.

Their language has deteriorated so much since the conquest, that the present generation barely comprehend a part of what one of the "old standards" say, when they speak the original tongue. There is now at San Gabriel an old woman named *Bona,* who takes a pride in speaking sometimes the "Court language" to the "young ones," to stultify their intelligence.

[LETTER No. 3]

Government, Laws and Punishments

THE GOVERNMENT of the people was invested in the hands of their chiefs; each captain commanding his own lodge. The command was hereditary in a family. If the right line of descent ran out, they elected one of the same kin, nearest in blood. Laws in general were made as required, with some few standing ones. Robbery was never known among them. Murder was of rare occurrence, and punished with death. Incest was likewise punished with death; being held in such abhorrence, that marriages between kinsfolk were not allowed. The manner of putting to death was by shooting the delinquent with arrows. All prisoners of war, after being tormented in a most cruel manner, were invariably put to death. This was done in the presence of all the chiefs, for as war was declared and conducted by a council of the whole, so they in common had to attend to the execution of their enemies. A war dance on such an occasion was therefore grand, solemn and maddening.

If a quarrel ensued between two parties, the chief of the lodge took cognizance in the case, and decided according to the testimony produced. But, if a quarrel occurred between parties of distinct lodges, each chief heard the witnesses produced by his own people; and then, associated with the chief of the opposite side, they passed sentence. In case they could not agree, an impartial chief was called in, who heard the statements made by both, and he alone decided. There was no appeal from his decision.

Whipping was never resorted to as a punishment; therefore all fines and sentences consisted in delivering money, food and skins.

If a woman proved unfaithful to her husband, and he caught her in the act, he had a right to kill or wound her without any intervention of chief or tribe. And anyone hurting *him* made it a crime for which he stood amenable to the captain. But what was more generally practiced, the injured husband informed the wife's paramour that *he was at liberty to keep her*. He then went and took possession of the lover's spouse and lived with her. The exchange was considered legal, and no resource was left to the offending party but submission.

Until the age of puberty, they were under the control of their parents; in default of these, of their nearest relatives. But from the age of puberty upwards, they came under the jurisdiction of the chief.

If a seer or wizard (they had no witches) was known or suspected of having made away with anyone, the chief had no jurisdiction over him, because he conversed with the *Great Spirit*. But other seers could do him the damage they saw fit, in their capacities as such.

[LETTER No. 4]

Religion and Creed

THEY BELIEVED in one God, the maker and creator of all things, whose name was (and is) held so sacred among them, as hardly ever to be used; and when used, only in a low voice. That name is *Qua-o-ar*. When they have to use the name of the Supreme Being on any ordinary occasion, they substitute in its stead, the word *Y-yo-ha-rivg-nain,* or *"The Giver of Life".* They have only one word to designate *life* and *soul*.

The world was at one time in a state of chaos, until God gave it its present formation; fixing it on the shoulders of *Seven Giants,* made expressly for this end. They have their names, and when they move themselves, an earthquake is the consequence. Animals were then formed; and lastly man and woman were formed separately from earth, and ordered to live together. The man's name was TOBOHAR, the woman's PABAVIT. God ascended to Heaven immediately afterwards, where he receives the soul of all who die.

They had no bad spirit connected with their creed; and never heard of a "Devil" or a "Hell" until the coming of the Spaniards.

It has been a current belief in this county, that the Indians of it worship the "bald-headed eagle," as a GOD. There is no such thing.

The Indians make "feasts" to the eagle on account of a tradition, which states it formerly to have been a *remarkably clever, industrious man,* chief of a large tribe, and who, when dying, told his people that he intended becoming an eagle, and that he bequeathed them his *feathers,* from henceforth to be employed at their feasts and ceremonies. Feasts are in consequence held *in honor of his memory;* and great reverence is shown to the bird.

Now, ten to one if an Indian at the present day be asked if they worship the eagle as a god, he will answer, yes! because he is accustomed to hear the whites make game of their ceremony, and he does not care about giving an explanation which he knows will be laughed at.

The porpoises were believed to be intelligent beings, created for the purpose of guarding the world, and whose duty consists in going round and round the earth to see that all is safe.

The owl was held in deep reverence, and supposed to predict death, by screeching near the residence of the doomed one. It was never killed.

The crows advised them when a stranger was coming on a visit.

They believed in no resurrection whatever; either in particular cases, or a general one; but the transmigration of the souls of wizards for a time into the bodies of animals, particularly of the bear, is firmly believed in.

Each lodge had a church, called *Yobagnar*, which was circular and formed of short stakes, with twigs of willow entwined basket fashion, to the height of three feet. This church was sacred, but was consecrated nevertheless every time it was used. This took an entire day, being done by the seers in a succession of different ceremonies. There was also an unconsecrated one used for the purpose of rehearsing in and teaching children, dedicated to this end, to dance and gesticulate. Having nothing to care about their souls, it made them stoical in regard to death. The only services performed in their churches were—asking for vengeance on their enemies; giving thanks for a victory; and commemorating the worth of their dead relatives.

The only ones admitted into the church were the seers and captains, the adult male dancers, the boys training for that purpose, and the female singers. But on funeral occasions the near relatives of the deceased were allowed to enter.

[LETTER No. 5]

Food and Raiment

THE ANIMAL FOOD in use among them was deer meat, young coyotes, squirrels, badgers, rats, gophers, snakes, raccoons, skunks, wildcats, the small crow, the blackbirds, hawks, ground owls, and snakes, with the exception of the rattlesnake. A few eat the bear, but in general it is rejected, on superstitious grounds hereafter to be mentioned. The large locust or grasshopper was a favorite morsel, roasted on a stick at the fire. Fish, whales, seals, sea otters, and shellfish, formed the principal subsistence of the immediate coast range of lodges and islands.

Acorns, after being divested of their shell, were dried, and pounded in stone mortars, put into filterns of willow twigs worked into a concave form, and raised on little mounds of sand, which were lined inside with a coating of two inches of sand; water added and mixed up.—Then filled up again and again with more water, at first hot, then cold, until all the tannin and bitter principle was extracted. The residue was then collected and washed free of any sandy particles it might contain. On settling, the water was poured off. After being well boiled, it became a sort of mush, and was eaten when cold. The next favorite food was the kernel of a species of plum which grows in the mountains and islands, called by them, *islay* (pronounced eeslie). Some Americans call it the *mountain cherry,* although it partakes little either of the plum or cherry. It has a large stone, to which numerous fibers are attached, pervading the pulp, of which there is very little. Its color, when perfectly ripe, inclines to black, and very much like what in Mexico is called the *ciruela.* This, cooked, formed a very nutritious, rich, saccharine aliment; and looked much like dry boiled *frijoles. Chía,* which is a small, gray, oblong seed, was procured from a plant apparently of the thistle kind, having a number of seed vessels on a straight stalk, one above the other, like wild sage. This, roasted and ground into meal, was eaten with cold water, being of a glutinous consistency, and very cooling. Pepper-grass seed was also much used, the tender stalks of wild sage, several kinds of berries and a number of roots.

All their food was taken either cold or nearly so, which, of course, tended to preserve the teeth. Salt was used very sparingly in their food, from an idea that it had a tendency to turn their hair *gray*.

The men wore no clothing, but the women in the interior had a deerskin wrapped round the middle, while those on the coast had sea-otter skins put to the same purpose. Their covering at night consisted of rabbit skins, cut square and sewed together in the form of a bedspread. Rings or ornaments of any kind were never attached to the nose, although all the Indians of Buenaventura and Santa Barbara used them. The men inserted a reed or a piece of cane through each ear; while the women wore regular earrings, each of which was composed of four long pieces of a whale's tooth, ground down smooth to a cylindrical form of eight inches in length, and half an inch in diameter. These were hung with the feathers of the hawk and turkey buzzard, from a ring made of the oblong shell. Their necklaces were very heavy and large, consisting of innumerable strings, of various lengths, of their money beads, of beads made of black stones, and pieces of whale's teeth, ground round and perforated. They used bracelets on both wrists, of very small shell beads.

During the season of flowers, the females and children decked themselves in splendor; not only entwining them in the hair, but stringing them with the stalks and leaves, making boas of them.

[LETTER No. 6]

Marriages

CHIEFS had *one, two* or *three wives,* as their inclinations dictated. The subjects only one. When a person wished to marry, and had selected a suitable partner, he advertised the same to all his relations, even to the *nineteenth cousin.* On a day appointed, the male portion of the lodge, and male relations living at other lodges, brought in a collection of money beads. The amount of each one's contribution was about twenty-five cents. All the relations having come in with their share, they (the males) proceeded in a body to the residence of the bride, to whom timely notice had been given. All of the bride's female relations had been assembled, and the money was equally divided among them; the bride receiving nothing, as it was a sort of purchase. After a few days the bride's female relations returned the compliment by taking to the bridegroom's dwelling baskets of meal made of *chía,* which was distributed among his male relations. These preliminaries over, a day was fixed for the ceremony, which consisted in decking out the bride in innumerable strings of beads, paint, feathers and skins. On being ready, she was taken up in the arms of one of her strongest connections, who carried her dancing towards her sweetheart's habitation. All of her family, friends and neighbors accompanied, dancing around, and throwing food and edible seeds at her feet every step, which were collected in a scrabble as best they could by the spectators. The relations of the man met them halfway, and taking the bride, carried her themselves, joining in the ceremonious walking dance. On arriving at the bridegroom's (who was sitting within his hut), she was inducted into her new residence by being placed alongside of her husband; while baskets of seeds were liberally emptied on their heads, to denote blessing and plenty. This was likewise scrambled for by the spectators; who on gathering up all of the *bride's seed cake,* departed, leaving them to enjoy their "honeymoon," according to usage.

A grand dance was of course given on the occasion, where might be seen warriors and hunters in full costume, making their various gestures in character, indicative of their respective callings. The old women took a part in the dance either as if carrying of game, or of dispatching their wounded enemies, as the avocation of their husbands called for. The younger portion of the women and old men sat around as singers.

The wife never visited her relations from that day forth, although they had undebarred leave to visit her.

In case her "lord" ill used her, and continued to beat her in a cruel manner, she gave advice of it to her kin, who in consequence collected together all the money which had been paid in at the marriage, and taking it in deputation to the husband's hut, left it with him, leading off the wife. They immediately married her to another.

The last case of bigamy or rather polygamy, was in one of the chief's from Santa Catalina; who was ordered by the priest to San Gabriel, and there baptized. He had *three* wives, the *first* of which was allowed him, and the others discarded. The priest joined him in the holy bands of matrimony according to the form of the Catholic Church; which to him appeared highly ridiculous. He is still alive and now resides at San Fernando; his name, as known at present, is *Canoa,* or *Canoe:* he is still a captain and accounted a great wizard.

[LETTER No. 7]

Births and Burials

IMMEDIATELY on the birth of a child, the mother and infant were *baked,* or in other words purified. In the center of a hut a large hole was dug; an immense fire was kindled therein, and large stones heated until red hot: when nothing but hot embers and the aforesaid stones remain, bundles of wild tanzy are heaped on, and then the whole is covered with earth, with the exception of a small aperture in the middle. The mother had to stand over this hole, with her child wrapt up in a mat, funnel fashion, while cold water was gradually introduced into the opening. This generated great quantities of steam, which was so hot at the commencement as to cause the patient to leap and skip not a little, while it produced profuse sweating afterwards. When no more steam was produced, the mother and child lay down on the heap of earth, and were well covered up until the steaming process was renewed. Three days was the term of purification, and morning and evening the times for sweating. No food was allowed to the mother during that time, and her drink (water) was warmed. She was now allowed to eat of everything at discretion, except animal food, which was debarred her for the period of two moons. Her diet at length completed, three pills were prepared, of the size of a musket ball, compounded of one part meat and one part wild tobacco. These were administered to her, swallowed, and from henceforth she was declared free to eat meats of any kind. But not until the child could run about was she privileged to share her husband's bed.

If a child was born to a chief, the old women immediately assembled, and washing it in water, drank the same, with great *gusto*. They then had a dance around the happy father, chanting all the while the future renown of the little one.

When a person died, all the kin collected to lament and mourn his or her loss. Each one had his own peculiar mode of crying or howling, as easily distinguished, the one from another, as one song is from another. After lamenting awhile, a mourning dirge was sung, in a low whining tone, accompanied by a shrill whistle, produced by blowing into the tube of a deer's leg bone. Dancing can hardly be said to have formed a part of the rites, as it was merely a monotonous action of the foot on the ground. This was continued alternately until the body showed signs of decay, when it was wrapt up in the covering used in life. The hands were crooked upon the breast, and the body tied from head to foot. A place having been dug in their burial place, the body was deposited, with seeds, etc., according to the means of the family. If the deceased were the head of a family, or a favorite son, the hut in which he died was burned up, as likewise all of his personal effects, reserving only some article or another, or a lock of hair. This reservation was not as a memento of the deceased, but to make a feast with on some future occasion, generally after the first harvest of seeds and berries.

Medicine and Diseases

THEIR MEDICAL MEN were esteemed as wizards and seers, and called *A-hub-su-voi-rot*. They not only cured diseases, but created them; they poisoned people with herbs and ceremonies, made it rain when required, consulted the good spirit and received answers, changed themselves into the form of divers animals, and foretold coming events. All of this was firmly believed by the people, and in consequence their seers were held in dread and deep reverence.

In regard to the diseases then prevalent, inasmuch as *syphilis* was unknown, *brandy* and its associates unused, and *high living* at a *low* ebb, their *nosology* was very limited. *Toothache* seldom or never troubled them, for which reason they carried the teeth perfect to the grave. *Rheumatism* was cured by applying a string of blisters to the part affected, each about the size of a ten-cent piece. The blister used was made of the fuzz of dry nettle stalks, rolled up and compressed, put on and made to adhere with spittle. Fire being applied, it burned like spunk, and when one went out another was lit. The blisters formed were immediately opened. *Lumbago* was cured by making the patient lay on his back for twenty or thirty hours on *hot ashes* and giving him sweating herbs to drink. *Fever* was cured by giving a bolus of *wild tobacco,* to insure vomiting, herbs administered and manipulations of the seer, accompanied by a song. *Local inflammation* was treated by *drawing blood* from the surrounding parts by scarifying with sharp pieces of flint. *Paralytic affections, stagnation of the blood, and loss of action in the limbs* were cured by *whipping* with bunches of *nettles;* as likewise by drinking the juice of the thornapple (*Datura stramonium*) which produced an ebriety of three days duration.—*Decline* (of very rare occurrence) was treated by giving, for a length of time, the meat of *mud turtles,* cooked.

They were well acquainted with lime in medicine, and made it from shells; but not aware of its presence in rocks. It was pounded up with wild tobacco and used immediately if intended to produce a nauseous intoxicating feeling, but in a more agreeable state it was powdered up well and kneaded into thick cakes, kept, and when required, a piece of the requisite size broken off and eaten.—Lime was supposed not only to clean the stomach, but likewise the bladder.

Strangury was cured by steaming the patient as in the purification of women after parturition; only that marshmallows were used instead of tanzy. Immediately after, a very large ball of masticated tobacco was given, which caused great depression and relaxation of the nervous system, oftentimes producing the desired effect. If not, blood was drawn by sucking the abdomen immediately over the region of the bladder. This operation was performed with many prior rites, such as smoking to the Great Spirit, pressure and rubbing of the part with the hands, and a song, every verse of which concluded with

> NOM IM MANOC, IM MANOC,
> NOM IM MANOC, IM MANOC.
> YOBARSE!
> I do, what I am doing,
> I do, what I am doing.
> Oh Church!

Even the name of the Deity was not invoked in this, but in the place of worship.

Bites of snakes were cured by the application of herbs and ashes to the wound; and herbs, ashes, and the fine dust found at the bottom of ants' nests given internally.

The hair was at times plastered all over with red clay, which was allowed to remain twenty-four hours on and was then washed off. This was supposed to impart a gloss and prevent it from splitting. To cure baldness, [chilicothes] were burned to a charcoal, ground to paste and rubbed into the grain of the scalp, morning and evening.

The seers (as medicine men) collected the poison used for dipping the heads of arrows.—Fire was supposed to destroy its hurtful properties; consequently the flesh of animals killed with poisoned arrows was eaten without any misgivings. The truth of the matter is that said poison contained nothing virulent, it being only *gall* boiled down to the consistency of honey.—The seers pretended not only to be acquainted with poison which destroyed life, by giving it internally, but also with others whose tact alone produced death, some being instantaneous, and others requiring one, two, or even twelve moons to operate.

[LETTER No. 9]

Customs

A GREAT NUMBER of their young men being hunters, they of course had their peculiar superstitions. During a hunt they never tasted food; nor on their return did they partake of what they themselves killed, from an idea that whoever ate of his own game hurt his hunting abilities. Before going on a hunting expedition they stung themselves all over with nettles, more particularly the eyes, the lids of which were opened to introduce the leaves.—This was done to make them watchful, vigilant and clear sighted. The skin of a deer's head and neck was put on their own, and on seeing game they would feign to be grazing—lifting up the head occasionally to stare about. By such means they approached so near as to make the first arrow generally "tell."

To make them hardy and endure pain without wincing (for cowardice as to corporeal suffering was considered, even among the women, as disgraceful) they would lie down on the hill of the large red ant, having handfuls of them placed in the region of the stomach and about the eyes. Lastly, to insure a full dose, they swallowed them in large quantities, alive!

A small string of buckskin was tied around the neck of those who were swift of foot.

When a girl came to the age of puberty, it was a joyful occasion for her relations. She underwent a purification in the same manner as women did at childbirth, accompanied by singing, and all were informed of her being marriageable.

The children were not without some education, for if an adult asked a boy or girl for a drink of water, they were not allowed to put it to their lips until the other had satisfied his thirst. If two persons were in conversation, a child was not permitted to pass between them, but made to go round them on either side. No male from childhood upward was allowed to call his sister *liar* even in jest. The word for liar being *yayare*.

The name of God, as before mentioned, was never taken

in vain, and the only exclamation amounting to anything like an oath was *niómare!* which simply means *bless me!*

Animosity between persons or families was of long duration, particularly between those of different tribes. These feuds descended from father to son until it was impossible to tell how many generations. They were, however, harmless in themselves, being merely a war of songs, composed and sung against the conflicting party, and they were all of the most obscene and indecent language imaginable.— There are two families at this day whose bad feelings commenced before Spaniards were even dreamt of and they still continue yearly singing and dancing against each other. The one resides at the Mission of San Gabriel, and the other at San Juan Capistrano; they both lived at San Bernardino when the quarrel commenced. During the singing they keep stamping on the ground to express the pleasure they would derive from tramping on the grave of their foes. Eight days was the duration of the song fight.

They saluted each other on meeting by saying *avá aha?* how are you? To which the other, if well, responded by answering *tehépko;* but if unwell, by *chainoc.* On parting they bid no *good bye;* the one merely said *yamu uimí,* I am going; to which the other answered, *mea!* go!

In regard to painting themselves, they had different grades according to the occasion.—Warriors and dancing parties were painted with different colors. Young females in "love" painted sparingly on the cheeks with red ochre. Women to the middle age and a little over, when required to be in the sun, put it on plentifully all over their features, to prevent their getting sunburnt.

Summer was considered to have commenced whenever the croaking of frogs was heard.—This, with the sun's declination north and south, served them to reckon long periods by; but short time was reckoned by days and months.

[Letter No. 10]

Customs (Continued)

Boys were trained to carry messages from one chief to another, and they continued in that service until worn out. It required a retentive memory.

They were not much given to travel, for they only relate of one traveler, who left his people and proceeded *north,* until he came to *where the geese breed.* And even *he* appeared to have possessed the organ ascribed to his genus; for on returning, he reported having fallen in with a nation whose ears reached to the hips! with another of diminutive stature; and finally, with a people so perfect, that they would take a rabbit or other animal, and merely with the breath *inhale the essence;* throwing the rest away, which on examination proved to be *excrement!*

They had only names for the four cardinal points of the compass, to wit:—

North . . . . *Fúmi*	South . . . . *Kitámi*
East . . . . . *Crúmi*	West . . . . *Páymi*

They were acquainted with the North Star, which was called *rómi.*

When a church feast was held—for instance in commemoration of the dead—they rehearsed with the tyros for eight days previous, in unconsecrated place of worship. All being ready, the seers took an entire day to consecrate the church; this done, the feast commenced on the second day. The singers (women) were seated in a circle around the church, leaving only the doorway free. The men and children, adorned with eagle and hawk's feathers, and a plentiful supply of paint laid on the face, neck, arms, and upper part of the body, proceeded to dance, being governed in the operation by numerous gestures, both of hands and feet, made by the seers. Each dancer represented some animal in his movements; but the growl given simultaneously at the end of each verse, was for the bear.

At the four quarters of the compass, poles of some ten feet in length were placed upright with a string at the end, on which feathers were filed, forming a sort of banner. Food was furnished the performers in abundance, at short intervals, and this continued six days and nights.

They sung songs in praise of the deceased, and sung others to the destruction of his enemies.

They danced to his memory, and did the same to the destruction of his foes.

On the eighth day the church was more adorned than before. When no more feathers could be stuck around, they placed them on their persons in profusion. The old women were employed to make more food than usual, and when the sun was in its zenith, it was distributed, not only among the actors, but to the spectators likewise. After eating, a deep hole was dug, and a fire kindled in it, when the articles reserved at the death of relatives were committed to the flames; at the same time, baskets, money, and seeds were thrown to the spectators, as in the marriage ceremony. During the burning process, one of the seers, reciting mystical words, kept stirring up the fire to ensure the total destruction of the things.—The hole was then filled up with earth and well trodden down. The feast was over.

[LETTER No. 11]

Traffic and Utensils

ALTHOUGH money in the strict sense of the word did not exist among them, they had an equivalent, consisting of pieces of thick rounded shells, less in diameter than a five-cent piece. These had a hole in the center and were strung on long strings. Eight yards of these beads (for they were also used as such) made about one dollar of our currency. Their mode of measuring consisted in meting from the knuckles of the left hand, to the point of the middle finger, thence round to the wrist, back again to the end of the finger, and thence round to one inch above the wrist. This quantity was called *pucú ponco,* and a *real* of Spanish currency received the same name. Double that quantity was called *wehé peca,* as also were two *reals;* three times the quantity was called *páhe ponco;* four times, *sayaco;* five times, *mahár ponco;* six times, *babahe paca,* and seven times, which was *watzá caviá* or *páhe motke,* finished their count. On account of their having no "eight times," they now adopt the Spanish economy, and say *puen peso,* one dollar. They had thereby a circulating medium and legal tender to transact business, when barter could not be employed. Considerable barter and trade was carried on between those of the coast and those of the interior, the latter furnishing deer

skins and seeds in exchange for money, fish, sea-otter skins
and soapstone pots.

Hemp was made from nettles, and manufactured into
nets, fishing lines, thread, etc. Needles, fishhooks, awls
and many other articles were made of either bone or shell,
although for cutting up meat, a knife made of cane was invariably used. Mortars and pestles were made of granite,
about sixteen inches wide at the top, ten at the bottom, ten
inches high and two thick. Sharp stones and *perseverance*
were the only things used in their manufacture, and so skill-
fully did they combine the two, that their work was always
remarkably uniform.

Their present clay pots were at that time unknown; the
Spaniards taught them their manufacture.

Their pots to cook in were made of soapstone of about an
inch in thickness, and procured from the Indians of Santa
Catalina; the cover used was of the same material. Their
baskets made out of split rushes are too well known to require description; but though waterproof, they were used
only for dry purposes. The vessels in use for liquids were
roughly made of rushes and plastered outside and in with
bitumen or pitch, called by them *sanot*.

[LETTER No. 12]

Sports and Games

THESE were few, and all of a gaming nature. The principal
one was *churchúrki* or *peón* as it is called by the Spaniards.
It consists of guessing in which hand a small piece of stick
was held concealed by another. Four persons on a side com-

posed a set, who sat opposite each other. They had their singers, who were paid so much a game, and an umpire who
kept count, held the stakes, settled disputes and prevented
cheating. He was paid so much a night, and had to provide
the firewood. He was provided with fifteen counters, which
were of reed and eight or ten inches long. The guessers never
spoke, but giving the palm of the left hand a sharp slap with
the right pointed with the finger to the side they guessed
contained the *peón*. Those who guessed right, won the *peón,*
and the others gained a counter each, and so on, until they
possessed all the counters or lost all the *peones,* when the
opposite side took the counting part.

The *peón* was white, of an inch or so in length; but they
had also a black one, which, to prevent fraud, they had to
remove to the other hand on changing, so as always to retain
one in each hand, to show when called upon.

This was their favorite game, and they sometimes bet their
all on it. It still continues to be their ruling passion to bet
at this game in preference to any other; for the bystanders
take as much interest and wager as heavily as those principally concerned.

Another game, called *chachaukel,* was played between
two. The counters consisted of 50 small pieces of wood, stuck
on end in the ground in a row, and two inches apart, with
a pointer for each player to show his stage of the game. Eight
pieces of split reed, with the under side blackened, were
thrown, points down, and as many white sides as came up,
counted to the thrower; but where all came up black, they
counted also. To throw eight, entitled the player to another
throw.

The adversaries counted from opposite ends, and if one's count came to that of the other, the rule was for the party caught to commence anew; which prolonged the game sometimes to a great length.

A game called *hararicuar* consisted in rolling a ring, and two persons threw long lances of reed, and if the ring lay on one or the other, so it counted. Three times constituted a game.

The last I shall mention is *wauri,* in which one person placed under a basket eight pieces of reed (painted on one side) as he thought proper; while another made corresponding marks on the ground. They were then compared to see whether the guess were right or not.

Football was unknown until after the conquest, when they learned it of the Indians of San Diego.

[LETTER No. 13]

Tradition

THERE WERE *seven brothers* married to *seven sisters,* according to their respective ages, who lived in a large hut together. The men went daily to hunt rabbits and the women to gather roots of flags for food. The husbands invariably returned first and on their wives' arrival invariably reported "bad luck" in their hunt, with the exception of the youngest, who, without fail, handed his wife a rabbit. Consequently the poor women fared badly as far as animal food was concerned. This continued, as a daily occurrence, for a long time, until in a conference held by the females they were convinced that they were cheated by their partners. Considering that it was so very strange that nothing was ever killed except by the youngest, they determined to arrive at the truth. Accordingly they agreed that the youngest sister should remain at home on the morrow, under pretext of having a pain in her jaw, and so watch the return of the party.—Next day the men as usual took their bows and arrows and set forth. The six sisters then departed, leaving the other concealed among the flags and rushes at the back of the hut in such a position as to command a view of everything transacted within.

Several hours before sunset the hunting party returned laden with rabbits which they commenced roasting and eating, except one which the youngest put apart. The others called him a fool and bade him eat the remaining one, which he refused to do, saying he still had some affection for his wife and always intended to reserve one for her. More fool you, said the others; we care more for ourselves than for these root-diggers. On the conclusion of the feast, the bones were carefully gathered together and concealed in a suitable place on the outside.

After some time had elapsed, the youngest wife arose and presented herself to the men in the hut, to their great surprise. On being asked where she came from, she answered: I have been asleep at the back of the house, having had to remain behind from a pain in the jaw, but am now better, as the sleep did me good. After a while the women came home, and running up to their sister, inquired after her health.

They soon found an opportunity to leave the hut and inquired the result of the espionage, besides visiting the deposit of bones. They cried a great deal and talked over what they should do. Let us turn into water, said the eldest. That would never do, responded the rest, for in that case our husbands would drink us. The second proposed being turned into stones, which was rejected on the ground of being trodden upon by the fraternity. The third wanted they should turn to trees, which was not acceded to because they would be used for firewood. Everything proposed was put aside on account of some defect until it came to the turn of the youngest. Her proposition to change themselves into stars was objected to on account of being seen, but overruled as they would be out of reach.

They proceeded to the lagoon, where they daily collected flag roots and constructed a machine (impossible to describe) out of reeds, and ascended to heaven and located themselves at the *Pleiads*. These seven stars still retain the names of the originals.

Only the youngest brother appeared to be vexed at the loss of his spouse, seeking her daily in the woods. One day, on going to the edge of the lagoon, bewailing his hard fate, the sisters had compassion on him. They instructed him how to use the machine they had made, and receiving him on high, placed him apart, as the constellation *Taurus* shows. The Indians still retain a song about these seven stars.

[Letter No. 14]

Tradition and Fable

Among the most curious of their traditions was the following:

[The Girl Enamored of the Lightning]

Four brothers and a sister lived together in a hut and were very fond of each other. The young men were principally engaged in hunting. The girl, whose name was *Chukit,* had refused many offers of marriage. After a while she became melancholy and fond of solitude and appeared to be *enamored of the lightning,* after expressing a desire to possess it.— Her eldest brother in the course of time perceived that she was with child, and taking the others into the woods, spoke as follows:

"Brethren, I perceive with sorrow that our sister has been harmed; she holds no intercourse with the young men of our village, therefore one of you has done this evil.—Which of you is it? Speak!"

The three declared themselves innocent, and each one mentioned his having had his suspicions regarding his fellows. They concluded at last to ask their sister, which was done.—"Who is the father of your child," said the eldest on their return to the hut. Bursting into tears, she denied ever having had any connection with man, but stated that about seven moons previous, having wandered into the woods saying ever and anon to herself "would that the lightning were mine!" that the lightning came out of a cloud and flashed over her, when she perceived a strange sensation of *cold* pass like a piece of ice through her brain into the abdomen.

That she had subsequent intercourse with it, always producing the same effect.

After some time the pains of labor commenced and a man-child was born. The midwife having asked for something to cut the navel string, to the astonishment of all, the child said, *"No! It will hurt me!"* According to the Indian custom all new-born children are given urine to drink for a medicinal purpose, and on a bystander's recommending the dose to be given, the child said, "No! It is bitter." He was called *Mactutu,* and every day became more and more wise, arguing with all the old men and seers on divers subjects, always to the discomfiture of their allegations and prostration of their wisdom. After gaining a victory he always told them it was useless to dispute with him, as he was the *Son of God*.

The chiefs and wise men of the tribe at length determined to put him to death. He was aware of it and bantered them continually by saying, "Put me to death, but in three days I will arise again!"

After many consultations his enemies hit upon a plan which destroyed him completely; for they said among themselves, if we burn his body, how can he rise again, seeing that he is consumed! He was accordingly burned alive, and his body dissipated. He never appeared more.

Some Indians after this said, "There is no God," because they had destroyed him; but the greater part said, "No! we have only destroyed his body, for his soul ascended to Heaven!"

The Coyote and the Water

A coyote, which, like all the rest of his kin, considered himself as the most austere animal on the face of the earth, not even excepting man himself, came one day to the margin of a small river. Looking over the bank, on seeing the water run so slow, he addressed it in a cunning manner, "What say you to a race?" "Agreed to," answered the water, very calmly. The coyote ran at full speed along the bank until he could hardly stand from fatigue, and on looking over the bank, saw the water running smoothly on.

He walked off with his tail between his legs and had something to reflect upon for many a day afterwards.

[Letter No. 15]

Legend

IN THE LODGE of *Muhuvit,* which lay behind the hills of San Fernando, once lived a chief connected with the following legend, who was a great wizard and enchanter. He had a son and daughter. The daughter was good-looking and possessed, as her father and brother did, a most astonishing head of hair, which, when loose, trailed on the ground. She however possessed a niggardly disposition, and moreover was lazy. After a while the chief of *Hahamogna* (Verdugos) asked her in marriage, and was accepted.

In due time she presented her husband with a daughter. Shortly after, she proved herself to be a glutton as well as parsimonious, for the people were commanded every day to bring rabbits, ready roasted, for her to eat, and she devoured the whole, without ever offering the lookers-on a single morsel. This caused universal discontent, so much so that the wise men of the village consulted together and at last urged the chief to send her home.

"Do with her as seemeth best," said the husband.

So, on a second consultation, the old men determined to put her to death instead of putting her away, fearing her father.

"What shall be done with the child?" asked the seers.

"Let it die with the mother!" answered the husband.

Orders were given the next day to have no water brought from the wells to their huts, but that all should go there and drink when so inclined. The rabbit-hunters were likewise instructed to stuff the game, before cooking it, with all kinds of reptiles. A large basket used for bringing water was placed in the last hut of the village and filled with urine. The hour having arrived for her to eat, the rabbits were presented, according to custom. On this occasion, however, she proceeded differently than in the habit of doing; for pulling out the leg of a toad, she enquired what it was. "It is part of a quail," replied someone. "Then eat it," said the victim. "No, eat it yourself," was the response. Pieces of lizards and other disgusting matter came to light, with the same result, until she finished the mess. This repast gave her great thirst, and she asked for water. Not procuring it there, she proceeded from one habitation to another in quest of it, with the same success. At last she arrived at the extremity of the lodge, and on receiving the proffered dish with eagerness, and at three draughts she finished it, with the exception of a little which she reserved for the child. For ten days did the same thing occur; at the end of which time, finding all the hair of her head and eyebrows gone—for it fell off by drinking the urine—and moreover that she was wasted in flesh and wrinkled, she determined on leaving and going to her father's. So taking her child in her arms, she left the hut secretly.

After proceeding some distance, she repented having done so, exclaiming, "What a fool I am to carry this burden, as if *he* liked me so much!" Throwing it away, she went on her road; but after going on a short way, she looked back and saw the infant, with its arms stretched out towards her; her heart relented at the sight, and returning, she again took it up, saying, "*Thou* hast committed no sin, that I should revenge myself upon thee." She went on and on, until extreme fatigue from her load brought her to stand; when observing a large rock close by, she took the child by the heels and dashed its brains out. The blood still exists, visible on the stone to this day. Still some Indians maintain that the child did not die, but turned into a squirrel. On she went, alone, sad and slow, until she came to where her mother preserved her seeds in the woods, and she crept into a large basket, called a *chamuca,* capable of containing about sixteen bushels.

Not long after her arrival, came the mother to procure a supply of seeds and acorns, and putting her hand in at the mouth, she touched her daughter, and not being aware what it was, gave a scream. "Yes!" said the daughter, "be afraid of me, after the injury you have done me in marrying me to a man who cared nothing about me!" The mother approached, but could scarcely recognize her own daughter, and heard from beginning to end the tale of her sorrows. The parent then said, "I will go to thy father and inform him," which she did.

The father being informed by his wife, secretly, he proceeded with her to the place of deposit, taking his daughter food and drink.—This they did day after day, and herbs were administered to her, to restore her, and purge her from the filth she had eaten. Her head was also cured by the oil from a black berry growing on the seacoast, called *hamisar*. In four moons the wrinkles had nearly disappeared from her face, and her hair reached to her waist.

At this stage of her cure, she was commanded by her father to go daily and bathe in her brother's bathing place. She did so, but the brother soon began to note how turbid the water was when he came to bathe. He became sad in consequence, and more so when he saw a hair in the water, which, on measuring with those of his own, was not one-third their length. He spoke to his mother on the subject, but she threw no light on the subject, being anxious to conceal with her husband the daughter's return until her shame and sickness had both passed away. The son, going to his bath one day sooner than usual, caught his sister in the water, but he knew her not. Taking her by the leg, he threw her out, saying, "So it is you who daily disturb my well. Begone!" In doing so, he beheld her nakedness, which caused her so much shame that she wandered off, and traveling to the seashore, drowned herself.

The brother, well satisfied with himself, returned home and told his mother of having found an unknown woman in his bath, how he had thrown her out and had seen her nakedness. The parents left the hut and went in search of the daughter, but without success.—"Shame has driven her away. Where can we find her?" said the wife. The husband answered not, but taking a willow twig, he made a

ring of it, covering it with buckskin; this he threw to the
north, but the ring returned to him. He then threw it south,
and back it came again; then east, with the same result;
but when he threw it west, it kept on. The father followed
it up in all its crooks and turns until he saw it enter the
ocean. "She has drowned herself from shame, but deeply
shall she be revenged," said he.

On arriving at home, he informed his wife, who cried bitterly, much to the astonishment of all the lodge, who knew
not what had occurred.

He called all of his people and told them to go a-hunting,
stop out all night, and take his son along. The son was then
advised of the party he was to join, and dressed in all his ornaments, finery and money beads. They set out and obeyed
orders, by sleeping in the mountains, having a large fire to
warm themselves at.

A little before daylight one of the old men let loose a
screech owl, which he had brought concealed and which
was no other than the boy's father. This caused general con-
sternation, and all fled save the young man himself. Immediately an enormous bird called by the name of *cuwot* (but
which was the father again) carried him up into the air. Seeing this, the people came running back, exclaiming, "The
cuwot has carried off the chief's son!" On coming to the
spot, his bones fell among them, which were gathered up
and buried.

A few days after this, a man was seen approaching the
village; the chief went and met him.

"Where dost thou come from?" asked the chief.

"From *Hahamogna*" (Verdugos).

"Ah!" said the chief, "how are they getting on there?"

"Very well, indeed; the captain there is about to take a new wife, and in consequence a great feast is progressing."

"Be it so," said he. "They have had their laugh, now I shall have mine, and we will all perish together."

He took the road to the village, and before arriving there, he fell in with all the women gathering prickly pears. He asked one of the women to do him the favor of sifting a basket full of *tunas* over his eyes. She objected and he persisted, until her companions told her to comply; but no sooner had she done so, than all of them commenced crying out and wailing in piteous terms—they were all stone blind! "Now it is my turn to laugh," said the chief, and he proceeded on towards their village.

Going to the west side of the lodge, he transformed himself into a huge eagle, and proceeded, flying close down to the ground. The cry was immediately raised among the people of "Catch the eagle!" But an old woman who was taking care of two children while their mothers were off, begged them not to do so, as it was not an eagle, but a wizard; at this they only laughed, but the old woman covered up the children with a basket to keep them from harm.

They soon caught it, and saying, "Let us pull its wings off," put it into execution. The moment its wings were separated from the body, a gush of blood poured out from one side, and another of green water from the other. Fever and bilious vomiting commenced, and killed all, save the old woman and children. The eagle soared, without his wings, to the clouds, and the chief was never heard of more by his people.

The old woman had to bury the dead, as she best could, and rested contented in raising the children, who consisted of a boy and girl.—When old enough, she made a bow with arrows for the one, teaching him how to use it, and a flat basket for the other, showing her how to clean seed for food. When of age, she married them, and they lived happily together.

The girl's disposition altered very much after her marriage, for her husband being a great hunter, she never lacked meat; and yet, with all, she refused to supply the old creature with animal food. The old woman, to be revenged, placed an awl made of deer's bone, with the point upwards, where the young one usually sat. It came near killing her, and it was again placed in her pool for bathing, with a like consequence. At last she informed her husband, telling him moreover that she expected to be made way with, in which case he would be apprised of it by a few drops of water falling on his left shoulder.

Being out a-hunting one day, the fatal sign was given. Throwing down his bows and arrows, he hastened home, and enquired for his spouse.

"Poor thing, she is dead!" answered the hag, "and I have buried her there," pointing to a grave.

"Bad woman, thou hast murdered her," said he, snatching up a billet of wood to kill her with, but she was too quick for him, for in a moment she was converted into a gopher, and burrowing in the earth.

For three days and nights did he lie upon her grave, lamenting her loss. On the third day he observed a small whirlwind arise from the grave and immediately disappear.

Shortly after another arose and exhausted itself quickly. A
third made its appearance, of a large size, and proceeded to
the south. This he followed up, and at every step he perceived it augment in its proportions. Still going on in pursuit, he at length saw footprints in the sand where it passed
over. "It is my dear wife," exclaimed he, and the more he
urged forward, until he had gone an immense distance.

A voice at length proceeded from the cloud saying, "Return back, husband mine, for I am not as formerly. No
earthly thing ever came where I am going; remember I
am dead to the world." He, however, could not be persuaded
and insisted on accompanying her. "I will risk it," said the
spirit, taking him up, "but forget not that no earthly eye
ever did, or ever will see us."

They passed over an immense sea, and ultimately reached
the land of spirits, where he heard myriads of voices in uni-
son say in sweet tones, "It smells of an earthly substance,
sister. What hast thou brought hither?" The wife spirit confessed having brought a human being. "Take him away," exclaimed the voices, which, though all around him, still he
saw nothing. She pleaded his being allowed to remain, on
the ground of superior qualities to the common herd, as
well as for hunting powers. "Let us try him," said the voices.
He was ordered to bring down a feather from the top of a
pole so long as hardly to be visible, which made him hesitate.
"Fear not," said the voice of his wife, "but look not down in
thy ascent." He accomplished it, and was given a long hair
to split from end to end. This likewise was a hard task, but
the wife told him to have faith. He had faith and the difficulty was overcome. Lastly, he was commanded to make a

map on the ground of the constellation of the Lesser Bear, and show the exact situation of the North Star. Now he had on earth often seen the seers draw the required map, but he knew nothing about doing it himself. His wife once more lent her aid, and he performed his job satisfactorily, for the spirits cried out, "Well done, our brother-in-law." Nothing now remained but to give proof of his hunting abilities; and in order to assist him, four spirits went along to drive the deer in his tract. It was not long before he heard the cry of "There they come!" but nothing could he see during the entire hunt, notwithstanding the number of advices he had. He was hooted at on his return, but allowed another trial of his skill which resulted the same as before. A third and last trial was allowed on the intercession of his wife, who told him he must now kill something. He declared it impossible if game could not be seen; to which she replied, "You have doubtless observed black beetles when a-hunting; these are deer, kill them!" He went out, the cry was raised as before, "Here they come." Beetles came swarming along, he killed one, and in an instant a fine buck was lying at his feet. Encouraged by this, he went on slaying, until voices bade him desist. All he killed was lifted in the air and carried home, but he saw nothing of the porters, though their shadows were visible on the ground. Great joy was manifested at his success, for he heard them saying, "Sister, no one, as thou knowest, was ever permitted to return to earth; death, thou art aware, exists not among beings in *Tucupar* (Heaven), but our brother-in-law is unable to participate in the pleasures we partake of, on account of the grosser materials of which he is composed. It is permitted out of compassion to him that thou return again to earth." And addressing the husband, the voices added, "Go thou with thy wife, but remember thou must not have intercourse with her until after three days; for a punishment awaits thee, if disobedient."

They left the spirit realms and traveled on earth; still she was invisible to him, until at night, having made a fire and lain down, he perceived a short distance off the outline of his wife, asleep. They travel the second day in the same manner, and he again made a fire, and on lying down, he saw her more distinct than the previous night. On the third night, she was perfectly plain. He could stand it no longer. "Wife of my bosom!" exclaimed he, and at the same time he clasped in his arms a billet of rotten wood! He remained a sorrowful wanderer on earth until the day of his death.

Here ends a legend, firmly believed in, which is selected from many others, as giving a good idea of their mode of thinking, belief, etc. It is faithful to the text, but the conversations, being tedious, are curtailed.

Some persons affirmed that the woman did not kill her child, but that it became a squirrel. This is reported as having caused much bloodshed between the contending parties of belief.

The bird called *cuwot* is strenuously believed in, at the present day. It is never seen, inhabits the mountains, and is nocturnal. Its cry is simply *cu,* and it often carried people away.

In regard to the woman's returning to life, they say it never *would* have happened, as the whole affair was merely a Heavenly ruse, out of compassion to the man, to get him back to earth, so as to appear again among them in his proper form as a celestial being.

[LETTER No. 16]

First Arrival of the Spaniards

THE INDIANS were sadly afraid when they saw the Spaniards coming on horseback.—Thinking them gods, the women ran to the brush, and hid themselves, while the men put out the fires in their huts. They remained still more impressed with this idea, when they saw one of their guests take a flint, strike a fire and commence smoking, having never seen it produced in this simple manner before. An occurrence however soon convinced them that their strange visitors were, like themselves, mortals, for one of the Spaniards leveled his musket at a bird and killed it. Although greatly terrified at the report of the piece, yet the effect it produced of taking life, led them to reason, and deduce the impossibility of the "Giver of Life" to murder animals, as they themselves did with bows and arrows. They consequently put them down as human beings, of a *nasty white color, and having ugly blue eyes!* This party was a small one, and soon left; having offered no violence, they were in consequence not disliked. They gave them the name of *Chichinabros,* or *reasonable beings.* It is a fact worthy of notice, that on becoming acquainted with the tools and instruments of steel used by the Spaniards, they were likewise called *Chichinabros,* which shows the estimation in which they held them.

Another event soon convinced them of their visitors' mortality, for shortly afterwards they received another visit from a larger party, who commenced tying the hands of the adult males behind their backs; and making signs of their wish to procure women—these having again fled to the thicket, at the first appearance of their coming. Harsh measures obtained for them what they sought, but the women were considered contaminated, and put through a long course of sweating, drinking of herbs, etc. They necessarily became accustomed to these things, but their disgust and abhorrence never left them till many years after. In fact every white child born among them for a long period was secretly strangled and buried!

The whites made them a number of presents prior to using any means to convert them; the presents were never refused, but only those consisting of goods were put to any use whatever. All kinds and classes of food and eatables were rejected and held in abhorrence.—Instead therefore of partaking of them, they were buried secretly in the woods. Two old Indians, not long since dead, related to me the circumstance of having once assisted when boys to inter a quantity of *frijol* and Indian corn, just received from the whites. Some length of time afterwards, being out in the woods amusing themselves, they came where the articles were deposited. Their surprise knew no bounds when they beheld an infinity of stalks and plants unknown to them, protruding through the earth which covered the seed.—They communicated the fact at home; it was ascertained to be the case, and the wizards pronounced it *white* witchcraft! Even *panocha,* of which they are now so fond, was declared to be the excrement of their new neighbors.

[Letter No. 17]

Conversion

Having now given a brief sketch of the manners and customs of the Indians, prior to their acquaintance with reasonable (?) people, and having noticed the first impression produced by their appearance on the aboriginals, I shall continue a letter or two more, so as to give an idea of the state they were brought to by the formation of the Missions of San Gabriel and San Fernando. Still the former shall serve as a guide in reference to everything; although on a smaller scale, the same will answer for the latter, or, in fact, any other establishment of the kind in California.

However, I may as well remark that no attention whatever will be paid to dates—and the text is as related by the old Indians, or as noted by the writer himself.

The site occupied by the principal building of the mission, the vineyards and gardens, was at the conquest of this country, a complete forest of oaks, with considerable underwood.

The water, which now composes the lagoon of the mill (one mile and a half distant), being free, like everything else, to wander and meander where it pleased, came down into the hollow nearest to the mission, on the Angeles road. This hollow was a complete thicket, formed by sycamores, cottonwood, larch, ash and willows; besides, brambles, nettles, palma cristi, wild roses and wild grapevines lent a hand to make it impassable, except where footpaths had rendered entrance to its barriers a matter more easy of accomplishment. This hollow, cleared of all encumbrance, served to raise the first crops ever produced at the mission, and although now a washed waste of gravel and sand, nevertheless, at that time it rejoiced in a rich black soil. On the side of this hollow, stood the lodge of *Sibagna* [San Gabriel]. Bears innumerable prowled about their dwellings and large quantities of deer sported in the neighborhood. The present site, however, was not chosen until some time after a building had been erected at the "Old Mission," which was intended to have been the principal establishment. The now San Gabriel River was named *El Río de los Temblores* [the River of the Earthquakes], and the building referred to, *La Misión de los Temblores*. Those names were given from the frequency of terrestrial convulsions at that time and for many years after. They were not only monthly and weekly, but oftentimes daily.

The brand for marking animals was a T with an S on the shank, like an anchor and entwined cable, to express *temblores*. Even after San Gabriel was founded, no other iron was ever adopted.

When the priest came to found the mission, he brought a number of vagabonds, under the name of soldiers, to carry out the proposed plan. Some of these were masons, carpenters, etc.—The priest having *converted* some few by giving them cloth and ribbons, and taught them to say *Amar a Dios,* they were baptized and coöperated in the work before them.

Baptism as performed, and the recital of a few words not understood, can hardly be said to be a conversion; nevertheless, it was productive of great advantage to the missionaries, because once baptized, they lost "caste" with their people, and had, *nolens volens,* to stop with the oppressor. This, of course, was put down by the padre as a proof of the influence of religion on their minds, and the direct interposition of the Virgin Mary! Poor devils, they were the *Pariah* of the West! Not one word of Spanish did they understand— not one word of the Indian tongue did the priest know. They had no more idea that they were worshiping God than an unborn child has of astronomy. Numbers of old men and women have been gathered to the dust of their fathers—and a few still remain—whose whole stock of Spanish was contained in the never-failing address of *"Amar a Dios!"* And whose religion, as Catholics, consisted in being able to cross themselves, under an impression it was something connected with hard work and still harder blows. Baptism was called by them *soyna,* "being bathed," and strange to say, was looked upon, although such a simple ceremony, as being ignominious and degrading.

We are, of course, unable to say that the severe measures adopted emanated from the priest; still there can be no doubt he either winked at the means employed by his agents, or else he was credulity personified! Baptism could not be administered by force to adults, it required a free act; so taking an Indian as guide, part of the soldiers or servants proceeded on expeditions after converts. On one occasion they went as far as the present *Rancho del Chino,* where they tied and whipped every man, woman and child in the lodge, and drove part of them back with them. On the road they did the same with those of the lodge at San José. On arriving home the men were instructed to throw their bows and arrows at the feet of the priest, and make due submission.—The infants were then baptized, as were also all chil-

dren under eight years of age; the former were left with
their mothers, but the latter kept apart from all communication with their parents. The consequence was, first, the
women consented to the rite and received it, for the love
they bore their offspring; and finally the males gave way
for the purpose of enjoying once more the society of wife
and family. Marriage was then performed, and so this contaminated race, in their own sight and that of their kindred,
became followers of Christ (?).

The Indians, from the beginning, never offered resistance
or flew to arms, although they had ofttimes distinguished
themselves in warfare with other tribes. At first, surprise
and astonishment filled their minds; a strange lethargy and
inaction predominated afterwards. All they did was to hide
themselves as they best could from the oppressor.

From the first misnamed conversion until the arrival of
Fray José María Zalvidea, they knew nothing about the various rites and ceremonies daily performed, and in which
they took a part. No explication was, or could be offered,
for the Indians only learned a few words of Spanish, and
the padres none of their language. The soldiers, it is true,
picked up a smattering of the Indian tongue, but such words
only as to enable them to gratify with more ease their lust
and evil propensities, and not to afford instruction.

But the Padre José María, who was a man of talent, and
possessed of a powerful mind—which was as ambitious as
it was powerful, and as cruel as it was ambitious—formed
a new era in their existence. In a short time he mastered the
language and reduced it to grammatical rules. He translated
the prayers of the Church, and preached every Sunday a

sermon in their own tongue. His translation of the Lord's Prayer, commencing with *Ayoinac* (Our Father), is a grand specimen of his eloquence and ability.

He gave them, thereby, an insight of the Catholic religion, but did not in one iota alter their own. His predecessors had done nothing of the kind, and his successors, Padre José Bernardo Sánchez and Padre Tomás Estenaga, contented themselves in having their sermons translated sentence by sentence, to the neophytes, through an Indian interpreter, named Benito. On the death of Padre Tomás, the custom ceased.

I shall have occasion to say more regarding their present religious state, before concluding this series of letters, as well as speak more fully of Padre José María.

[LETTER No. 18]

First Missionary Proceedings

HAVING, at length, a sufficiency of neophytes to build with, ground was cleared and laid off; *adobes* were made and laid up; timber, cut in the neighboring mountains, was hauled; and at last a proper covering being required, *tule* or flags were put on, tied with nettle hemp made by the Indians, which formed a thatched roof suitable for present exigency. The church had a steeple to it, which was afterwards taken down, having sustained damage during an earthquake. The present belfry was substituted instead.

In after years, not only were other buildings erected, but tile manufactured, and placed on all of the edifices, including four rows of new double houses, forming three streets for the married portion of the community. Living in houses, however, did not suit their tastes; they were always vexed and annoyed with them, and debarred the satisfaction of burning them up according to usage, when their observances demanded it.

All this while, the former small stock of animals were carefully herded and were augmenting greatly.

Vine slips, fruit trees, and pulse, etc., were procured from Lower California. The first vineyard planted consisted of 3000 vines. It retains the name of *Viña Madre,* and from it sprang all the present generation of vineyards.

A better class of people than the low vulgar soldiers, both men and women, were induced to emigrate from Sinaloa and Lower California. They were a great acquisition, as were likewise a few Indians from the latter place, who had been well instructed by the "Jesuits" in various arts. The men among the newcomers served as *mayordomos* and overseers in the different branches of industry carried on. And being likewise well acquainted with agriculture, and some of the required trades, their services were invaluable.

The women were no less useful, for they taught the young female Indians to sew, and they became most expert at the business. Last and not least in the eyes of many besides priests, they instructed the older heads in the art of cooking, making of chocolate paste, preserves, and other edible knickknacks unknown for some time previous to our missionary friends.

Water was brought to irrigate the crops, from numerous little streams, and more produce was raised than necessary for the sustenance of all. The neophytes were supplied with blankets and some few cotton goods, but not to any great amount.

Indians of course deserted. Who would not have deserted? Still, those who did had hard times of it. If they proceeded to other missions, they were picked up immediately, flogged and put in irons until an opportunity presented of returning them to undergo other flagellations. If they stowed themselves away in any of the *rancherías,* the soldiers were monthly in the habit of visiting them; and such was the punishment inflicted on those who attempted to conceal them, that it rarely was essayed. Being so proscribed, the only alternative left them was to take to the mountains, where they lived as they best could, making occasional inroads on the mission property to maintain themselves. They were styled *huídos,* or runaways, and at times were rendered desperate through pursuit, and took the lives of any suspected of being traitors. They were always well informed of all passing at the mission.—They sometimes, when things got too hot, went as far as the Tulares.

A considerable quantity of books, to compose a library, were brought from the College of San Fernando, in Mexico, and a number of additional contributions were received during the time of Zalvidea and Sánchez, from the same source, and also, some by purchase from Lima. I cannot say much for the collection—it being nothing to compare with remnants of the Bibliothekes I have examined in Lower California, in the missions established there, which are now, I am sorry to say, reduced to ashes.

The more valuable part of the works consisted of those treating on Theology and Law, with a scanty number of

rather curious, quaint manuscripts; the balance being anti-
quated and erroneous productions on natural history, geography, etc., imparting little or no information. The best of
the library has, long ere this, either been stolen or destroyed,
and the refuse at the present time, consisting of some three
or four hundred volumes, is mere rubbish.

[LETTER No. 19]

New Era in Mission Affairs

ON THE ARRIVAL of Padre José María Zalvidea, cattle were
plenty, as were likewise horses, mares, sheep, and hogs. Cultivation was carried on to considerable extent, but it was to
him that the after splendor of San Gabriel was due. He it
was who planted the large vineyards intersected with fine
walks, shaded by fruit trees of every description, and rendered still more lovely by shrubs interspersed between—who
laid out the orange garden, fruit and olive orchards—built
the mill and dam—made fences of *tunas* (*Cactus opuntia*)
round the fields—made hedges of rose bushes—planted trees
in the mission square, with a flower garden and sun dial in
the center—brought water from long distances, etc., etc.

He likewise remodeled the general system of government, putting everything in order and to its proper use, and
placing every person in his proper station. Everything under
him was organized, and that organization kept up with the
lash!

Thus people were divided into various classes and stations.
There were *vaqueros* [cowboys], soap makers, tanners, shoe-
makers, carpenters, blacksmiths, bakers, cooks, general serv-

ants, pages, fishermen, agriculturists, horticulturists, brick and tile makers, musicians, singers, tallow melters, *viña-deros* [vineyard keepers], carters, cart makers, shepherds, poultry keepers, pigeon tenders, weavers, spinners, saddle makers, store and key keepers, deer hunters, deer and sheep-skin dressmakers, people of all work, and in fact everything but coopers, who were foreign; all the balance, masons, plasterers, etc., were natives.

Large soap works were erected; tanning yards established; tallow works, bakery, cooper, blacksmith, carpenter, and other shops; large spinning rooms where might be seen 50 or 60 women turning their spindles merrily; and looms for weaving wool, flax and cotton. Then large storerooms were allotted to the various articles which were kept separate. For instance, wheat, barley, peas, beans, lentils, chickpeas, butter and cheese, soap, candles, wool, leather, flour, lime, salt, horsehair, wine and spirits, fruit, stores, etc., etc.

Sugar cane, flax and hemp, were added to the other articles cultivated, but cotton wool was imported.

The *ranchos* belonging to the mission were put on another footing, as were the sheep farms. A house was built at San Bernardino, and other exterior operations carried out.— The principal *ranchos* belonging at that time to San Gabriel were San Pasqual, Santa Anita, Azusa, San Francisquito, Cucumonga, San Antonio, San Bernardino, San Gorgonio, Yucaipa, Jurupa, Guapa, Rincón, Chino, San José, Ybarras, Puente, Misión Vieja, Serranos, Rosa de Castilla, Coyotes, Jabonería, Las Bolsas, Alàmitos and Cerritos.

A principal head *mayordomo* commanded and superintended over all. Claudio López was the famed one during

Padre Zalvidea's administration, and although only executing the priests' plans, in the minds of the people he is the
real hero. Ask anyone who made this, or who did that, and
the answer on all sides is the same: *El difunto Claudio!* And
great credit is due him for carrying out, without flogging,
the numerous works set before him. There were a great
many other *mayordomos* under him, for all kinds of work,
from tending of horses down to those superintending crops,
and in charge of vineyards and gardens.

It is strange no medical man was kept on the establishment, as the number of people was great, and the stock
of medicines very large.—They were provided not by the
pound, but by the quintal! Not in gallons, but in barrels full!
Still all the dependence for medical aid (with the exception
of midwives) was either on a casual foreigner passing, or on
the stupidity of some foreigner employed on the premises.
I know not why, but an Anglo-Saxon in those days was synonymous with an M.D. Many an *extranjero* who never before possessed sufficient confidence in himself to administer
even a dose of Epsom, after killing, God knows how many,
has at length become a tolerable empiric. One thing in favor
of the sick was, that after a lapse of years, the greater part
of the drugs lost their virtue.

Indian *alcaldes* were appointed annually by the padre, and
chosen from among the very laziest of the community; he
being of the opinion that they took more pleasure in making
the others work, than would industrious ones! From my
own observation this is correct. They carried a wand to denote their authority, and what was more terrible, an immense scourge of rawhide, about ten feet in length, plaited

to the thickness of an ordinary man's wrist!—They did a great deal of chastisement, both by and without orders. One of them always acted as overseer on work done in gangs, and accompanied carts when on service.

The unmarried women and young girls were kept as nuns, under the supervision of an abbess, who slept with them in a large room.—Their occupations were various; sometimes they sewed or spun, at others they cleaned weeds out of the gardens with hoes, worked at the ditches or gathered in the crops. In fact, they were jacks or jennies of no trade in particular.—The best-looking youths were kept as pages to attend at table and those of most musical talent reserved for church service.

The number of hogs was great and were principally used for making soap. The Indians, with some few exceptions, refused to eat pork, alleging the whole family to be transformed Spaniards! I find this belief current through every nation of Indians in Mexico. Why should they, without being aware of it, have each selected the hog more than any other animal to fix a stigma upon? It probably may be from its filthy habits; or, can something appertaining to the Jews be innate in them?

At San Francisquito, near the mission, were kept the turkeys, of which they had a large quantity. The dovecote was alongside of the soap works, and in an upper story, affording plenty of dung to cure leather and skins with.

The padre had an idea that finery led Indians to run away, for which reason he never gave either men or women any other clothing (including shirts and petticoats) than coarse frieze (*xerga*) made by themselves, which kept the poor wretches all the time diseased with the itch. If any hand-kerchiefs or cotton goods were discovered among them, the same was immediately committed to the flames.

He was an inveterate enemy to drunkenness, and did all in his power to prevent it, but to no purpose. He never flogged, however, while the influence of liquor lasted; but put them into the stocks, under care of the guard, until sober. Finding the lash alone was of no avail, he added warm water and salt to the dose, which was given until it ran out of the mouth again! It was of no use, the disease was as incurable as consumption.

Having found out the game practiced in regard to destroying the children born to the whites, he put down all miscarriages to the same cause. Therefore, when a woman had the misfortune to bring forth a stillborn child, she was punished. The penalty inflicted was, shaving the head, flogging for fifteen subsequent days, iron on the feet for three months, and having to appear every Sunday in church, on the steps leading up to the altar, with a hideous painted wooden child in her arms!

He had no predilection for wizards, and generally (as some one or another was always reporting evil of them), kept them chained together in couples and well flogged. There were, at that period, no small number of old men rejoicing in the fame of witchcraft, so he made sawyers of them all, keeping them like hounds in couples, and so they worked, two above and two below in the pit.

On a breach occurring between man and wife, they were fastened together by the leg, until they agreed to live again in harmony.

He was not only severe, but he was, in his chastisements, most cruel. So as not to make a revolting picture, I shall bury acts of barbarity known to me through good authority, by merely saying that he must assuredly have considered whipping as meat and drink to them, for they had it morning, noon and night.

Although so severe to the Indians, he was kind in the extreme to travelers and others.—There being so much beef, mutton, pork, and poultry, with fruits, vegetables and wines, that a splendid public table was spread daily, at which he presided. Horses to ride on were at their service, and a good bed to sleep on at night. Whenever ready to start either up or down the coast, horses and a servant were at command to go as far as the next mission.

Having brought the establishment, and everything connected with it, to the climax of perfection, he had still calculated on doing more. He purchased large quantities of iron, with the intention of railing in all of the vineyards and gardens. But, alas! even Catholic societies are not proof against the "capital sins" they so strongly condemn. Envy and jealousy stepped in and prevailed. He was ordered by his superior to the Mission of San Juan Capistrano. The loss of his favorite hobby capsized his reason, and after lingering for many years in a disturbed religious state of mind, he at length expired, regretted by all who knew his worth and gigantic intellect.

Better Times

THE PADRE José Bernardo Sánchez had, for some time previous, been a colleague of Zalvidea but attended only to matters connected with the Church. On the translation of Padre José María to San Juan he became his successor. He was of a cheerful disposition, frank and generous in his nature, although at times he lost his temper with the strange, unruly set around him.

He was a great sportsman and capital shot, both with rifle and fowling piece. Although no one could complain of Zalvidea, in regard to his kind treatment, still there was a certain restraint in his presence, arising from his austerity and pensiveness, which even custom did not erase from the mind. Padre Sánchez was different; his temper was governed according to circumstances. In ecclesiastical affairs, his deportment was solemn; in trade he was formal; in the government of the mission, active, lively and strict; in social intercourse he was friendly, full of anecdote, fond of a joke, even to a practical one. Picnic parties were of weekly occurrence and generally held at the mill, when, independent of a yearling heifer baked under ground, many other good things reigned on the table.

I cannot refrain from relating an anecdote connected with those parties of pleasure, as it shows the relish the old man had for anything ludicrous. A few of the actors are still alive, but the greater part have been gathered with the padre, to the dust they sprang from.

Don J. M. M., an old Spaniard, who had large commercial

relations with the mission, having a negro cook, called Francisco, who was science itself in all relating to the kitchen, the priest and M. made up a plan to carry out a joke at the expense of their guests. So having procured a fine fat little puppy, he was stuffed and roasted in a manner that would have tempted the most fastidious epicure to "cut and come again." This was brought on as a last course under the name of lamb, with an excellent salad to correspond.

All ate of it and praised it much, with the exception of the two concerned in the joke.—After concluding with a glass of wine, the old man enquired of his guests how they relished the dog? No one would believe it, until the negro made his appearance with the head and paws on a plate. Then a mixed scene ensued, which brought tears into the old man's eyes, while he nearly killed himself with laughter. All, of course, were squeamish, but while the quiet portion retired to ease themselves, in discharging the detested food, the pugnacious remained to fight M. first, and do the other afterward. The padre eventually procured harmony, but for many a day after, roast lamb and salad were viewed with suspicion by the former partakers of his cheer.

The same regulations which had been observed by his predecessor, were still in force under him, but more lenity was shown to the failings of the neophytes. Although the lash was ever ready, yet many other modes of chastising were adopted in its stead for minor offenses.

The general condition of the Indians was rendered better, and a more healthy state prevailed even in their morals. Many an Indian who had previously stolen and committed other acts of insubordination, from a vindictive spirit, now refrained from such deeds, through the love and good will held to their spiritual and temporal ruler.

The purchases made at one time seldom exceeded $30,000, consisting of domestics, bleached, brown and printed; flannels, cloth, *rebozos,* silk goods, and, in fact, everything; besides supplies of sugar, *panocha,* rice, hosiery, etc. These goods were fitted up in two large stores for the accommodation, not only of the public, but for the necessities of servants and use of the neophytes.

The females had their frieze (*xerga*) converted into sweat-cloths, and more suitable garments provided them. This measure effected a great change, for now of a Sunday might be seen coming out of church, women dressed in petticoats of all patterns and colors, with their clean chemise protruding from the bosom, with a 'kerchief round the neck and *rebozo* round the shoulders; while the men had their pants, jacket, trousers, hat and fancy silk sash. Even the children sported in a white or fancy shirt, with a handkerchief tied around the head.

This was, indeed, a transformation, and one for which they felt grateful. It elevated them to better thoughts and principles, and made them esteem themselves more than probably anything else would have done. Nor did the reformation stop here. The married people had not only sheets provided for their beds, but even curtains. It was the duty of the *mayordomo* to visit each room weekly, and see that every article was kept clean and report accordingly. The priest paid a monthly visit for the same end.

On coming out of Mass, the whole community was assembled and rations given to families for the ensuing week.

Besides, each man received half a pint of spirits, and the women a pint of wine. *Panocha,* molasses and honey were distributed, and if required, clothing; as also two or three dollars each on occasions.—Although rations were given as stated, yet the mission provided daily food for the laborers.

The mission bell, on being rung, roused the *alcaldes* from their slumbers, who in loud voice soon set all the world agog. Mass was heard, and again the bell rang to work. At eleven its notes proclaimed dinner, when in they flocked with their baskets to receive *posole* and a piece of beef. *Posole* consisted of boiled beans and corn or wheat. At twelve o'clock they were again warned to their labors, which concluded a little before sundown to afford them time to receive supper, which consisted of *atole* or mush. If a gang were at a distance, a copper kettle and attendant accompanied to provide food on the spot.

After twelve o'clock on Saturdays, soap was distributed, and all the world went a-washing of clothes and persons, to make a decent appearance at church on Sunday. Saturday night was devoted to playing *peón,* and with few exceptions, none slept, for whites and Indians, men, women and children, were generally present.

After service, on Sunday, football and races were on the carpet until the afternoon, when a game called by the Scotch "shinty," and I believe by the English, "bandy," took place.— One set being composed of all men and one of all women. People flocked in from all parts to see the sport, and heavy bets were made. The priest took a great interest in the game, and as the women seldom had less than half a dozen quarrels, in which hair flew by the handful, it pleased him very much. The game being concluded, all went to prayers, and so ended the Sabbath.

He died in 1833, regretted by all the community, and leaving everyone who knew him sad at his loss.

His course was a good one, yet probably Padre Zalvidea's was equally so. It was required in his time, no doubt, and the step from the one to the other had a more beneficial tendency than had he from the first carried out measures such as those of Sánchez. He was succeeded by Padre Tomás Estenaga.

[LETTER No. 21]

Decay of the Mission

THE MISSION, as received by the Padre Tomás, was in a flourishing condition, but in 1834 (I think it was) the Mexican Congress passed a law secularizing all of the missions, by which each Indian was to receive his share of land, gardens, and stock; but immediately on the top of it a change was effected in the general government, and instead of carrying out the law, they abolished it. They, however, secularized them and ordered administrators to have charge instead of the clergy. These facts being known to the Padre Tomás, he (in all probability by order of his superior) commenced a work of destruction. The back buildings were unroofed and the timber converted into firewood. Cattle were killed on halves with people who took a lion's share. Utensils were disposed of, and goods and other articles distributed in profusion among the neophytes. The vineyards were ordered to be cut down, which, however, the Indians refused to do.

It did not require long to destroy what years took to estab-

lish. Destruction came as a thief in the night. The whites
rejoiced at it. They required no encouragement, and seemed
to think it would last forever. Even the mere spectators were
gladdened at the sight, and many of them helped themselves
to a sufficiency of calves to stock farms.

It is not the intention here to give a detail of all that
occurred, as our line, as marked out from the first, relates
merely to the Indians, and to other persons and things only
so far as they are connected with them.

General Figueroa, having been appointed political chief
and commandant general of the territory, arrived, and his
adjutant, Col. Nicolás Gutiérrez, received the mission from
the Padre Tomás, who remained as minister of the church
with a stipend of $1500 per annum from the establishment,
independent of his synod from the Pious Fund in Mexico.

As a wrong impression of his character may be produced
from the preceding remarks, in justice to his memory, be it
stated that he was a truly good man, a sincere Christian and
despiser of hypocrisy. He had a kind, unsophisticated heart,
so that he believed every word told him. There has never
been a purer priest in California. Reduced in circumstances,
annoyed on many occasions by the petulancy of administrators, he fulfilled his duties according to his conscience, with
benevolence and good humor. The nuns, who when the secular movement came into operation had been set free, were
again gathered together under his supervision and maintained at his expense, as were also a number of the old men
and women. Everything he got was spent in charity upon
those of the *ranchería* whom he considered as worthy of it
and they remember him with gratitude and affection.

The Indians were made happy at this time in being permitted to enjoy once more the luxury of a *tule* dwelling, from which the greater part had been debarred for so long; they could now breathe freely again.

Administrator followed administrator, until the mission could support no more, when the system was broken up. I shall make no remarks here on their administration; it is to be presumed they complied either with their instructions or their own ideas.

The Indians during this period were continually running off. Scantily clothed and still more scantily supplied with food, it was not to be wondered at. Nearly all of the Gabrielenos went north while those [neophytes] of San Diego, San Luis and San Juan overran this country, filling the Angeles and surrounding *ranchos* with more servants than were required. Labor in consequence was very cheap. The different missions, however, had *alcaldes* continually on the move, hunting them up and carrying them back, but to no purpose; it was labor in vain.

This was a period of demoralization. People from Sonora came flocking in to assist in the general destruction, lending a hand to kill off cattle on shares, which practice, when at last prohibited by government orders, they continued on their private account.

These Sonoreños overran this country. They invaded the *ranchería,* gambled with the men and taught them to steal; they taught the women to be worse than they were, and men and women both to drink. Now we do not mean or pretend to say that the neophytes were not previous to this addicted both to drinking and gaming, with an inclination to steal, while under the dominion of the Church; but the Sonoreños most certainly brought them to a pitch of licentiousness before unparalleled in their history.

[LETTER No. 22]

Finis

HAVING given a sketch of the Angeles County Indians from the time they were free, natal possessors of the soil, living contented in a state of nature, until these civilized times of squatting and legislative oppression, in which not only they but those bearing their blood in a fourth degree are included, to the shame of this our country, and disgrace of the framers of such laws, I shall now conclude them, with a very short review of how far their ancient manners and customs remain in force among the handful left of a once happy people.

Their former lodges are not now in existence, and most of the Indians remaining in the county are from other parts—from Santa Ynez to San Diego. A few are to be found at San Fernando, San Gabriel and the Angeles. Those in service on *ranchos* are a mere handful. You will find at present more of them in the county of Monterey than in this, excluding the three places named above. Death has been busy among them for years past, and very few more are wanting to extinguish the lamp that God lighted!

The Indians from the northwest coast killed great numbers years ago on the Islands. Those of San Clemente, the remains of which some eighteen years since were collected in caves on the Island, showed the whole of them to have been possessed of double teeth all round, both in the upper and under jaw.

I have previously mentioned that their language has deteriorated much since the conquest. Numerous causes affect all languages, and one of the many which did so to theirs was the want of their former councils held so frequently, in which their wise men spoke with eloquence suited to the occasion, using more dignity and expression, which naturally elevated the minds of all and gave a tinge of better utterance even in ordinary conversation.

They have at present, *two* religions—one of custom and another of faith. Naturally fond of novelty, the Catholic one serves as a great treat—the forms and ceremonies an inexhaustible source of amusement. They don't quarrel with their neighbor's mode of worship, but consider their own the best. The life and death of our Savior is only, in their opinion, a distorted version of their own life. Hell, as taught them, has no terrors. It is for whites, not Indians, or else their fathers would have known it. The Devil, however, has become a great personage in their sight; he is called *Zizu,* and makes his appearance on all occasions. Nevertheless, he is only a bugbear and connected with the Christian faith; he makes no part of their own. The resurrection they cannot understand, but a future state of spiritual existence is in accordance with their creed.

Their chiefs still exist. In San Gabriel remain only four, and those young. There are more, but of tribes formerly from the direction of San Bernardino. They have no jurisdiction more than to appoint times for the holding of feasts and regulating affairs connected with the church. No standing church remains nowadays; it is made yearly and consecrated when required, on any spot they choose to select.

Their food continues the same, with the addition made to the list of what the Spaniards introduced.

Their clothing is of course distinct, and a cloak made of rabbitskins has within this year or two become a novelty among themselves.

For a long time back, marriage has been performed in the Catholic church; and only one instance of its fulfilment in their own *alone,* exists in the case of a young girl who contracted matrimony about three years ago. Marriage vows, I am sorry to say, are not very binding, although many examples of strict fidelity exist.

Women undergo the same purification after childbirth as formerly, with the exception of such as were in the service of whites at their first parturition.

The seers have declined very much in their ability both of predicting events and doing harm; although instances of sickness occasionally occur of which they stand the blame. In performing cures, however, they still take the precedence of the other members of the faculty known as M.D.'s.

Ten years ago shell-bead money was current in the mission, not only between Indians, but between them and the whites. It is now extremely scarce, and hoarded from one year to another to use at their church ceremonies, and repurchased again for double its value.

I have refrained from touching on politics. The administrators I have left to work out their own salvation—and dates, with statistics, I leave to those possessed of abler pens to furnish an account of, and of which there is a fine field open to write about—confining myself entirely to the title of these letters.

If these sketches of Indian character have been at all interesting to the readers of the "Star," I shall consider myself amply paid for the time occupied in writing them.

NOTES

Preface

[1] *Paisano* (feminine, *paisana*) means an inhabitant of a Spanish-speaking country, *país* being the Spanish word for country. Idiomatically, *paisano* is an appellation given by soldiers to any man not in military service; hence, a civilian. *Hijo* or *hija del país*—literally, son or daughter of the country—has a wider significance, including the military.

[2] An *adobe* is a large brick made of mud mixed with straw and baked in the sun. Often the word is used to denote a house built of *adobe* bricks. All the residences in California during the period of Spanish and Mexican occupation were *adobes,* with the exception of Indian *jacales* (brush shelters).

[3] *Hacendado* can be translated as landholder, and *hacienda* as estate. *Hacendado* is differentiated, in the Spanish mind, from *ranchero*. The latter may mean the owner of a small farm, whereas *hacendado* describes the land baron, who once owned thousands of acres in California, under Spanish and Mexican grants.

[4] Don Juan was the son of Don José Bandini. Born in 1800 in the family home at Lima, Peru, and educated there, Don Juan came to California as a young man, settling in San Diego. He married twice, each time into an important California family—Estudillo and Argüello. By Dolores Estudillo he had five children—Arcadia, who was first married to Abel Stearns and later to Robert S. Baker; Ysidora, who was married to Colonel Cave J. Coutts; Josefa, the wife of Pedro Carrillo; José María, whose wife was Teresa Argüello; and Juanito. Don Juan's second wife, Refugio, who became a great friend of the Indian woman Victoria Reid, was a niece of that famous beauty, Concepción Argüello, beloved of the Russian prince, Rezánov. Refugio also was the mother of five Bandini children—the sons Juan de la Cruz, Alfredo, and Arturo; and two daughters, who were married to Charles R. Johnson and Dr. James B. Winston. All Don Juan's daughters were famous for their beauty. As rarely to be noted of the old California families, the succeeding generations have retained a considerable amount of the founder's ability and fortune. Various members of the Bandini family still hold important positions in California social and political circles. Don Juan himself was one of the most widely known of Hugo Reid's contemporaries, interesting himself especially in politics. A synopsis of events in his active life can be found in the Pioneer Register section of Bancroft's *History of California* (Vol. II, pp. 709–710). Don Juan died at Los Angeles, in 1859.

[5] *Compadre* is the title by which a godfather (*padrino*) or godmother addresses the father of the godchild. The father (*el padre*) and the mother (*la madre*), in turn, may address their child's godparents as *compadre* or *comadre*. Occasionally these titles were used in an extended sense, as terms of affection for intimate friends.

[6] A league was the common measure of distance in early California—approximately three miles. The extent of property was commonly computed in square leagues, rather than acres, a square league comprising approximately 4430 acres.

As a smaller measure, *una vara*—the Spanish yard of thirty-three inches—was used; for instance, in computing the frontage of a city lot.

[7] *Poco tiempo*—an idiomatic expression hard to translate. An attempt is made on p. 11.

[8] Before 1863–1864, the winter of the great drought in California—when not enough rain fell to start the spring growth of grass, and a million animals, mainly cattle and horses, are said to have starved to death,—Don Abel Stearns either owned or had an interest in the following large cattle ranches in southern California.

	Approximate acreage
Los Alamitos	23,000
La Jurupa	33,800
La Laguna	13,300
Los Coyotes	48,800
La Habra	6,700
San Juan Cajón de Santa Ana	26,600
Las Bolsas y Paredes	35,500
La Bolsa Chica	8,000
La Sierra	17,800
Total	213,500

Stearns also claimed title to two large *ranchos* in Baja California, which he never developed:

Guadalupe	43,700
San Rafael	36,400
Total	80,100

Stearns's own loss of cattle at the time of the great drought has been estimated as between 40,000 and 50,000 head. And by the end of the famine his vast acreage was mortgaged for $50,000. Don Abel's interesting career has been exhaustively detailed by Pearl Pauline Stamps, in a serial entitled "Abel Stearns—California Pioneer," which ran during the months of May, June, July, and August, 1926, in the *Grizzly Bear Magazine*.

[9] Henry Dalton, a business partner and lifelong friend of Hugo Reid, told his nephew Charles Jenkins—still living in Los Angeles—that Reid was in the midst of a promising college career at Cambridge, England, when he left the Old Country forever, owing to an unhappy love affair. Dalton himself was an educated Englishman, and the information that he gave Jenkins is substantiated by William Heath Davis in a manuscript account of the Reid family preserved in the Huntington Library and quoted, in part, on pp. 70–73 in the present book.

[10] Hawaii was often called the Sandwich Islands a hundred years ago; and Kanakas, Sandwich Islanders. Much trading was done between the Islands and ports in the Americas; and Sandwich Islanders were in demand as sailors on trading vessels of various nationalities, being regular seadogs. Intense cold they could

not stand, however, and frequently, on winter voyages around the Horn, they fell sick and died. Richard Henry Dana, Jr., in *Two Years Before the Mast,* often mentioned the good nature and physical prowess of Kanaka crews manning such vessels as the *Ayacucho,* under direction of European or American officers.

[11] The *Los Angeles Star,* first newspaper printed in southern California, was a four-page weekly "published every Saturday, opposite Bell's buildings, City of Los Angeles," by John A. Lewis and John McElroy. The first issue appeared on May 17, 1851, and was printed partly in English and partly in Spanish. At the time of Hugo Reid's affiliation with the paper, as "San Gabriel correspondent," from February, 1852, until his death in December of the same year, William H. Rand was acting as editor and part-time printer. The complete series of Hugo Reid's *Letters* to the *Star* readers, which consisted of twenty-two well-written and well-informed essays on the California Indians' nature, customs, legends, and history, is reproduced in Appendix B of the present work, from clippings in the Bancroft Library.

[12] Both the Gaffey and the Davis collections of Californiana repose in the Huntington Library; the Pío Pico Collection, in the Bancroft Library; and the Antonio Coronel manuscripts, in the Exposition Park Museum, Los Angeles. Mr. Wagner has made valuable gifts of manuscript material to the Huntington Library, but he retains possession of the greater part of his collection.

[13] "The Coronels told Mrs. Jackson the story of Hugo Reid, his marriage to the Indian woman, and of [María] Ygnacia."—C. C. Davis and W. A. Alderson, *The True Story of Ramona,* p. 149. Don Antonio was a man of intelligence and wealth who aided Hubert Bancroft in his compilation of the monumental *History of California.* In the Pioneer Register, Bancroft made acknowledgment: "In '77 he [Don Antonio] dictated for my use his *Cosas de California,* or recollections of early events, a ms of 265 pages, and one of the best narratives of its class in my collection. He also gave me a valuable col. of Doc. Hist. Cal. from his family archives."

[14] *Journal of John McHenry Hollingsworth, 1844–1850.* The First New York Volunteers was a regiment of adventurous young men "of good habits . . . and various pursuits," organized in New York and commanded from the first by Colonel Jonathan D. Stevenson, a colonel of militia, ward politician of New York City, and former member of the legislature. Its purpose was twofold: active participation in the war with Mexico, and the subsequent colonization of California. The regiment came round the Horn in three ships, arriving at San Francisco in March, '47. Details of its personnel and achievements may be found in the section, "New York Volunteers and Artillery Company, 1846–1848," in Bancroft's *History of California,* Vol. V, Chap. XIX. Hollingsworth was in Company G of the N.Y.V., commanded by Captain Matthew R. Stevenson, son of the colonel.

[15] "After completing *Ramona,* Mrs. Jackson became resolved to write the true story of María Ygnacia Reid, but died before starting it."—*The True Story of Ramona,* p. 149.

[16] Charles Jenkins is a stepson of George Dalton, Henry Dalton's brother. As a young man, before coming to California, Hugo Reid went into partnership with Henry Dalton, first in a mercantile house in Lima, Peru, where Don Enrique

lived for a number of years, and then in Hermosillo, Mexico, where Hugo established a branch of Dalton's trading company. In '45, Henry Dalton followed Hugo Reid to California and settled in the vicinity of San Gabriel, becoming grantee of three large *ranchos,* San Francisquito, Santa Anita, which he bought from Reid in '47, and Azusa. In his *Notes* of '45, Thomas Larkin described Don Enrique as an educated Englishman, "forty years old, a man of property, intelligence, and local influence."

[17] Laura Evertson, the child "Lalita," whose relationship with Señora Victoria Reid is depicted in Chapter Eight, later married the distinguished judge, Andrew J. King, and lived in Los Angeles. For the Historical Society of Southern California she wrote a number of sketches of early life in San Gabriel at the time of her arrival by covered wagon in the fall of '49. A particularly vivid character sketch entitled "Hugo Reid and His Indian Wife" was read before the society on March 7, 1898.

[18] The rambling *adobe* residence, in the vicinity of the Los Angeles Plaza, which Stearns built for his child bride at the time of their marriage.

[19] For a more complete description of this early transition period, consult Hugo Reid's *Letters* reprinted in Appendix B.

[20] According to Miss Mary Foy, still living in Los Angeles, who has known many members of the Bandini family and also was an intimate friend of "Lalita" King. Miss Foy owns an exquisite example of Victoria Reid's beadwork, a small table runner, presented to her long ago by Lalita, who had received it from Doña Victoria herself.

[21] The Huntington estate includes portions of each of the original Reid *ranchos:* Santa Anita and Huerta del Cuati, the latter of which was known as Lake Vineyard after Don Benito Wilson bought it from Doña Victoria in 1852. Refer to the map of early southern California land grants, following p. 200.

Chapter One: The Land of Poco Tiempo

[1] The evidence that Hugo Reid arrived in California on the *Ayacucho* is circumstantial. The date of his first visit, given as the summer of 1832 in a political *carta*, or passport, signed at La Paz in 1834 by the Mexican *jefe político*, Poliano Monterde—preserved in the Pío Pico Collection—coincides with the time spent by the *Ayacucho* in the course of that year, trading in California ports. Both John Wilson, the captain, and James Scott, supercargo, had known Reid while he worked in Lima as Henry Dalton's partner. At the time of Reid's marriage to the Indian woman, Scott acted as one of his character witnesses, and Wilson was a lifelong friend, even being one of those who signed the invitation to the funeral of Don Perfecto in '52. It is scarcely possible that Reid could have come to California overland from Mexico, at such an early date, without receiving great acclaim for so hazardous a feat; and among the six or seven vessels entering San Pedro "harbor" that summer, it is natural that Reid would have chosen the one commanded by his friend and fellow countryman.

[2] Reid's residence was given in his passport as Hermosillo, Capital of Sonora, Mexico. There he managed the branch office of Henry Dalton's Lima trading company, according to Charles Jenkins.

[3] Los Angeles having been planned as a typical Spanish *pueblo* (town), most of the important buildings fronted on a central square, or public park, called the Plaza.

[4] With the Patties, father and son, Nathaniel Miguel Pryor—called *Miguel el Platero* by the *paisanos*,—had been in the first party to come to California by the Gila route, and also first to come overland from the Mississippi River. Pryor was imprisoned in San Diego with other members of his party, and there Sylvester, the older Pattie, died. James Ohio, the son, detailed their adventures, a few years later, in his *Personal Narrative*. Pryor was twenty-seven years old at the time of Reid's arrival, and had been living in Los Angeles for two years. He made a fair living by mending clocks, and even more by otter hunting. For many years his home was a popular meeting place, performing the multiple function of hotel, men's club, and bar, in a community where there were, as yet, none of these institutions. As late as the Mexican War, Pryor's place retained its importance as a social center, serving as official headquarters for the New York Volunteers. Don Miguel died in '50.

[5] John Roger Cooper, known in California as *Don Juan el Manco* because of a contracted left arm, was a native of Alderney Island, and his mother, by a second marriage, became the mother of Thomas Larkin. He was engaged in all manner of trading ventures in partnership with his half brother Larkin. They were two of the best-known men of the day, associated with everything noteworthy that happened in Monterey during their lifetimes. Captain Cooper lived to the age of eighty. He had come to California in 1823, and died there, in San Francisco, in '72.

[6] Richard Laughlin also had a Spanish nickname, being called *Ricardo, el Buen Mozo*. Born in Kentucky in 1802, he had turned trapper and accompanied Pryor on the Pattie expedition across the wilderness to California. Later, in Los Angeles, he became a viticulturist, being one of the pioneers who found a new use for

their beaver traps—the steel springs were of just the right shape to be forged into pruning knives. Laughlin died in '46, in the Mexican War.

[7] Hugo Reid's *Letters* in Appendix B contain a full account of the accomplishments of Sánchez and Zalvidea in transforming San Gabriel into the Pride of the Missions.

[8] Engelhardt, *San Gabriel Mission and the Beginnings of Los Angeles*, p. 4.

Chapter Two: Trial and Error

[1] *Anchetas:* goods collected for exportation by a person not engaged in trade.

[2] *Gente de razón:* members of the gentility—a term commonly used to distinguish Spanish and Mexican residents from the American Indians.

[3] The reference is to a poetic passage in one of Hugo's letters quoted on p. 95.

[4] This quotation and those in the next three paragraphs are from Letter 21, Appendix B.

[5] According to Henry Dalton, William Heath Davis, and Antonio Coronel, Hugo Reid's wanderings were first occasioned, when he was eighteen, by the fickleness of a Scotch girl named Victoria with whom he thought himself deeply in love. A promising career at Cambridge University had been interrupted by Hugo's abrupt departure from Liverpool for the New World.

[6] *Ranchería:* a collection of huts, like a hamlet. In a California *ranchería* like the one near San Gabriel occupied by members of Victoria's family, the huts would be called *jacales.*

[7] Jacob Primer Leese was an energetic and able business man whose career was blotted by bitter feuds with business associates and members of his family. After leaving Los Angeles in '36, he went to Monterey and formed a partnership there with two prominent northerners, Nathan Spear and William S. Hinckley. At the end of that year he became a naturalized Mexican and moved to Yerba Buena (San Francisco), where he soon married Rosalía, a sister of the renowned General Mariano Guadalupe Vallejo, much against Vallejo's will. The partnership with Spear and Hinckley lasted only two years, dissolving in a quarrel over $13,000 in profits. Leese engaged in various business projects, some successful and some not. His career reached a climax when he was thrown into jail by Frémont at the time of the Bear-Flag Revolt. From a prison window he jotted down the notes for an eyewitness account of the revolt, and this account, says Bancroft, "is one of the best narratives extant on the subject." He shared that prison chamber with his brother-in-law Vallejo and with Victor Prudon, with whom he was scarcely on speaking terms.

[8] General Santa Ana had been a great military hero in Mexico, but from this date ('36) he was a fallen idol. In an early battle, in the days of his phenomenal popularity, Santa Ana lost a leg and had a wooden one made as a substitute. The emotional Mexicanos continued to revere this appendage, as a symbol of past glory, long after they ceased to love the general himself. When their former leader died in disgrace, burial was refused his remains in the Catholic cemetery of Mexico City, where other national heroes lay in peace—but a funeral was celebrated for his wooden leg with all possible pomp and glory! (According to John Gaffey.)

[9] *Home Sweet Home* was written by an American actor and author, John Howard Payne, in 1830, as incidental music to a play called *Clari; or, the Maid of Milan.* By the end of '32, more than 100,000 copies—an unprecedented number—of this song had been sold, and it was still growing in popularity.

[10] The 1844 census says that Victoria's son Carlos, who by that time had taken the name of Reid, was born at San Gabriel in 1836.

Chapter Three: The Festal Wedding

[1] The Spanish manuscript detailing these "marriage investigations" is preserved in the Gaffey Collection. Each *extranjero* who underwent the baptismal rite received a Spanish name in addition to his own.

[2] Since the Indian woman's name appears only as Bartolomea in the mission records preceding 1837, and as Victoria from then on, it has been suggested that Hugo Reid renamed her to suit himself—either in honor of his sovereign, the young Victoria, who ascended the British throne that same year, or in recollection of the Scotch girl named Victoria who had been his first love. References in letters and reminiscences to the woman Reid married invariably entitled her Doña Victoria.

[3] Santiago (James G.) Dove was a young Englishman, twenty-three years old, who had lived a roving life as a sailor on the whaler *Kitty;* as a carpenter in Lima, Peru; and recently as a trapper in the wilderness of the great Southwest.

Julian (William) Pope was an American trapper, a friend of Pryor and Laughlin, who had accompanied them to California in the Pattie party. Like them, he stayed on the coast and eventually married *una hija del país*. He died suddenly in '43, from severing an artery with an axe.

Joaquín (Joseph Gilbert) Bowman, a much older man than the others, admitting to fifty-six years at this time, was a native of Kentucky who had accompanied Jedediah Smith to the coast as early as '26. Shortly thereafter, he settled in San Gabriel as a miller, and remained in charge of the public mill (now known as the Old Mill, in the city of Pasadena) for many years. He was respected by the padres and became one of Reid's intimates. Hugo usually referred to him affectionately as "Old Bowman," and became deeply distressed when his friend, for some mysterious reason, attempted to take his own life, in 1842. See p. 96.

[4] This information about Victoria has been supplied by Thomas Temple after an intensive search in the San Gabriel Mission records for items about her age, parentage, Indian husband, and children.

[5] Durán succeeded Sánchez as *padre presidente* of the Alta California missions, on May 26, 1830.

[6] Since an eyewitness account of Hugo's marriage to Victoria could not be found, contemporary descriptions of a typical wedding among the *gente de razón* have been drawn upon. Passages from Don Alfredo Robinson's *Life in California* proved especially valuable in recreating what must have been a gay and colorful scene.

Chapter Four: The Indian Wife

[1] The Rancho de Santa Anita was described by Judge Hoffman, in his *Reports of Land Cases,* as comprising three square leagues and being situated in Los Angeles County. See map following p. 200. La Huerta del Cuati, or de Quati, was a small *rancho* of 128.26 acres, also in Los Angeles County. It was renamed Lake Vineyard by Don Benito Wilson, when he purchased it from Doña Victoria in 1852.

[2] William Heath Davis, *Seventy-five Years in California,* p. 143.

[3] Volumes could be written about the part that Thomas Oliver Larkin played in the history of early California. He was a man of tact and good sense, a native of Massachusetts born at the turn of the century (1802), who came to Monterey in '32 at the invitation of his half brother, Captain Cooper. At first he was employed by Cooper as a clerk, but soon he went into business for himself, starting with a capital of $500 a small store for the sale of "groceries, grog, produce, and drygoods." By the time of the Mexican War he had made a fortune. He kept a careful record of each year's profits, as follows:

January 1, 1835	. . .	$ 2,650	January 1, 1841 . . .	$21,493
1836	. . .	4,708	1842 . . .	37,958
1837	. . .	5,626	1843 . . .	49,147
1838	. . .	11,013	1844 . . .	46,505
1839	. . .	13,788	1845 . . .	60,175
1840	. . .	15,895	1846 . . .	66,644

Unlike most of his friends, Larkin never sought to become a Mexican citizen, but in '36 obtained a *carta* which was renewed from year to year. From '43 to '48 he served as United States consul in Monterey, and Bancroft is right in saying that "nothing like just credit has hitherto been given for his public services in '45–'46 [the years of the war with Mexico]." In '48 he was elected to represent Monterey at the constitutional convention. Larkin died, greatly respected, in '58. He left a mass of manuscripts—personal letters, official documents, and business communications—of which full use has never been made. Many of them are in the Bancroft Library, and many more in the Huntington Library.

[4] *Tapado* means constipated. Several remedies for this common condition, like rhubarb laxative and magnesia, are mentioned in notes penned either by Hugo or Felipe Reid to Don Abel's clerk, William Howard, who apparently was the nearest approach to a pharmacist that Los Angeles could offer.

[5] La Jurupa: a *rancho* comprising seven square leagues in San Bernardino County which, at Bandini's death, came into the possession of his son-in-law, Don Abel Stearns.

[6] According to J. M. Guinn, "The Old Pueblo Archives," Southern California Historical Society *Publications,* Vol. IV, p. 37, 1897–1898, "*Rúbricas* were intricate flourishes of loops, circles, and zigzags" following a person's name, and taking the place of a seal on a Spanish document. Everyone had one, as distinct as a cattle brand, and as necessary, since a signature was not legal without one. "Only people of illimitable patience in a land of *poco tiempo* would go through life constructing such wonders." It is to the reminiscences and research of Mr. Guinn

that the author is indebted for the greater part of the description of Los Angeles
as it was when Reid first came there in the 'thirties (Chapter Four).

[7] For a full and interesting account of "Early Postal Service of California," see
the article by J. M. Guinn in Southern California Historical Society *Publications,*
Vol. IV, p. 18.

[8] William Edward Petty Hartnell was born in Lancashire, England, in 1798.
Undoubtedly, Hugo Reid first knew him when he was working for Dalton in
Lima, Peru, because—until '29—the Englishman was a member of the firm McCulloch, Hartnell, and Company, agents both of Begg and Company, headquarters
in Lima, and of the Brothertons in Liverpool and Edinburgh. Hartnell first came
to California, after several years' residence in Lima, on the *John Begg* in 1822;
and thereafter traveled several times between California and Peru, trading miscellaneous cargoes for mission produce. However, Hartnell was not a business man
by nature, and he dissociated himself from the partnership in '29, settling down
in northern California to live a *hacendado* life on the Alisal *rancho,* of which he
was grantee. There he established his Seminario de San José, a boys' school which
did not last more than a few years. Hartnell was a scholar and linguist, speaking
and writing fluently the Spanish, French, and German languages in addition to
his own. At the time when Reid wrote to him concerning the Santa Anita grant,
Hartnell was serving, by Governor Alvarado's appointment, as *visitador general*
of Alta California missions, at a salary of $2000 a year. Although he never made
much money, he exercised a fine influence over a great many people. Throughout
his lifetime, he maintained an interesting correspondence with men of education
and prestige, all over the world. In '25 he married María Teresa de la Guerra,
daughter of the Santa Barbara patriarch Don José de la Guerra y Noriega, and,
by her account, they had twenty-five children—twenty sons and five daughters.

[9] From the San Gabriel Mission records.

[10] Hugo Reid's *adobe* still stands by the lake at Santa Anita. One of the last
people to occupy it was that fabulous character, "Lucky" Baldwin, who, after
"striking it rich" at the Comstock Lode, came south and transformed the quiet *hacienda* of Santa Anita into a pleasure resort, complete even to a carriage house and
casino. Yet Baldwin, after living in fantastic luxury, chose to die in the modest
bedroom once occupied by Hugo and Victoria Reid, in the low *adobe* whose
simple lines emphasized the flamboyance of its close neighbor, the turreted "gay
'nineties" casino.

[11] This description of Davis's and McKinley's visit to Santa Anita has never
before been published. It is preserved only in manuscript form in the Huntington
Library, Davis Collection.

[12] William Davis Merry Howard came to California as a cabin boy on the
California in '39, at the age of twenty, having been sent to sea by a Boston mother
who thought he needed discipline. For a time, he served as clerk to Don Abel
Stearns in Los Angeles and was extremely popular, being "a large man, of fine
personal appearance; jovial, generous, and humorous; fond of practical jokes,
late suppers, and private theatricals; but always attentive to business. He had
no political ambitions, but was fond of helping his friends into office." In '42, as
supercargo on the *California,* he sailed to the Sandwich Islands and carried away

a wife from there, Mary Warren—the adopted daughter of Captain Grimes,—who had just returned from school in Boston. In '45 Howard started a store in Yerba Buena, in partnership with Henry Mellus, and they made a fortune at the time of the Gold Rush. Howard died in '56, at the age of thirty-seven.

[13] The Gaffey Collection includes the complete "marriage investigations" (Spanish manuscripts) of Hugo Reid, Abel Stearns, Juan Leandry, and Richard Laughlin, each containing information about these characters and their witnesses which cannot be found elsewhere. Thomas Temple owns a copy of the Pryor investigation. Pryor's young wife lived only until September 4, 1840, when she died giving birth to a son, christened with his father's two names, Spanish and American—Miguel Nathaniel.

Chapter Five: Cargoes and Contraband

[1] Of the *Guadalupe,* Michael White (Don Miguel Blanco), in his memoirs acquired by Bancroft, said: "We built another schooner for the Mission San Gabriel. She was named the *Guadalupe* (after Joseph Chapman's wife, Guadalupe Ortega) and put in command of William Richardson, then living at the mission. She made a trip to San Blas and came back, and then I took charge of her myself, some eight days after having married María del Rosario Guillen [a daughter of Señora Eulalia Pérez], on November 22, 1831. I went in her to Mazatlán and San Blas. Richardson and another man named Manuel Somali went as supercargoes. Her cargo consisted of dried tongues, olives, wine, drief beef, soap, mission *aguardiente,* and other trifles; also two priests, not of the missionaries here, one of them Father Jesús Martínez, who had married me. The *Guadalupe* was a top-sail schooner of 99 90/100 tons burthen, and carried a cargo of 150 tons. I was away less than a year. My mother-in-law, Doña Eulalia Pérez [supposedly a hundred years old!], married during my absence Don Juan Mariné."

[2] According to Pearl P. Stamps's biography, "Abel Stearns—California Pioneer," published in the *Grizzly Bear Magazine,* May–August, 1926.

[3] Keith returned to his practice in Hermosillo immediately after Hugo Reid's wedding, in the fall of '37.

[4] Jonathan Trumbull Warner, known in California as Don Juan José, was a native of Connecticut, born in 1807, who adventured to St. Louis and New Mexico in '30, acting as clerk to Jedediah Smith when that renowned trail blazer was killed by Indians in New Mexico, a year later. Warner then joined Jackson's party of trappers on their way to the coast. He set his traps the length and breadth of California, before settling in Los Angeles in '34. After five years of community life he commenced to grow restless again and started east, by way of Acapulco, and thence overland to Vera Cruz. When in New York, he delivered a lecture on the Far West, stressing the need for a railroad to the Pacific. The return trip he made round the Horn on the *Julia Ann.* In '43 he asked for a license to hunt goats and seals on the Santa Barbara Islands. The next year, having become naturalized, he obtained a grant to the Agua Caliente *rancho,* near San Diego, where he lived with his family until '57. His home became known as Warner's Ranch, and he acquired, in addition, the neighboring Camajal y el Palomar *rancho.* Here Kearny's men camped in '46, before the fight of San Pascual. Warner, like Stearns, Leidesdorff, and Leese, acted as Larkin's confidential agent during the Mexican War. See Larkin's secret circular letter addressed to these men, reproduced on pp. 132–133.

[5] Micheltorena. See pp. 100–101.

[6] See Bancroft, *History of California,* Vol. IV, p. 565: "Vessels of 1841–1845; *Esmeralda* . . . Hugo Reid, master."

[7] This version of the Jones incident is based on notes made in the course of a conversation with John Gaffey, who heard the story of the Micheltorena ball from Doña Arcadia herself.

[8] In July, 1842, Don Abel had purchased the Los Alamitos *rancho* of six square leagues, and all its livestock, from Don Francisco Figueroa for $6000. The live-

stock consisted of: cattle, 900 head; sheep, 1000; horses and mares, 240. Average prices were: cattle, per head, $3; sheep, 75 cents to $1; mares, $2 to $2.50; horses, $7 to $8. The Alamitos, Stearns's "home" ranch, was the foundation of his landed wealth.

[9] *Arroba*: equal to 25 pounds.

[10] Dr. Richard Somerset Den was a finely educated Irish physician who lived in Los Angeles for a few years, arriving in '43. He took Keith's place as the Pueblo doctor (there were others, like John Marsh, who came and went in the late 'thirties and 'forties), and had a tremendous practice. According to Newmark (*Sixty Years in Southern California,* pp. 108–109), "he was seldom seen except on horseback, in which fashion he visited his patients, and was, all in all, somewhat a man of mystery. He rode a magnificent coal-black charger, and was himself always dressed in black. He wore, too, a black felt hat; and beneath the hat there clustered a mass of wavy hair as white as snow. . . . His standing collar was so high he was compelled to hold his head erect, and he tied around his collar a large black silk scarf. Thus attired and seated on his richly caparisoned horse, Dr. Den appeared always dignified, and even imposing. . . . He was on intimate terms with Don and Doña Abel Stearns, acknowledged social leaders. Dr. Den was fond of horse racing, and had his own favorite race horses sent here from Santa Barbara, where they were bred." Dr. Den served, in 1847–1848, as chief physician and surgeon of the Mexican forces during the Mexican War. The following year he left for the gold mines, where he sometimes made as much as $1000 a day in fees paid by sick miners.

[11] The Huntington Library possesses the only complete file of the *Southern Vineyard* (1858–1859), published weekly in Los Angeles and edited by J. J. Warner.

[12] See Reid's inventory of his own vines and orchard trees, pp. 113–114.

[13] William Heath Davis, *Seventy-five Years in California,* p. 121.

Chapter Six: Calamity at the Mission

[1] *Uba cimarrona:* the grape that grew wild in California, of which the giant vine at San Gabriel is an example.

[2] See Letter 22, Appendix B, esp. p. 283.

[3] Quoted from the *Master Key,* monthly publication of the Southwest Museum, Los Angeles, November–December, 1937.

[4] The Santa Anita *rancho* passed through many hands before becoming the residential district, between the towns of Pasadena and Arcadia, which it now is. The site of Hugo Reid's *adobe* is reserved out of the subdivision, for a public park. In the park area are included the lake and buildings erected by "Lucky" Baldwin after he acquired the *rancho* in the 'seventies. Santa Anita was originally occupied by the Indians, who called this territory *Aleupkigna.* It became church property at the coming of the Spaniards. Hugo Reid was the first individual to obtain a grant to Santa Anita. He sold it to Henry Dalton, in 1847, for 20 cents an acre, estimating the acreage at 13,500. Dalton sold it to Joseph A. Rowe for $33,000—an increase of $6000 over Reid's selling price. Rowe sold out to William Corbitt and Albert Dibblee, who soon disposed of a portion of the large *rancho* to Leonard J. Rose, 2000 acres, at $2 an acre. In '65, Corbitt and Dibblee sold the remainder of Santa Anita to William Wolfskill, already a large landholder. Louis Wolfskill, who had married a daughter of Henry Dalton, inherited Santa Anita from his father. He sold 1740 acres to Alfred B. and Katharine S. Chapman in '69; they paid $19,500 for this property, which then adjoined the L. J. Rose Sunny Slope estate and now includes the Chapman Park subdivision. In 1870, Wolfskill offered his ranch at $9 an acre; in '71, at $10; and in '72, sold out for $10.50, to Harris Newmark. By this time, Santa Anita was reduced, through previous sales, to 8000 acres; so Newmark's purchase price was $85,000. Three years later, on a visit to southern California, Elias Jackson Baldwin became enchanted with Santa Anita, and resolved to have it at any price. Newmark asked, and got, $200,000. The *rancho* stayed in the Baldwin family until its recent purchase by a syndicate headed by Harry Chandler of Los Angeles, which is developing a residential subdivision on the land once owned and loved by Hugo Reid and his Indian wife.

[5] Don Benito's diary has been inherited by his granddaughter, Miss Anne Patton, living in San Marino.

[6] *Albaceas:* testamentary executors.

[7] Don Juan Temple adventured far from his home in Massachusetts to the Sandwich Isles and, finally, to California—on the *Waverley,* in '27. He was a good business man and made a great deal of money in real estate and other deals. Perhaps his most notable coup was a profitable lease of the Mexican Mint, in Maximilian's time. In the annals of '46 and '47, Temple is named as the creditor of missions in the southern district—to which fact Hugo is referring.

Chapter Seven: War Clouds

[1] According to John Gaffey, Bandini and Stearns were angry because Victoria took away special trading privileges which they had enjoyed for some time. They asserted that Victoria did not intend to stop the practice of special privilege merely to favor better friends of his. Don Juan and Don Abel often became embroiled in politics, sometimes advantageously and sometimes disastrously. In this matter of Victoria, they succeeded in arranging his deportation and retaining their own "rights" under his friendly successor, Don José Figueroa.

[2] P. T. Hanna, *California Through Four Centuries,* p. 76.

[3] William Alexander Leidesdorff was living proof that California provided an opportunity for any enterprising man, whatever his original station in life. Leidesdorff, a native of the Danish West Indies, was the illegitimate son of a Dane by a mulatto. He came to the United States as a boy and, through application, acquired so much skill in navigation that he was in demand as master on vessels plying the trade route from New York to New Orleans. He sailed to California as master of the well-known *Julia Ann,* in '41, and made a number of trips on her between coast ports and the Sandwich Islands. In Yerba Buena he engaged in business deals which brought him a fortune; and also became a respected member of the council, treasurer, and member of the school committee. He introduced the first steamship, the *Sitka,* to San Francisco Bay, in '47. His little-known correspondence with Larkin is a mine of information to students of American history. Leidesdorff, who might have been a social outcast in other countries, so deeply appreciated the democracy of his adopted country, California—and with her, America,—that he poured all his energies into the formation of the new state. He was interested, above all, in the establishment of a public school system. It was a great loss to California when one of her most progressive spirits died—in '48, at the early age of thirty-eight—Leidesdorff having been born the same year as Hugo Reid.

[4] According to John Gaffey, who provided the writer with much of the material for this chapter—either copies of the Larkin correspondence, or the original letters in his own collection.

[5] Now in the Bancroft Library.

[6] The old Mexican woman was Doña María Clara Cota de Reyes.

[7] See Bancroft, *History of California,* Vol. V, pp. 588–589.

Chapter Eight: The Flower of San Gabriel

[1] Felipe's fine hand and complex *rúbrica* often appear in the San Gabriel Mission records. Several letters, mere *cartas de orden,* are preserved in the Gaffey Collection.

[2] Only when driven by desperation would Victoria touch a pen—the symbol, to her, of tragedy-dealing "education." Her two letters were both written to Don Abel, one when María Ygnacia was dying, and the other, a few months before Hugo's death, when she knew he was ill and yet he had gone off in retreat to write his long-planned Indian essays without telling her where. See p. 194.

[3] The story of Doña Victoria and the child "Lalita" is based on Laura Evertson King's reminiscences, read before the Southern California Historical Society, in 1898, when the sensitive child had become a middle-aged woman and the wife of a judge.

Chapter Nine: Gold and Dross

[1] This version of Marshall's discovery is based on a pamphlet of thirty-two pages in the author's possession. Anonymous, simply called *California,* it was issued by Chambers in London, in 1894, without a title page.

[2] Felipe, of course, is Reid's stepson; but also his *compadre,* because Hugo had stood as *padrino* to one of Felipe's children.

[3] Frederick Henry Teschemacher was a close-mouthed German trader who came to San Francisco in '42, achieved great financial success, and was an early mayor of the city. Mystery surrounds his personal life. Indeed, as Bancroft says, "for so prominent a pioneer, there is a remarkable lack of information about him."

[4] *Vapor:* Only a few months before this letter of Reid's, the *California* had been the first steamer to be placed in service on the West Coast run of the Pacific Mail Steamship Company. This company carried mail and passengers on the route from New York to Chagres, thence across the Isthmus of Panama, and from Panama to San Francisco. Bringing 365 passengers, a crew of 36, and many bundles of mail, the *California* left Panama on the first day of February, and arrived in San Francisco on the last. She was followed by the *Oregon* and the *Panamá,* sister ships, which arrived in San Francisco on April 1, 1849, and June 4, 1849, respectively. Reid's letter is dated July 14, and he already seems to take steamer service as a matter of course, although he observes that "the steamer due on the first and advertised to leave San Francisco on the fifteenth has not made her appearance." See p. 173.

[5] For the vital part that Riley played in California history, see pp. 184–187—a description of the convocation of the constitutional convention.

[6] William Money was an eccentric Scotchman, self-styled "doctor, artist, and philosopher," who had recently settled in San Gabriel, near Uva Espina. Money filled immense volumes with his "pioneer reminiscences," which nobody would buy or listen to—not even Bancroft. When Hugo Reid returned to San Gabriel, he often resented intrusions of his privacy by the old bore, Money, who felt that they had a great deal in common—both being Scotchmen and men of letters.

Chapter Ten: "Old Reid"

[1] Published by Robert Semple and Walter Colton, it first made its appearance as a weekly, at Monterey, August 15, 1846.

[2] The *California Star* was the second newspaper published in California, its first issue appearing in San Francisco, January 9, 1847. The publisher was Samuel Brannan, and the first editor, E. P. Jones.

[3] See Lindley Bynam's *Laws for the Better Government of California, 1848,* a pamphlet reprinted from the *Pacific Historical Review* of September, 1933.

[4] See Reid's letter of July 14, 1849 (p. 173), containing an anecdote about Governor Riley and the Hon. Thomas Butler King.

[5] Typical claims made and lost by Captain Sutter appear as follows, in Judge Hoffman's *Reports of Land Cases Determined in the United States District Court (Northern District):*

"743: John A. Sutter, claimant for surplus lands of New Helvetia, 22 square leagues, in Yuba and Sutter Counties, granted February 5, 1845, by Manuel Micheltorena to John A. Sutter; claim filed March 2, 1853. Discontinued.

"759; 369: John A. Sutter, claimant for Town of Sutter, in Sacramento County; claim filed March 2, 1853, rejected by the Commission, July 17, 1855, and appeal dismissed for failure of prosecution, February 23, 1857."

[6] See *Report* of the debates in the convention of California on the formation of the state constitution, in September and October, 1849, by J. Ross Browne.

[7] *Ibid.*, p. 24. Hugo Reid was admitted as a member of the constitutional convention on September 5, 1849—afternoon session.

[8] The complete list of "members of the convention of California" is reproduced in Browne's *Report,* pp. 478–479. Each man had to give his name, age, birthplace, last state residence, the district in California that he was representing, his home town or post office, length of residence in California, and profession. Hugo Reid answered the form questions as follows, lopping a year off the age he had given at the time of his wedding: "Hugo Reid, 38, Cardross, Scotland, Angeles, San Gabriel, sixteen years, farmer."

[9] Bancroft, in his Pioneer Register, describes Peter H. Burnett as "one of the luckiest men of the time." A native of Tennessee, born in 1897, he had been a farmer living in Oregon at the time of the discovery of gold at Sutter's Fort. Joining the world and his brother, Burnett spent a few months at the mines and acquired some land near Sacramento "cheap," in a transaction with Captain Sutter. Within a year Burnett rose so far from the ranks of newcomers as to become judge of the supreme court; to sell a portion of his Sacramento property for $50,000; to move to San José, and be elected governor of the new state!

[10] See introduction to Appendix B.

[11] The Hacienda Rosa de Castilla occupied the site of the present Halfway House on Mission Road, between Los Angeles and Pasadena, according to Miss Mary Foy, who can remember that "at this point there was water. It was a general stopping place for eating and resting."

[12] Charles Jenkins told the author of his visit to Uva Espina. A hale and interesting old man, he still lives in Los Angeles.

[13] See *Annals of Los Angeles*, p. 67, for Gregg Layne's account of the San Gabriel murder of General Joshua H. Bean by members of the Joaquín Murieta gang—wherein he includes Felipe Reid.

[14] See note 11 to Preface.

[15] The invitation to Señor del Valle is from Thomas Temple's private collection of Californiana.

[16] Padre Anacleto Sestrade.

[17] From Hoffman's *Reports of Land Cases (Southern District)*: "468; 47; 486: Victoria Reid, claimant for 200 *varas* square, near San Gabriel, in Los Angeles County, granted May 15, 1843, by Manuel Micheltorena to Serafín de Jesús; claim filed, November 8, 1852, rejected by the Commission, November 29, 1853, and appeal dismissed for failure of prosecution, October 24, 1855." Since Victoria lost her claim to the land and her house fell down in the same year, undoubtedly she returned to live with the ancient Señora Eulalia Pérez y de Mariné, who did not die until '78, at the reputed age of 140.

BIBLIOGRAPHY

Archives of the *Ayuntamiento*. Original Spanish manuscripts, in the City Hall, Los Angeles, California.

Archives of California, 1844–1850. Departmental state papers, in the Bancroft Library, University of California, Berkeley, California.

BANCROFT, HUBERT HOWE. Pioneer Register, in *History of California* (San Francisco: The History Company, 1886), Vols. II–V.

BYNUM, LINDLEY. *Laws for the Better Government of California, 1848*. Pamphlet, reprinted from the *Pacific Historical Review* of September, 1933.

California (London: Chambers Publishing Company, 1849), anonymous pamphlet.

Californiana, Collection of Antonio Coronel. Manuscripts in Exposition Park Museum, Los Angeles, California.

Californiana, Collection of William Heath Davis. Manuscripts in Huntington Library, San Marino, California.

Californiana, Collection of John Tracy Gaffey. Manuscripts in Huntington Library, San Marino, California.

Californiana, Collection of Pío Pico. Manuscripts in Bancroft Library, University of California, Berkeley, California.

CLEVELAND, E. L. *The Gold of California* (New Haven: J. H. Benham, 1849), pamphlet.

CLELAND, ROBERT GLASS. *Pathfinders* (Los Angeles: Powell Publishing Company, 1929).

[DANA, RICHARD HENRY, JR.] *Two Years Before the Mast: A Personal Narrative of Life at Sea* (New York: Harper and Brothers, 1840).

DAVIS, C. C., and ALDERSON, W. A. *The True Story of Ramona: Its Facts and Fictions, Inspiration and Purpose* (New York: Dodge Publishing Company, 1914).

DAVIS, WILLIAM HEATH. *Seventy-five Years in California (1831–1906)* (San Francisco: John Howard, 1929).

ELLIS, ARTHUR M. *Hugo Reid's Account of the Indians of Los Angeles County* (Privately Printed. Los Angeles, 1926).

ENGELHARDT, FR. ZEPHYRIN. *San Gabriel Mission and the Beginnings of Los Angeles* (Mission San Gabriel, 1927).

FORBES, ALEXANDER, *California: A History of Upper and Lower California from Their First Discovery to the Present Time* (London: Smith, Elder, and Company, 1839).

HANNA, PHIL TOWNSEND. *California Through Four Centuries* (New York: Farrar and Rinehart, 1935).

HOFFMAN, OGDEN (district judge). *Reports of Land Cases Determined in the United States District Court (1853–1858)* (San Francisco: Numa Hubert, 1862).

HOLLINGSWORTH, JOHN MCHENRY. *Journal: 1848–1850* (San Francisco, 1923).

JACKSON, HELEN HUNT. *Ramona—A Story* (Boston: Little, Brown, and Company, 1901).

LAYNE J. GREGG. *Annals of Los Angeles (1769–1861)* (San Francisco: California Historical Society, 1935).

Matrimonios, 1774–1855. Record of marriages in San Gabriel District. Parchment tomes preserved in the San Gabriel Mission.

NEWMARK, HARRIS. *Sixty Years in Southern California, 1853–1913* (New York: Knickerbocker Press, 1916).

Newspaper files consulted in the Bancroft Library: *Los Angeles Star, Pacific, San Francisco Herald.*

Pasadena (Los Angeles: Title Guarantee and Trust Company, 1935), pamphlet.

Publications of the Historical Society of Southern California (Los Angeles, 1844–1933), Vols. I–XV.

Report of the Debates in the Convention of California on the Formation of the State Constitution in September and October, 1849, by J. Ross Browne (Washington: John T. Towers, 1850).

[ROBINSON, ALFRED.] *Life in California: During a Residence of Several Years in That Territory . . . by an American* (New York: Wiley and Putnam, 1846).

STAMPS, PEARL PAULINE. "Abel Stearns—California Pioneer," *Grizzly Bear Magazine,* May–August, 1926.

WILSON, BENJAMIN D. Diary of "Don Benito." Manuscript owned by Miss Anne Patton, San Marino, California.

INDEX